CATHERINE JASEK

This is a work of fiction. All of the main characters appearing in this work, including Nick Pratt and his family, friends, and foes are fictitious. However, Bodie was actually an important gold-rush town in the 1870s and 1880s, and many of the townspeople mentioned in this book were actual citizens of Bodie.

Print ISBN: 978-1-66786-485-3
eBook ISBN: 978-1-66786-486-0

Printed in the United States of America

BUCK UP

AN ADMONITION TO TOUGHEN UP AND BE BRAVE.

I dedicate this book to my family with love.

CHAPTER 1

"So, do you have a wife?" Jodie asked his new friend.

"A wife?"

"Sure, a special lady you live with."

"Well, I do have someone special in my life," Nick acknowledged.

"Is she pretty?"

"No, not pretty, but she's cute. She has big brown eyes and red curly hair. She and I have been together a long time."

"What's her name?"

"Cindy."

Susanne, a fellow passenger, watched this exchange with interest. She knew Nick well, and she knew he had no wife; Cindy was his dog.

"What do you like best about Cindy?" Jodie asked.

"She loves me and is always glad to see me. Not everyone is." Nick grinned.

"Is there anything you don't like about her?"

Nick leaned forward confidentially and said, "She snores."

Jodie giggled. Susanne suppressed a smile.

Nick held his finger up to his lips. "But if you meet her, don't tell her I said that."

"It's our secret," Jodie promised.

Nick smiled at the boy whose incessant chatter had kept him awake during most of the long journey. A Thomas Hardy novel rested on Nick's lap but had mostly been unread. Instead, Nick had listened to the young boy and had even encouraged him by asking him questions.

Nick had not married and had no children of his own, but he seemed protective of the boy as an elder brother would be. He had seen that the boy had eaten when the stagecoach had stopped to change horses at the home stations. He had covered him with a blanket in the night when he slept. No one had gotten much sleep on the journey, especially those passengers sitting upright on the middle bench with no back support. Nick's back ached, but he didn't mention it. Nick had been so solicitous of both Susanne and Jodie that passengers entering the coach at various stations had incorrectly assumed the three were a family.

Four other passengers now shared the coach. One, a slovenly shopkeeper, had slept most of the way when he wasn't taking a nip from the flask he kept in his pocket. Only once did he look up and admonish Jodie. "Stop that danged ruckus." Then he fell back asleep. Nick looked at him sprawled in the corner taking up more room than he should. Nick found his soft snoring oddly comforting and hoped he would not awaken again before they reached their destination.

Susanne, the only woman in the group, had also started her journey in San Diego. She had enjoyed listening to the banter between Nick and his new, young friend. Nick was quick witted and quick with his words, but the boy also had a sharp mind and had readily traded barbs. Susanne had been in San Diego on business; she owned a photography studio in Bodie and was on her way home. She knew that Nick was also in San Diego, and although they had not planned to meet there, she was pleasantly surprised when they had ended up on the same stage for the return journey. The trip had been uncomfortable and tedious. Even the leather coach shades couldn't keep the dust out, and Susanne could feel the grit inside the collar of her dress. She looked forward to a cleanup and a change of clothes. Now that the stage approached Bodie, the uneven road had become even rougher, and the passengers all held on and braced themselves. All except the shopkeeper who slept on. Whiskey is an effective sedative.

Jodie opened his mouth to speak, but Nick sidestepped his upcoming question with one of his own. "So, Jodie, you never did answer me. Why are you traveling alone? Who will meet you when you arrive?"

"My Aunt Tess is going to meet me. Or rather, I am to go find her. I don't think she knows I'm coming. At least not yet. My mother told me to go find her and Annabelle."

"Annabelle?"

"My cousin. I've never met her because she's only four. She is Aunt Tess's daughter."

"When did you last see your aunt?"

"Not since I was a baby in Montana. It's been years and years, so I know I won't recognize her."

"She won't recognize you either," Nick pointed out.

"Right. Tess is my mother's younger sister. My mother put me on the stage and told me to find her in Bodie. I am to stay with her for a few months."

"Nick," Susanne interrupted. "You know so many people in town. Do you know this aunt of Jodie's?"

Nick looked at Susanne. Then he looked at the boy as if he were making up his mind. Nick did not normally lie, but he lied now.

"I do know your Aunt Tess. Listen, Lad, I'm sorry to tell you this, but she isn't in Bodie right now. She went away to visit friends and took Annabelle with her."

Jodie looked alarmed. "How can that be? My mother specifically told me to stay with her until Mom gets better. She's sick."

Susanne leaned over and put her hand on Jodie's shoulder. "Sick how? What's the matter with her?"

Jodie looked unsure of himself now. "She has consumption. It's a lung disease. She coughs a lot, and sometimes she spits up blood. Doc Murray is making her check into one of those hospitals called a sanitarium. He was going to drive her there himself. We had no idea where I should go, so Mom finally told me to go find my aunt in Bodie."

Susanne asked, "Don't you have other relatives to take you in?"

"No," Jodie replied, "only my aunt."

"Where is your father?" Nick wanted to know.

"I don't know. He went off to the gold fields almost a year ago. He was going to find lots of gold, and we were going to be rich. He was going to get me a dog, and we were going to buy our own house." Jodie sighed. "But we haven't heard from him."

Nick shook his head. "A year is a long time."

Jodie wiped a tear away. "I'm afraid something has happened to him. He would have come home if he could have. He would never leave us because Mom depends on him so. He's a great guy, but we haven't heard from him."

From the coach window, they could now see the bustling town of Bodie, and they could hear a thunderous roar. It was late afternoon, and the sun had begun to weaken on the high plain of this booming mining town on the California border.

"What's that awful noise?" Jodie asked.

"It comes from the stamp mills. You are hearing the huge steel rods, called stamps, that fall and pound the ore after it is taken from the mines. By crushing the ore, it is easier to extract the gold. Look over there." Nick pointed in the distance. "That's the Standard Mill. It alone has twenty stamps."

"When will the mill close for the night?" Jodie wanted to know. He was tired and knew he wouldn't be able to sleep with all that noise.

"Sorry, but the mill never closes. That pounding noise will go on all the time you are here."

Jodie looked bewildered. He knew nothing of mining, but he was naturally inquisitive. "How do the miners raise the heavy stamps, so they can fall on the ore?"

"It's all done with a steam engine that lifts the big stampers. So, if you guessed that it requires a lot of water for the steam engine, you're right."

"And wood," Susanne said. "Twenty cords of wood a day are needed to keep it working."

Nick gazed at Susanne now as she sat next to Jodie. "Susanne, will you do me a favor? This young lad needs a place to sleep. Will you take him to the Manor and make sure he gets some dinner and a bed for tonight? I have a quick errand to run, but I will be along directly. I'll take your bag and leave it off at your place. My errand is important. Do you mind?"

Susanne nodded her assent. "Sure, I'll visit with Mary Kay and help her make up an extra bed. She will probably put Jodie in with Tristan." Susanne handed Nick the key to her studio. Normally, she did not lock her door, nor did the townspeople lock their houses. However, a huge influx of men had converged on the town recently hoping for jobs in the mines. The pay of four dollars a day was good, even if the twelve-hour shifts were long. Unfortunately, there were more miners than jobs and not enough lodging to accommodate them all. Men could be found sleeping in doorways and under billiard tables. So, Susanne had locked up when she left town.

Nick thanked her and turned to Jodie. "You heard all that? What do you think? Mind bunking with us until we get your situation worked out?"

"No Sir. I would be greatly relieved. You're nice to help me."

"Yeah, yeah. I'll do what I can."

Jodie looked hopeful. "Maybe you can find my aunt. Otherwise, I'm not sure where to go."

The stagecoach stopped on Main Street. The weather was pleasant for April, and hundreds of residents congregated on the board sidewalks and out into the streets. Teams of mules, pulling a variety of freight, jammed the muddy streets. Saloons were busy as barkeeps poured shots of whiskey to men standing three-deep at the bars and as blackjack dealers shuffled cards. Nick could hear talking and laughter, and every so often he recognized voices he knew. Normally, he would have been right there with them drinking beer and telling stories.

Nick helped take the baggage down from the roof of the coach, thanked the driver for a safe trip, and picked up his bag and Susanne's. Then, he knelt down in front of Jodie, put his hands on the boy's shoulders, and looked him in the eye.

"Listen to me, Jodie. I have a piece of advice for you. You are a little boy. I think you said you were eleven on your last birthday. So, I need you to hear me. There are lots of kids in town. Many are older and tougher than you. Are you listening?"

Jodie nodded.

"So, here's what I want you to do. You can't go around with a name like Jodie. Jodie is a fine name, but not here. 'Jodie from Bodie' — It won't work. Those tough boys will make fun of your name. They might even beat you up and leave you in a slump behind Silas Smith's store. Kids here are tough and need no excuse for shenanigans. So, I want you to change your name while you live in Bodie. Do you have a middle name?"

Jodie shook his head.

"Okay then. What if we just call you 'J?' Or better yet, we'll call you 'Jay'—'J A Y.'"

Jodie shook his head. "No, I don't want to do that. I just want to be called Jodie. I don't want any trouble, but I want to keep my name."

"Yeah, okay. We'll do it your way. You've got enough trouble. But I want you to buck up because I'm afraid you may face some hard times while you are here. Go with Susanne now."

Susanne handed the boy his weathered suitcase. "Come on, Jodie, let's walk this way."

Nick hefted his and Susanne's bags and walked in the opposite direction toward Bonanza Street— a street he would warn Jodie never to go near.

Nick walked north on Main Street, site of all the commercial establishments. He passed a dry-goods store, a saddle shop, and several saloons and chop houses. He dropped Susanne's bag off at her studio and walked on. He ran into John Wagner coming out of the tobacco shop. John offered to buy him a drink. Nick was sorry to turn him down because John was a level-headed guy, and he enjoyed chatting with him. Nick spent a lot of time drinking beer in his saloon.

"No time tonight, John, but thanks. Got an errand to run. I'll stop by tomorrow." Nick hurried on.

He passed a brewery, a bakery, and a barber shop; all businesses that hadn't been there four years before when Nick had first arrived in town. Nick had come to Bodie a few months before Mary Kay and had liked it immediately. The people were friendly, beer was plentiful, and the price of property was still cheap. Nick had beaten the boom here all because he had heeded the advice of an old timer he ran into in a bar in Nevada. A miner he would never meet up with again, but with whom he had enjoyed spending the afternoon swapping stories and lies. The old man had asked Nick if he had heard of a place called Bodie. Gold had been discovered there in '59 but nothing had come of it. But now the old miner thought it might, and he urged Nick to look into it. Nick couldn't say if he had heard of the camp. He didn't think so, but at the man's insistence, he decided to check into it. He found out Bodie was located about a hundred miles from home. So, he rode over, took a look, and decided to buy property and settle there. In Virginia City, he had been at loose ends for a long time. So, why not? What did he have to lose?

Nick had lived in Virginia City, Nevada, for several years. He had moved there from Grass Valley, California, at the invitation of his brother Ed. Ed and Mary Kay Pratt had settled there shortly after their wedding in '68. Off on an adventure, away from home for the first time, these young Cornish youngsters had never looked back. Ed, used to hard-rock mining, found a job immediately. Mary Kay kept a tidy house, perfected her cooking skills, and had Ed's babies. Nick joined them within a year. He opened a carpentry shop and never lacked for customers. In a town of 25,000 people, someone always needed something built or rebuilt. The friendly attitude of the Pratts and their many kindnesses to those they met attracted others to them. It wasn't long before they had many friends.

They all liked to dance and went to many social events. Square dances were held out at Hoffman's place. Ed particularly enjoyed these dances and thought he might even become a caller.

"Someday, I'm going to call some of these dances myself," he told his friends. "Lefty is going to show me the ropes."

"With your big, husky voice, you won't have to call too loud," they had retorted.

"You calling me a big mouth?" he had asked. The answer was a resounding, "Yes."

Ed good naturedly took their ribbing. He was built like Paul Bunyan and was often teased about his size. But it was his laugh that made people smile. Ed liked a good joke, and his guffaw brought people running, so they too could share in the fun.

Like most young women, Mary Kay sewed. She made Ed a shirt to match her navy, calico dress, and they wore these on Saturday evenings when they formed squares in Hoffman's barn. Ed proudly wore his shirt but liked to tease his pretty wife.

"Say, are we wearing those fancy dancing duds tonight?" he would ask her. "We look like a pair of matched bookends."

Mary Kay would scoff and say, "You, Mister, are fortunate to be both paired up and matched up with me. Only the angels in Heaven know just how blessed you are. So, go get dressed. I don't want to hear another word."

When these two teased each other, Ed always replied, "Yes, Dear. As you wish, Dear."

Then, he would hug Mary Kay tightly. Ed loved his wife.

Some evenings, they attended performances at Piper's Opera House or at another venue. All three enjoyed theatrical productions and saw some fine performances by prominent actors of the day. Mary Kay regretted having missed Mark Twain when he had spoken there, but that was before her time. She often thought about him when she passed the *Territorial Enterprise*, his old newspaper office. She was an avid reader and had read all his stories.

Ed wasn't much of a reader; he said he couldn't sit still that long. Like many Cornish men, he enjoyed wrestling and competed against others in various matches. He looked forward to the Fourth of July celebration when many contests took place. Nick had built him a shadow box to display his many medals.

On Sunday mornings, Ed and Mary Kay attended the Methodist church services and participated in its many activities. Whenever the minister or the minister's wife asked for help, Mary Kay's hand shot up first. She was like a zealous student with the correct answer.

"I'll do it. I'll bake a cake. I'll gather garments for the poor. How can I help?"

The minister was always happy to let her help.

No persuasion on Mary Kay's part could convince Nick to join them in church. He had always attended services at home because he had been expected to, but with no parental authority in Virginia City, Nick was taking a break from religion. Ed, not one to boss his younger brother about religion or anything else, remained mum. Mary Kay gave it her best effort but eventually stopped badgering Nick. She knew it was a lost cause but worried that Nick's soul would be lost to the devil. She was devout enough to be concerned, but finally, she held her tongue and appreciated Nick for his good qualities and did not dwell on his bad. She and Nick had been in the same class at school and had been friends for a long time. They were indeed family. And so, the three young Pratts enjoyed life in this large, busy mining town of Virginia City, proud to be part of the Comstock Lode. Life was good for several years, and then suddenly, it wasn't.

CHAPTER 2

When Ed died in Virginia City, Mary Kay returned home to Grass Valley. Her dad and uncle came and got her, her baby daughter, and Ed's body and took them home. Her young son stayed with his Uncle Nick until Nick could make arrangements for his business, and then they followed two days later.

Ed was buried in the Methodist cemetery in his hometown on the following Tuesday. It rained all through the funeral, and the twenty-three-year-old widow sobbed all day. Mary Kay and Ed had been happily married for six years, and Mary Kay couldn't imagine a future without him now. They had courted at an early age and had been neighbors and friends long before that. They had attended the same school, although Ed was two years older. He had carried her schoolbooks as they walked home each afternoon. Sometimes Nick walked with them, but on days when he stayed for track practice, Ed liked to pull Mary Kay behind Mrs. Carey's lilac hedge and kiss her. It was behind this hedge that he had told her he loved her for the first time. Such sweet memories! But now Ed was gone, and Mary Kay was lost.

After the grave-side ceremony and burial, Mary Kay had endured an afternoon of well-wishers who crowded into her mother-in-law's house. All wanted to talk with her and console her, but she had no words to offer in return. When she could finally excuse herself, she walked to her parents' home and crawled into bed in her old bedroom. She noted the yellow-flowered wallpaper, a gift from her dad on her twelfth birthday. Her dad had liked Ed and had willingly given his blessing to their marriage. This memory brought her to tears again, and once in bed, she stayed. Her large, extended family had taken baby Nessie in tow and were passing her around to the various aunts. Nessie's grandmothers would take care of her later. Four-year-old Tristan understood that something terrible had befallen his dad. His Uncle Nick was still here though, and this comforted the little boy who never left Nick's side. And so, this was the beginning of a world without Ed.

Mary Kay refused to budge from bed, and at first her mother could not convince her that she would feel better if she were up and dressed. But Ellen would not be deterred, and after four days, Mary Kay could stand her mother's nagging no longer. When Saturday came, family members awoke to the aroma of coffeecake baking in the oven. Soon, two apple pies cooled in the larder. Mary Kay had bathed, dressed, and changed the bed linen. She was indeed up as her mother had requested. Baby Nessie too was cared for, sitting in the old family highchair watching her mother's every move and banging a wooden spoon on the tray in front of her. Mary Kay found comfort in being with her daughter and in baking for the family. "I can do this," she told herself. "I must be strong for the children. Ed would want me to be strong."

When she finished in the kitchen, she moved out to the garden where she spent the rest of the day. She wanted no company and was content to prune, weed, and trim. She carried bouquets of agapanthus into the house and arranged the blue and white blossoms in her mother's good Waterford vases. She scattered lavender in the parlor, revived by the pungent smell it emitted. Gardening and flower arranging also brought her comfort. "I can do this," she kept telling herself.

Ellen was encouraged by this industry on her daughter's part, but she knew it would be a long time before Mary Kay's grieving would end. Mary Kay had always been a talker, and she had an opinion on all activities around her. But not now! Although she was up and about and doing, she was silent. She offered no comments and responded lethargically to questions put forth by others. She did not engage in informal conversation, not even with her children. Tristan was used to her prattling on about everyday matters, so he was confused by this quiet mother who did not tease him or sing to him.

Nick had returned to Virginia City shortly after his brother's funeral. He had jobs to complete there and could not renege on his work commitments. He had hated to leave both Mary Kay and his mother who were grieving, but he was equally reluctant to stay at home where every room reminded him of Ed. Nick too was in pain. Before he left, he hugged Tristan and told him he would one day come back for him. In the meantime, Tristan was to take care of his mother and baby sister. Tristan had nodded solemnly and had agreed to do as his Uncle Nick asked.

Ellen realized that Mary Kay was depressed. This depression continued for some months. Ellen had expected Mary Kay to gradually come out of her shell and embrace life again. When she did not, Ellen decided a change of scenery was in order. She arranged for Ed's mother, Rose, to care for the children, packed Mary Kay on to the train, and they headed for Oakland to visit a dear friend, Ina Coolbrith.

Ina had always been literary; she wrote poems and had some of her work published. Her first poem was published when she was just eleven years old. Sixty years hence, she would become California's first Poet Laureate, but that was years in the future and not even a dream yet.

Ellen and Mary Kay had visited Ina once before, in San Francisco— three months before Mary Kay's wedding. They had traveled to the city to buy Mary Kay's wedding dress and had stayed with Ina. Although Ina had worked as an English teacher then, she still made time to socialize. She had many friends who gathered at her home for stimulating discussions. San Francisco, a fine-arts Mecca for the educated and cultured, attracted talent from afar. Ina considered Ellen and Mary Kay to be her kindred souls. She had known them for years, and many a cup of tea had been shared while they discussed books.

Sometimes, Josephine Clifford had joined them. She was a cherished friend of Ina's who worked on *The Overland Monthly* as the secretary. Ina and her friend Brett Harte published the paper and depended on Josephine who had both common sense and a good listening ear. Josephine liked to visit with "The Girls," as she called Ina's friends from Grass Valley. San Francisco had been quite the experience for Mary Kay, who as a young woman had enjoyed meeting such charming people.

Now, six years later, Ina lived in Oakland and worked at the library there. She would work there for many years and even mentor young Jack London, but when Ellen and Mary Kay came to visit, she was new at the job. Ina was grateful to have this good job even though it paid little.

"Goodness knows, I am the breadwinner of the family what with both mother and my sister in poor health. I also have my niece and nephew living with me. No, the library salary isn't much, but it is sufficient. And look at all the interesting people I shall meet! "

Mary Kay was impressed that Ina knew Samuel Clemens, who had taken the pen name of Mark Twain. "Í like his story about the frog," she told Ina. "Twain has quite the imagination."

"Remember, that tale is based on a true story. Twain heard it from an old prospector up in Calaveras County." Ina told her. "A Nevada newsman, Jim Townsend, also contributes ideas that both Mark and Brett use."

Ellen spoke up. "Twain's book *The Innocents Abroad* will always be my favorite. I like Twain's subtle sense of humor, and yet he is still able to get his point across. Twain can make historical events look absurd, and he is no kinder to religion. He makes the Church look positively greedy and uncaring of the poor."

"Twain reminds me of Dickens in that he points out the ills of society," Mary Kay added.

Ina told Ellen and Mary Kay her latest news of Twain. "Mark is working on a new book. It's a story of a mischievous young boy who lives in Hannibal, Missouri along the Mississippi River. That's all I know, but I look forward to reading it."

Now In Oakland, Ellen had booked herself and her daughter into a hotel. Ina's new home was filled with family members, both young and old, and Ellen would not consider inconveniencing them. While Ina worked long hours at the library, Ellen and Mary Kay shopped, read, and strolled in a nearby park. The sunshine rejuvenated Mary Kay.

They went to Ina's in the evenings and on Sundays when the library was closed. Ina had hired a cook, and Ellen and Mary Kay were invited to dinner every evening. They were both talented bakers, and the cook graciously allowed them in her kitchen to make tasty desserts for the family. After dinner, Ina's many friends would join them, and their times together were lively. Ina's new friends enthusiastically embraced Ina's Grass Valley friends, and new bonds were formed. These new companions knew that Mary Kay was a recent widow, and so they showed her every kindness— with one exception. When it came to cardplaying, consideration did not show its pretty head. Whist was the favorite game.

"Cutthroat," someone would exclaim as money exchanged hands. Laughter prevailed and good-natured shouting could be heard. Some partnerships lasted. Others did not. Often, two or three card tables filled Ina's front parlor, and games went on all evening.

At other times, guests put on their best manners and came for book discussions. Leo Tolstoy, the Russian novelist, was a favorite author. Ina's book club had read *War and Peace* and had picked it apart, discussing both the spirituality of the characters and the family relationships. They had enjoyed learning about Russian society as it struggled against Napoleon's army. Russia was on their minds, and since Alaska had recently been purchased from the Russians, that topic always evoked lively talk. Ambrose Bierce called the Alaskan Purchase, "An unfortunate decision."

Joaquin Miller asked, "What was William Seward thinking?" and a heated debate followed. Some considered Alaska a vast wasteland. Others thought perhaps it would provide resources such as lumber to the nation. Those with a political bent suggested that its residents could as least be taxed. Everyone had an opinion.

After the guests departed each evening, Ina, Ellen, and Mary Kay would kick off their shoes and meet for one more cup of tea in the kitchen. Even though Ina had an early morning the next day, she needed this quiet time alone with her old friends. Now the talk was more intimate, and she was able to share her troubles. She was particularly worried about her sister who was seriously ill. The doctors were not encouraging.

Ina talked of her mother, Agnes, and what an interesting life she had led. She had married Don Carlos Smith, the brother of Joseph Smith, the Mormon leader. Carlos died of malaria only four months after Ina was born. Ina's mother, now a widow, had been expected to marry Carlos's brother, and she did so, becoming Joseph Smith's seventh wife.

"So, was your last name really Smith when you were born?" Mary Kay asked.

"Yes. My real name was Josephina Smith. Ina is a shortened version of Josephina. We were Latter Day Saints, Mormons. My mother had been married to my Uncle Joseph Smith for a couple of years when he was murdered by an anti-polygamist group in Illinois, where we lived."

"How terrible for your family!" Mary Kay had exclaimed.

Ina had told Ellen this story years before, so Ellen sat quietly now as Ina recounted her early life to Mary Kay. Most people did not know Ina's connection to the Mormon group, and Ina preferred it that way.

"I thought Joseph Smith claimed to have only one wife," Mary Kay said.

"Yes, that was his claim. He was legally married to Emma Hale, but he had several wives who were his 'spiritual' or 'religious' wives. He certainly did not publicize those. My mother was a widow for only five months when she was wed to Uncle Joseph. She said Brigham Young, the present leader, attended their wedding ceremony."

"Was your mother always a Mormon?" Mary Kay asked.

"No. She joined the church in Boston when she was in her early twenties. She met and married Carlos, my father, in Ohio. After Uncle Joseph was shot, she gave up the Mormon religion, changed her name back to her maiden name, Coolbrith, and moved to St. Louis."

"How did you end up in California?"

"In St. Louis, my mother married again. This time to a printer named William Pickett. They soon had twin sons, and when I was ten years old, we all moved to California. Have you ever heard of a man named Jim Beckwourth?"

"Yes," Mary Kay replied, "he was the renowned mountain man."

"Indeed, he was. He led our wagon train across the mountains, and I sometimes rode on his horse with him. There is a pass in the Sierra Nevada Range named for him."

"You certainly have met some famous people," Ellen mused.

"I have. Fortune has been good to me. I will add one more name to the list. My family settled first in Los Angeles. When I was still a child, I met Pio Pico, the last Mexican governor of California. I danced with him."

"You should write a book describing all the people you have known," Ellen suggested.

"No, I think I will stick with poetry. I enjoy writing that. Besides, I don't have time to write much of anything presently. Now, let me tell you about this braggart who came into the library today." And with that, Ina changed the conversation from assassination and multiple wives to that of foolish men and their foibles. Soon, all three ladies were trying to hold down their laughter as they wiped their eyes with their hankies. Sometimes, late-night chats were just what the doctor ordered. Ina couldn't help her ailing sister, but she knew to take care of herself.

It was in this friendly atmosphere that Mary Kay finally perked up. She enjoyed playing cards and had played since she was a child. She joined in the literary discussions. Gradually, some of the chatter and laughter were hers. When the month-long vacation ended, Ellen was pleased with the change in her daughter.

And then it was time to board the train and return home to the children. Both Ellen and Mary Kay were sad to leave Ina whose sister was so ill. Also, Ellen was reluctant to withdraw her daughter from the stimulating company that had benefitted her. But Mary Kay missed her children, so it was time to go. They hugged Ina and told her they would continue to pray for her family, and then they were gone.

When they arrived in Grass Valley, Nick was there waiting for them. He had an idea to tell to Mary Kay.

"Have you ever heard of a place called Bodie?" he asked.

CHAPTER 3

No, Mary Kay had not heard of Bodie because she had been consumed by other matters, namely learning to live life without Ed. She was to learn about Bodie; however, because Nick was eager to tell her all he knew.

"A fellow named William Bodey traveled from New York to the gold fields. He found gold in '59, but a brutal blizzard then cost him his life. In the early '60s, a mining district was formed there in his name, and several mines began operating. No one found enough gold to make it worthwhile though, and by '68 there were only a couple of dozen miners who stayed on.

"Besides the miners who remained, there was a Negro named William O'Hara who operated the boarding house for the Empire Company and acted as watchman there. He actually owned a mine for a while because of debts owed him, but he didn't want it and eventually sold it to miners Lockberg and Essington. They owned the mine when it caved in, exposing a treasure in gold. Word got out, and that began the rush to Bodie! Fortunately, I had already bought my property there when the cave-in occurred.

"The old timer who first advised me to check out Bodie also told me to look O'Hara up when I got there, and I am glad I did. He is a good friend of mine now. He is an exceptional man and a fine cook. He and his wife Charlotte owned a successful restaurant in California before she died. I hear that she was the best of women in that she went out of her way to help others. O'Hara is so well liked in town that people call him Uncle Billy. I call him that too. He has been in Bodie longer than almost anyone. I will be happy to introduce him to you, and maybe you and he can swap recipes."

"Are there any women in town?"

"Oh, sure. You will like Marietta Horner. She and her husband Rodger have been there since '67. In fact, their son Daniel was the first baby born in Bodie. I think he is Tristan's age. I will introduce you to Ben Butler too. He and his brother are the town blacksmiths. Marietta is their sister."

"Any other women?"

"Marietta has a sister there, Elizabeth Ann. She is married to Robert Kernohan, a miner. The Butlers, Horners, and Kernohans are all prominent families there, and they are all related by marriage."

"Any other women?" Mary Kay asked.

Nick was not about to mention the Ladies down on Bonanza Street. Instead, he said, "Sure, but I don't know everyone. You will like Marietta. Like you, she is an expert seamstress. She has a sewing machine that is the envy of the Indian women around there. They think it has magical powers."

Mary Kay could see how earnestly Nick wanted her to like Bodie. He was her best friend, and she knew he had only her best interests at heart. And so, she and her children had moved to Bodie with Nick. Although both had families in Grass Valley, neither wanted to live there where every place and every person reminded them of Ed.

Here in Bodie, Nick had built Mary Kay a boarding house; his finest work, he claimed. He had bought four lots that day when he shopped for real estate after talking with the old miner. Two lots were in the southern part of town and adjoined each other. The boarding house now sat on one. Nick had begun construction on another large house next to it. His carpentry shop sat on a side street near the center of town. On the fourth lot, he had built a store on Main Street and had it rented to a tin smith. It was to the boarding house that Nick had sent his young friend Jodie. And now Nick was on his way to do the errand he had mentioned to Susanne on the stagecoach earlier that afternoon.

It wasn't to a brothel that Nick went but to a saloon around the corner from it. From there he sent word that he wanted one of the ladies to meet him as soon as possible. Nick was finishing a beer and exchanging gossip with Sully, the bartender, when Tess came in. Nick gave her a peck on the cheek, ordered her a sarsaparilla, and moved with her to a table, so they could talk undisturbed.

"Where's Annabelle?" he asked.

"Sophie is watching her. What's going on?"

"I just returned from San Diego and had a traveling companion all the way. It was your nephew, Jodie."

Tears formed in Tess's eye. "My God, Jodie is here? I thought I had more time."

"More time? So, you were expecting him?"

Tess pulled an envelope from her pocket and handed it to Nick. "This came in the mail yesterday, but I didn't think Jodie was coming yet. I was trying to figure out what to do. I can't have him here. You know that."

Nick opened the envelope, extracted the letter, and slowly read it.

April 7, 1878

My Sweet Sister Theresa,

It is with a heavy heart that I pick up my pen to write to you today. I just returned from seeing Doctor Murray. You were right to urge me to go. My nagging cough has not stopped, and the doctor informed me that I have consumption— a severe case. He insists that I go away for some months to a sanitarium where I can get fresh air, nourishing food, and proper medication. Otherwise, he says I won't recover. He also wants me to stay away from Jodie, so Jodie won't get this disease. Frankly, I'm surprised he isn't sick already. The doctor has arranged for me to leave on Saturday. I am sorry to impose, Tess, but I feel I must send Jodie to you in Bodie. I have no one else to keep him. My neighbors are decent, kind people, but I can't expect them to care for my son for months. As you know, I have no idea where my wanderlust of a husband is. It's been nearly a year since he went off to find his fortune, so I can't send Jodie to him. I'm sorry not to give you more notice of Jodie's arrival. I will put him on the stage this week. He is a smart boy and will be able to find you easily, I am sure. You should know though that he does not want to leave San Diego. He expects his dad to come home, and he doesn't want to miss him. I have tried to talk with him about the reality of the situation, but he is stubborn. I do hope he can be of help to you and little Annabelle. I will write again when I know more and know the address of the hospital. Thank you in advance for your generous heart.

Your loving sister, Jeannie

Nick folded the letter and shook his head. "You certainly are in a pickle," he said. "Obviously, your sister doesn't know your circumstances, or she wouldn't send her boy to you."

"Obviously," Tess said dryly.

"Well, she knew where to find you. What occupation does she think you have?"

"Seamstress."

Nick laughed. "Can you sew?"

"Actually, I can. Mother taught both Jeannie and me, and we sew expertly. I can do accounting as well."

Nick looked Tess in the eye. "Then what in the hell are you doing working for Sophie?"

Tess looked back at him. "You know my story. When I ended up here in Bodie, I had no money and no friends. I had a newborn daughter who needed to be fed every day. Sophie took us in and has been very good to both of us. I couldn't have made it without her help. So, don't you judge me, Nick!"

"I'm sorry, Tess. I get it. I'm not judging you. And I understand your loyalty to Sophie. But by God, she's a businesswoman. She runs a successful brothel, but you don't have to work for her forever."

"I don't intend to. But until I pay Sophie the money I owe her and have money to pay rent somewhere, I'm stuck there. I need to get out before Annabelle is old enough to know about such things. But back to my immediate problem, where is Jodie now?"

"I sent him up to the Manor with instructions for Mary Kay to feed him and find him a bed for the night."

"What's Jodie like, Nick? I haven't seen him in years, and he's already eleven years old."

Nick chuckled. "Talkative little bugger. Chattered away all the way from San Diego. Got on the nerves of one of the passengers. But not Susanne. You remember my telling you about Susanne? She's a good friend of Mary Kay's, and of mine as well. She was also on the stage and helped Jodie pass the time. It was a long trip for a little boy."

"He didn't get on your nerves?"

"Nah, I like kids."

"I know you do. And they like you. Annabelle adores you."

"Yeah, yeah. I'll tell you what. I'll keep Jodie with me at the Manor until you can get your life in order. But it can't be for long. Mary Kay has her hands full already. She has three boarders besides her kids and me."

"I understand."

"Tess, why don't you just let me pay off your debt? I will gladly do that for you. You know I have offered before."

"Not a good idea, Nick. I don't want to owe anyone anything, not even you. It would change things between us, and I don't want to ruin this friendship we have. But thank you again for the offer."

Nick was disappointed, but he nodded. He understood.

"What will you tell Jodie?" Tess asked now.

"I told him I thought you and Annabelle had gone to visit friends and wouldn't be back here for a while. I will tell him we don't know when to expect you back. In the meantime, he is to stay with me."

"You're a good friend, Nick."

"Yeah, yeah, I know. But see what you can do to get away from Sophie."

"I will. But I can't get out yet. The good thing is that if I run into Jodie on the street, he won't recognize me, won't realize I am his aunt."

"True. But you must be careful not to run in to him because if he sees Annabelle, he'll know. How do you think I figured it out?

Jodie kept talking about his cousin Annabelle. I don't know another four-year-old here in Bodie named Annabelle."

"How long do you think Jodie will be here?"

"I don't know, but months I imagine. Tuberculous doesn't have a quick fix."

"I'll pay for his food."

"No, you won't. Get your debt paid off, so you can find another place to live. You can always take in sewing from your home; you won't need to pay rent in a shop."

Tess sighed. "No, but I will need sewing supplies."

"Yeah, yeah, I know. We'll figure it out."

"Thanks, Nick, for everything." Tess stood up. She squeezed his shoulder, and then she was gone.

* * * * * * * * * *

Nick watched Tess leave and knew he also had to get going. But he sat there looking at the chair she had vacated. Lost in thought, he was reminded of the first time he had met her. He had not known where she worked when he stood behind her in line at the butcher shop. Annabelle had not been with her that morning four years ago. Tess was alone and had smiled shyly at him when he spoke to her. He thought she might be the prettiest girl he had ever seen, and he was just coming from Virginia City where beautiful women were in abundance.

Nick was a talker. It was almost as though he could not stand a quiet room and needed to fill the space with words, no matter how insipid. So, he used his words and at times accompanied them with sweeping gestures and animated motions. At the butcher shop that morning, he talked with everyone including the petite Spanish woman who stood in front of Tess in line.

"Que Paso, Senorita. Coma esta?" The woman bestowed a huge smile on him. And then she rattled off a chain of sentences that Nick, with his rudimentary knowledge of Spanish, could not understand. He smiled at her and held up his hands in surrender.

"Poquito! Poquito! I speak very little Spanish and do not understand what you said. I am sorry. Spanish certainly is a beautiful language but *no comprende!"*

She laughed delightedly, and they were compadres. She spoke English to him as they chatted in line, and she nodded to him and smiled as she walked away a few minutes later, package in hand. Weeks later, Nick would build a backbar for her saloon-owning husband. She had put in a good word on his behalf. Her husband later recommended Nick to his friends, and so Nick's business flourished.

Nick also spoke to the miners who had lined up behind him. Nick's cheerful demeanor drew people to him. On that dull Monday morning, with the long week stretching out before them, the townspeople liked Bodie's newest citizen. They found him to be entertaining, and each secretly hoped he might run in to him again. Nick made several friends that morning at the butcher shop including the butcher himself. Tess was one of his new friends. He did not know her story then or that she had a young daughter who would soon capture his heart. He was new to Bodie, had been there only long enough to rent a room and go in search of groceries.

When Nick had first arrived in Bodie, he had seen how inhospitable the land was. Set in the Sierra Nevada Mountain Range at an elevation of over 8,000 feet, Bodie lay above the tree line. So, the Bodie Hills sported no trees and few blades of green grass. Tuffs of dry brush clung to the ground between the volcanic rock. Sage was prevalent. Sometimes, when the fierce winds blew, the sagebrush would whirl through the air at a great speed. Why, Nick wondered, were all mining camps located in such desolate terrain? Virginia City had looked much the same.

Nick had grown up in Northern California where the trees grew tall and lush and smelled of pine and cedar. Colors changed there, and residents were assured that the winters would see snow. Snow would certainly fall here in Bodie as well, but as Fred Bechtel, the postmaster, would later tell him,

"Snow, yes! — Many feet of incapacitating snow! Followed by slush and mud and dirt and grime."

So, it wasn't the physical charms that lured men and women here to Bodie. They came for the gold. They stayed, hoping for great wealth from one of the thirty mines in operation. Miners believed that if they stayed just one more day, endured the rigors of the mine for just one more shift, then all would work out. That was the promise of America. One worked hard and was rewarded. And so, the miners stayed. They endured multiple hardships and backbreaking work. A miner who went deep underground sometimes did not emerge again, or if he did, he was never the same physically or emotionally. Mining accidents resulted in broken bones, severed limbs, or premature death. Winter weather saw frostbitten ears and noses. But people worked on, and some were indeed rewarded as they struck paydirt. When the riches died out, they moved on. Always, news came of another strike, another bonanza, another dream.

The first to arrive at the mines, almost as soon as the prospectors themselves, were the support groups: the merchants with their high-priced goods; the laundresses; and of course, the Ladies. These groups followed both soldiers and miners because they filled a need.

Nick's thoughts often wandered to the people who occupied such places as Bodie. He and his pals Casey and Lex sometimes discussed philosophical topics as they nursed their brews after work.

"I just find it interesting that people from so many different places and backgrounds all converge on a single place at the same time," Nick would speculate.

"Yeah, people who would never have known each other otherwise," Lex agreed.

Nick nodded. "Exactly. They would never have met, and yet, some become lifelong friends."

"Or worst enemies," Casey pointed out.

"Yeah, that too. Some even marry each other, and children are born who never would have otherwise come into this world."

"There are so many men out here in the West," Lex added. "Because they're lonely, they are attracted to women they never would have looked at back home."

"And vice versa," Nick said. "The War Between the States left so many widows. If the ladies want to marry again, sometimes they have to settle for men they would never have considered before."

Casey looked down at his beer. "Some men and women hurt each other in irreparable ways and then simply move on." His thoughts went back to another time, another place.

Nick looked at his friends. "I am intrigued because I don't find any of this to be random."

"What do you mean?"

"That people from so many places all happen to be here at the same time seems random, but instinctively, I know there is a design to it. That we were meant to be here. Hell, you know I am not religious, but I can't help but think there is a divine hand at work here,"

"It sounds like you have given this some thought," Lex said.

"Yeah, yeah, I have," Nick told him. " I love it here in Bodie. When I first got here, it felt like I was coming home. This place energizes me. It gives me hope somehow."

"How long do you think you'll stay?" Casey wanted to know.

"No telling," Nick said. "You know I came here thinking I'd do something to help Mary Kay. Build her a boarding house maybe—anything to get her out of her depression! She was so happy with Ed. I wish you both could have known him. He was such a great guy. Not a day goes by that I don't miss him."

"You're not so bad yourself," Casey told him. "Perhaps someday, when Mary Kay has had enough time to grieve, she'll turn to you."

"Nah, not happening. We've been best friends since we were kids, so we definitely aren't thinking about romance."

"Do you reckon she would consider me then?" Lex asked. "I think she's pretty cute with her long red hair and all."

"Her red hair and her fiery temper! But she sure can cook. You could do worse."

"Not much of an endorsement, but I'll take it." Lex grinned. "Let me know if you think she will ever allow another man in her life, will you? I would treat her right, Nick."

Nick grinned back at his good friend. God, how he loved Bodie and everyone in it. Sure, it was the gold that lured people here. But it wasn't about the gold; it was the people who mattered. It was they who panned the rivers, built the mine shafts, and assayed the nuggets. It was the people who had tales to tell afterwards. Unlike the gold, which was fleeting, the stories remained. They became legend and part of family lore. Everyone had a story to tell, and Nick wanted to hear them all. He had enjoyed Virginia City but had truly lost his heart to this wind-swept mining town. He considered Bodie his town, and he did his best to bring joy to it.

Nick shook himself out of his reverie. Time to go home. He had committed himself to a young boy, and he needed to get home and take charge. He thought of Mary Kay. It was a good thing she liked children since he had neglected to ask her if she wanted another one, although temporarily.

CHAPTER 4

No one played cards at the boarding house on Sunday evenings. Mary Kay was too religious to allow games or anything else except singing on a Sunday. But the rest of the week was fair game. On Tuesday evenings, whist began right after supper. Nick partnered with Mary Kay, while Wiley and Thornton played as a team. These two older men were mining engineers who had been college room- mates and had remained close friends. They had boarded with Mary Kay for two years and were now considered part of the family. Both whist partnerships were evenly matched, and so neither pair could claim victory too often. But this was a competitive game, and brag- ging rights were involved. A ledger was kept to record the wins and losses. So, Tuesday was Whist Night.

On Fridays, Susanne joined them, and the five of them played another trump-playing game called Back Alley. This time, they played without partners. If Coosie was available, he often played too. Bids were made or lost, and money regularly traded pockets. Of all the players, Mary Kay was the most serious. She delighted in triumphing over these men in her life. The fellows would never have deliberately thrown the game in her favor; she would have been insulted if they had. But she did not need their help because she played both skillfully and strategically. A deuce prize was part of the game, and Mary Kay often pocketed that too.

Mary Kay's religion discouraged card playing. Mary Kay agreed that public gambling at the saloons was sinful, and she was grateful that Nick had no interest in it. It was bad enough that he drank alcoholic drinks, another vice frowned on by the Methodist Church. However, she could not believe that card playing at home threatened her moral or spiritual life. It was her main form of entertainment after a heavy day's work. She had the money, so that was not a consideration. If she lost on Friday, she probably regained the money the following week. So, in her mind, card playing was not an evil.

But Sundays were off limits for card playing. Sunday was the day of worship. Mary Kay had two young children to raise, and she had every intention of teaching them the love of God and His Ten Commandments. Children also needed to learn scripture. Sometimes, she missed Virginia City. When she allowed herself the pain of recalling her married life there, she also remembered the church that had been the center of her life. Virginia City had boasted a healthy community of Methodists who had enjoyed worshipping together on Sunday mornings and studying the Bible together on other days of the week.

Mary Kay came from a long line of Methodists. Her family in Grass Valley were devout churchgoers. John Westley and his tenets influenced their decisions. Both faith and good- works were emphasized, and so Mary Kay believed in community service and could often be seen helping others in Bodie less fortunate than she. She missed having a church though— something Bodie did not have. A shopkeeper had once explained it to her.

"Bodie is a community of men, not of families. These miners get one day off a week, and they don't want to spend Sunday morning anywhere but sleeping off Saturday night's excesses. No, you won't find a church here in Bodie."

Mary Kay had been distressed about this lack of religious commitment when she had first settled here, but eventually she found other like-minded women, and they organized Sunday services in their homes. They also met at the Odd Fellows Hall. Finally, they were blessed to have Reverend Hinkle, a circuit-riding preacher, assigned to Bodie. George Hinkle, a quiet, scholarly man, arranged for services in the new Miner's Union Hall. Somehow, the Catholics managed to obtain the better time slot on Sunday mornings for their masses. So, the Methodists gathered together on Sunday afternoons to worship. Mary Kay and her children attended regularly.

Nick had not attended religious services in Virginia City, but after Ed's death, he had turned completely away from the church. He did not understand a God who could so blithely take away his brother, a young family man in his prime. Nick wanted nothing to do with religion. He was quite willing to help Mary Kay raise her children, but their religious training was not part of the deal. So, Mary Kay guided her children to the Miner's Union Hall alone every Sunday to listen to Reverend Hinkle deliver his weekly sermon. Afterwards, she walked home feeling rejuvenated. This also was a chance to visit for a few minutes with the other women who attended the service. Mary Kay enjoyed this social aspect as well. The women chatted while the young children chased each other playing tag.

"Don't get dirty. Don't ruin your Sunday clothes," the mothers would perfunctorily call to their offspring as they ran by. The husbands also formed groups and talked of mining and stock trades. Mary Kay loved it all. Sundays were important to her.

Mary Kay served dinner to her family and boarders at noon on Sundays before she went to the religious service. Usually, she roasted beef or pork. Sometimes, she fried chicken. Always, she served their favorite pies. Wiley and Thornton cleaned up the kitchen for her while she was gone. They emptied the ash from the cast iron stove, brought in firewood, and prepared the kitchen for the coming week. They were paying customers, to be sure, but they liked Mary Kay and appreciated her many thoughtful gestures toward them. They felt like honorary uncles to her children and enjoyed helping her. At the Manor, Sundays were sacred— a time for worship and a time for family. No games of any sort were allowed. Certainly, no one played cards on Sunday evenings.

So, when Nick mounted the steps to the boarding house this Sunday evening after talking with Tess, all was quiet. Wiley and Thornton sat in the parlor, each reading a book. Susanne sat at the kitchen table waiting for him. Mary Kay stood at the window, looking out but seeing nothing, lost in her thoughts. Supper had been put on the back burner, and Jodie was nowhere to be seen.

"I suppose you've been at Wagner's Saloon, 'Wetting your whistle.' Isn't that what you call it?" Mary Kay was in a temper.

"No, I wasn't at Wagner's. I had an errand. Didn't Susanne tell you?"

Mary Kay scowled at Nick. "So, we'll be taking in young boarders now, is it?"

Nick was unprepared for this hostility. He couldn't imagine where Jodie was or why Mary Kay was so angry. He set his bag down and turned to her.

"What's happened?"

"Disrespectful, he was. Came in, took one look at me and laughed in my face. Then he said, 'I know a secret about you. You snore."

Susanne spoke up, "I hadn't yet had a chance to introduce Jodie."

"Then he said that I must be Cindy. He thought I was a dog!" Mary Kay spit the words at Nick.

"Ah, there's been a great misunderstanding here. I made a joke in the coach about Cindy. I'm sure the boy meant no harm. He just didn't know your name, that's all."

"I know he doesn't actually think I'm a dog," she snapped. "It was his discourtesy. I don't think he respects women, or he wouldn't have spoken so. I don't like him, and I don't like his attitude. I put him in the guest room and told him to stay put until you got here."

Nick picked up his bag. "I'll take care of it," he said.

He took the stairs two steps at a time. He opened the bedroom door and to his surprise found Jodie fast asleep with Cindy curled up next to him. Cindy thumped her tail when she saw him but did not get up. Nick left them there and went into the dining room. The others were just sitting down to eat, and Nick joined them. "It smells delicious. Thanks for waiting for me." During supper, Nick filled Mary Kay and the two boarders in about Jodie's predicament. Susanne chimed in once to clarify a point Nick was making. Mary Kay listened without comment until he finished. Then she asked, "Did you find his aunt? Was that your errand?"

Nick felt uncomfortable having to lie to her, but he certainly couldn't tell her that Jodie's aunt lived in a house of prostitution. He was too much of a gentleman to even consider such a conversation with Mary Kay and Susanne in the room. So, he repeated the story he had spun earlier about the aunt and cousin leaving town. Aunt Tess was expected back, but no one knew when.

"So, Mary Kay, you'll agree that the lad has nowhere to go." Nick grinned now. "And you being such a good, upright Christian woman; you certainly can't throw him out on the street. You are much too soft hearted for that. I'll take charge of him. You won't have to do a thing."

"I don't care for the boy, and I don't care for his attitude. I understand the joke about the dog. That's not it. It was the disrespect that offended me," Mary Kay said.

"Yeah, yeah. I know, and I get it. Jodie could be impertinent on the coach too, but in all fairness, I probably encouraged him. We bantered back and forth the entire trip, and he probably thought it was okay to be flip here too. I'll set boundaries with him. Now, to the point: I'm certain the aunt wouldn't have gone had she known her sister was sick and the boy was coming to Bodie. Can't you see the sadness in this situation? I'll make every effort to locate the aunt. What do you say? May he stay with us?"

And so, because Nick never asked her for anything, and because she could see the boy's predicament, Mary Kay reluctantly agreed to give Jodie a home for a while. "Not forever, mind you, just for a while."

* * * * * * * * * *

Later that evening, Nick sat alone at the kitchen table working on his business accounts. He knew how fortunate he was to work in a mining town and not ever have to go down into the mines. He often thanked his dad for teaching him the many carpentry skills he knew and used daily. As a carpenter, he made a good living and did it all above ground. He was friends with many miners and never knew if he would see them again when their shifts were over. So many things could go wrong in a mine.

Of all the dangers down in the mine shafts, fire was the most feared. Miners worried they would burn to death or die of asphyxiation. Sometimes a miner would suffocate from the poisonous fumes of the blasting powder. The expression "Fire in the Hole" was a warning to take cover; blasting was to begin. When an object unexpectedly fell down the shaft, miners knew to cover their heads, or to duck into a hole to get out of the way. Sometimes it was the men who fell. A miner, fatigued or absorbed in his work, would forget where he was, step back off a ledge, and fall hundreds of feet to his death. Miners who escaped accidents were always susceptible to pneumonia or silicosis from breathing the ore dust in the warm mines. Miners were considered worn out and old by age thirty-five.

Many miners were frustrated by the dangerous working conditions. They felt they took all the chances while the capitalists sat in board rooms and raked in fortunes by the miners' labor. Many were willing to strike for higher pay or better working conditions. The Miner's Union did what it could for the men. However, mining was often the only occupation a man knew, and if he quit, a number of others were in line ready to take his place. Miners continued to pour into Bodie despite the danger and harsh working conditions. Nick was happy he was not one of them.

Jodie poked his head in the kitchen and smiled. Nick closed his ledger and smiled back. Cindy skidded into the room and began running in circles around the table and then jumping up on Nick.

"You fool dog, I missed you too." Nick leaned down and gave his dog a hug.

"Feeling better?" he asked Jodie.

"I didn't know I was so tired."

"Are you hungry? I saved you some dinner."

"Famished."

Nick heated up the pot roast, poured the boy a glass of milk, and then sat down to watch him eat. Jodie thanked Nick when he finished.

"What are your plans?" Nick asked.

"What do you mean? You told me I could stay here."

"Yes, I did. For tonight. Where will you go tomorrow?"

The smile left Jodie's face. "I hoped to stay here. Unless you found my aunt?"

"No, I didn't find her. Why would you think you would be welcome to stay here after the rude way you treated my sister-in-law?"

"I was only kidding."

"Is that what you call it? You will find that Mary Kay is one of the best people on God's earth. She works hard to keep this place running. We have three boarders whom she cooks for and cleans up after. You disrespected her. What were you thinking?"

"Aren't women supposed to cook and clean? Isn't that their job? And besides, I told you I was just kidding."

"You are a young boy. You do not get to talk disrespectfully to women. In fact, you will not talk in a hurtful manner to anyone. Certainly, you do not speak like that to your mother, do you?"

"She doesn't mind."

"What do you mean?"

"My dad always talked to her like that. She never said anything, so I knew she didn't care."

Nick sighed. "You would be surprised. Just because someone doesn't protest means nothing. Look, I'm disappointed in you. I brought you here into my own home. My sanctuary. And this is how you treat the people who are most important to me! This is a warm, caring home where we all look out for each other, and we are willing to look out for you. But not if you act like you did this afternoon. Do you hear me? I hope you're paying attention, damn it! I love Mary Kay. She's been through a lot. She is a sister to me, and I won't allow you to mistreat her. Do you understand? "

Jodie nodded. "I didn't know she was your sister. I thought she was your wife."

"Wife! I don't have a wife. What in the hell would I do with a wife?"

"I just thought you said your wife snored . . . " Jodie's voice trailed off.

Nick looked at him for a long moment. Then he said, "You won't treat anyone disrespectfully: not a relative, not the Queen of England, not the hired help."

"Really? Not even the hired help?"

Nick wanted to wring his neck. He didn't think he was getting through to the boy. Was Jodie obstinate or did he really not get it? "You still don't understand. If she had been the hired help, I would have expected you to treat her even more kindly."

Jodie paused before replying. "Okay, Nick, but in my defense, I didn't know. The men I know in San Diego don't usually talk decently to their wives or lady friends. Or to each other for that matter."

Nick looked at him steadily. "Don't be that man."

"Man?"

"The man whom women fear and talk about with loathing when they're alone together. Don't be that man. Instead, help women."

Jodie looked Nick in the eye and then nodded. "Okay, I'll try, Nick. Can I stay?"

"Yes, you may stay here, but clean up your attitude."

Jodie nodded.

"Okay, now go to bed. You will go to work with me tomorrow, and we'll have an early start."

CHAPTER 5

Sometimes, Nick forgot to be polite. He could be short tempered when frustrated and was too practical to always be patient. And yet, people liked him. They liked his gregarious nature, and his willingness to put other people's needs in front of his own. They liked that he was pragmatic and always measured twice. Friends and acquaintances alike appreciated his ability to speak directly and get to the point. He did not always soften bad news.

He knew how to make tough decisions. His brother Ed had taught him to view both the pros and the cons of major decisions and then make up his mind and stick to it. No looking back and wondering, "What if?" Ed had told him that with every decision, man chooses a path. With that path, he eliminates all other paths and the futures those paths might have held for him. Nick took his brother's advice and knew that decisions have consequences. Ed had also cautioned him not to make decisions by indecision. He was to step up and make his own decisions, or someone would certainly do it for him. Nick sighed when he thought of Ed. Not a day went by that he didn't miss him. Nick had three other brothers and a good relationship with each of them but not the closeness he and Ed had shared.

Ed had also taught Nick the value of keeping his word. "You don't have to promise anyone anything," he had advised, "but the minute you take on that commitment, you must adhere to it. A promise is a contract. So, it's better not to commit to it in the first place if you haven't thought it through."

Nick was thinking about this as he and Jodie walked to Nick's carpentry shop the next morning. Nick had given his word to Tess that he would take care of Jodie until she could do it herself. Nick felt that responsibility now. It could be a while until Tess was in the position to take over Jodie's upbringing. Nick thought about Jodie's mother. He didn't even know her name or where she was. What if the mother never recovered and never sent for the boy? Add to this the fact that Mary Kay did not like the boy and didn't want him around. Nick had a lot to think about.

Jodie did not realize it at the time, but the stars were aligned on the day he met Nick on the stagecoach. Things might have turned out differently for the young boy had Nick not come along. But Fate likes children and often treats them kindly. Jodie certainly wasn't an orphan, but he had no parents looking out for him in his new town.

His dad had left home promising to return as soon as he made a bundle in the mines. He had not made a bundle, nor had he been to the mines. In the meantime, he had not written. Because Jodie had not heard from him, he naturally thought the worst. Jodie tried not to think that his dad was dead somewhere; it was too frightening to even consider. But Jodie had not given up hope. He idolized his dad, and it never occurred to him that his dad had deserted him and his mother and had simply moved on. How could Jodie know that his dad had tired of his responsibilities and had decided his family could count him out? But his mother knew. In her heart, she realized she had married a scoundrel. She hadn't known it at first, but as Billy had grown more discontented and restless, she sensed it. He was not the life companion she thought she had married, the one who had made her promises. Instead, he was the one who had taken her away from her family and then deserted her hundreds of miles from home.

The first time Billy had hit her, they both had been surprised. He blamed it on too many drinks at the bar. But he had done it again. He was frustrated with his job he had told her. She knew this was an excuse.

They had come to a mountain town north of San Diego, so Billy could connect with his best friend. Billy must have misunderstood; however, because the friend had not been happy to see him, and the expected job offer was not forthcoming. After heated words, the friend wanted nothing more to do with him and told him to move along; he was not welcome there. The friend had several cousins who also encouraged Billy to hurry along. So, Billy had moved his family farther south to San Diego where he then tended bar in the new section of town. He worked nights, slept late in the day, and spent little time with his family. Jeannie had wanted to go to work to help pay the bills, but Billy would not hear of it. And then he left.

Jodie had not wanted to go to Bodie when his mother became sick. San Diego was his home now, and he had made friends there. Ian was his best buddy, and they lived next door to each other and attended the same school. Why, Jodie had wondered, couldn't he stay and live with Ian until his dad returned? Jodie had practically invited himself to move in with Ian's family. Ian's mother, Maura O'Hara, had had to tell him no; it wouldn't work. She had too many children already, and with a deadbeat husband, one more mouth to feed was out of the question. Jodie had sulked then and had argued with his mother.

He wasn't a bad boy, but he was selfish as many eleven-year-olds are. He knew his mother needed treatment, but he couldn't leave San Diego and chance missing his dad. What would Dad think if he arrived home to find the house had been rented to someone else? He wouldn't know where the family had gone. Besides, it was baseball season, and Dad had promised to take him to a game this year. So, Jodie couldn't leave. He tried to wear his mother down. Perhaps she could delay treatment. It was the doctor who settled the matter.

"No, young man, your mother will not be delaying anything. Go pack your bag. You are getting on the stage this morning, and I'll be taking you there myself."

Jeannie was relieved. She needed to get well, so she would be there while Jodie grew up. Billy wasn't coming back, so she was the only reliable parent. She did what she considered the responsible thing and sent Jodie to her sister. She had no way of knowing Tess couldn't take him in. So, Jodie was a fortunate boy when Nick crossed his path enroute to Bodie. Jodie just didn't appreciate it at the time.

Nick's carpentry shop, just off Green Street, was not a large place but was sufficient for Nick's work. He had built it himself when he first moved to Bodie. An organized man, Nick kept a tidy shop. Tools were in place, hanging on walls or laid on shelves. His ledger was in order, and his bills were paid. Nick worked diligently and ran a profitable business. He was not only a carpenter but also an all-around handy man. A thin layer of sawdust covered the floor of his shop, and the woody aroma of it wafted through the place. When Nick opened the window, light streamed in and dust particles floated throughout the shop. Once in the shop, Cindy headed for the two large wooden bowls in the corner, one filled with dog food, the other filled with fresh water. Nick took good care of his dog as well as his shop.

Nick and Jodie stayed just long enough for Nick to grab the tools he needed. He had to repair a back porch because he had promised Hal Peterson he would be there as soon as he returned to town. The job would take only a couple of hours. Jodie sat on the

Peterson's steps and watched Nick work, annoyed by the constant thumping of the stamp mills in the background. Cindy sat next to him. She had found a new friend.

"Jodie, after we finish here, we need to go back to town. I'll give you a quick tour, so you will know your way around. But then I need to get back to the shop because I have a load of wood arriving today, and Lee won't leave it if I'm not there to pay him."

"Then what?"

"I'm building a back bar for a new saloon that's opening on Main Street. I'll need to go there and work until supper time. Here's an idea; how about if I leave you at the shop this afternoon? You could wait for the wood delivery, pay the man, and then even put it away for me. I'll show you where to stack it. It would be a great help. Would you mind?"

Jodie shook his head.

"Tomorrow, we'll register you for school."

Jodie liked school and was good at learning, but he hadn't considered going to school while in Bodie. "Can't I stay and work with you instead?" he asked.

"No, school it is! Summer vacation will be here in five weeks. You can work for me then. I'll pay you, so you'll have walking-around money. What do you think?"

Jodie shook his head. "I really can't stay in Bodie, Nick. You've been good to me. I know that. But I have to go home. My dad is going to show up eventually, and he won't know where to find me."

Nick put his hammer down and leaned against the porch rail. "When did you see him last?"

"Dad left in July, right after the Fourth. He took Mom and me to the parade and to the picnic down by the bay. We had a great day.

We were supposed to go to the baseball game too, but Dad changed his mind because he had to pack. He left early the next morning."

"When did you last hear from him?"

"We haven't."

Nick crossed his arms before asking, "Not even at Christmas?"

Jodie looked wistful. "No, not even then. Mom and I both thought he would come home for the holidays. But he didn't come, and we were pretty lonely for sure. That's why I'm worried about him. He wouldn't have missed Christmas if he could help it. Mom hasn't said much. She never talks bad about Dad, but I know she thinks he deserted us. That's what the pastor thinks too. But Dad wouldn't do that. He really is a great guy. You would like him."

"I'm sure I would." Nick smiled at Jodie, but his heart was sad. He too thought it possible that the dad wasn't coming back. After all, he had made no attempt to contact them.

"Tell me about your mother," he said now.

"Her name is Jeannie."

"What's your last name?"

"Burke."

"Go on."

"Well, Mom is just Mom. She cooks and cleans and does all the stuff mothers are supposed to do. She did go to college to become a teacher. Dad didn't go to college because of the war. He never wanted Mom to work. Said he was the breadwinner. Mom did have to get a job after Dad was gone awhile though, so she could pay the bills. She taught school until she got sick. Then the principal sent her home because of her cough."

"Is your mother from San Diego? Were you born there?"

"No, Mom was born in Montana. Me too in a place called Butte. She and my Aunt Tess grew up there. My grandfather owned a bar, and my grandmother cooked and served food there for the Irish miners. Everyone thought she was a terrific cook. I barely remember my grandparents because we moved away when I was only three years old."

Nick picked up his hammer. He didn't want to look at Jodie. He suddenly felt sorry for both Jodie and his mother. "Is your dad from Butte too?" he asked.

"Nah. From the South, but I don't remember which state. Georgia, maybe. He and a buddy went up to Montana after the war. He met my mom at the family bar and married her. After I was born, we moved to a town in California named Julian. We weren't there too long and then moved down to San Diego. But Dad always promised Mom that they would go back to Butte. She always wanted to go home."

"Did you ever go?"

"No, but Dad promised her, so I know we would eventually go back. She desperately wanted to go home, but in the meantime, she got sick."

"It's tuberculosis?"

"Yes. She's pretty sick. I feel bad leaving her alone because she depends on me. Toward the end, all she did was cry. So, you can see why I have to go home."

Nick moved over and sat down next to Jodie. "I understand that you have no relatives in San Diego. Is that right?" he asked.

"Right. No relatives."

Nick smiled at him. "So, you have no one there to stay with?"

"No." Jodie shook his head.

Nick put his arm around the young boy. "So, let's say that you go back to San Diego. You have no one to stay with. Your mother is unavailable. It's also possible that you dad won't or can't return. What do you do then?"

Jodie hung his head. "I'm counting on him coming back."

"Yeah, yeah, I know you are, Lad, but let's reason this out. In San Diego, you have no one to help you. If your mother found out you were there living on the streets, her condition could possibly worsen. She doesn't need that. You dad wouldn't like you being on your own either."

"I don't know what to do. My dad doesn't know where we are."

"Jodie, you have no choice, so why not let me help you? You stay with us, and I will see what I can find out about your dad. I will send inquiries to San Diego. I have friends there."

Jodie nodded. "Okay, I'll stay. But do I have to go to school?"

"Of course, you do. I do not associate with illiterates. Do you know what an illiterate is?"

"Someone who can't read?"

"Exactly. And you need to stay out of trouble. This is how you can help your parents. You have to grow up sometime. This is the time."

CHAPTER 6

Nick and Jodie finished up at Hal Peterson's place and returned to the shop. It was lunchtime, and Jodie was surprised when Nick grabbed a tin pail off the desk and handed it to him. Lunch! It seemed that Nick had thought of everything, and as usual, Jodie was hungry. He thanked Nick.

"Yeah, yeah. You're welcome. Make sure you thank Mary Kay though. She's the one who made this for you."

"Okay. Where's your lunch?"

"No time for lunch today, Lad. I promised to be at Shay's by early afternoon. You should see the bar I'm building. The wood is mahogany and what a beauty it is! I love wood! I love everything about wood. I love the texture of it and the way it smells. Did you know that different woods give off different aromas? You should smell cedar! But I especially like working with mahogany. It has excellent workability because it is hard and durable. And the color is magnificent. Truly magnificent! Its reddish-brown color darkens over time. I love to polish it. Yes, I'm eager to get to work. Repairing a porch is one thing, but getting to actually build things is much more fun."

Jodie looked at Nick. He had never heard a man talk like this about wood or anything else. It was almost poetic. He wasn't sure what his dad would think of Nick but knew he would consider him corny or odd. Jodie couldn't think of the correct word, but he instinctively knew his dad would not like Nick.

Dad was masculine and tough. He was tall and good looking and walked with a swagger. Proud of his former military career, he disparaged those who hadn't fought for the South. He could talk intelligently on a variety of subjects, but Jodie couldn't imagine him ever discussing the characteristics of wood.

Dad could be lively and fun. Jodie had seen that side of him, but after the family had left Julian, his dad's lively spirit had seemed to leave him. Dad brooded and was angry most of the time. Jodie had been careful to maneuver around him, even though Dad didn't seem to know or care that he was in the room. And then his dark mood would lighten and he would acknowledge Jodie's presence. He would be kind to both Jodie and his mother for a while until the broodiness set back in. Although it kept Jodie off kilter, Jodie loved his dad. He liked his new friend, Nick, but Nick was nothing like his dad.

Nick reached in his pocket. "Here is the money to pay for the wood that Lee will deliver this afternoon. Pay him and then stack the wood over here near the back door."

"Okay."

"This is important, Jodie. I'll need the wood for tomorrow. I greatly appreciate the help."

"No problem."

"When you finish putting the wood away, you can go explore the town, go on home, or do whatever you want to do. Just make sure you are home in time for supper with your hands washed and your hair combed. We eat promptly at 6:00 o'clock. Any questions?"

Jodie shook his head. "No, I'll be fine."

"Okay then. I'll see you back at the Manor. Come on, Cindy." And Nick was gone.

After Nick left, Jodie wandered around the shop eating his pasty while he looked at Nick's things. He smiled when he came across an embroidered wall hanging nailed over Nick's desk. Someone had stitched these words:

"Lord, Give Me the Strength to Put Up with All the People Who Are Going to Annoy Me Today."

Jodie did not know Nick well, but he could certainly imagine that some people could irritate him. Jodie hoped to never again be one of them. He had already experienced Nick's annoyance last night.

Another work of embroidery hung on the wall near the front door. This one said:

"Old Age and Treachery Will Soon Overcome Youth and Skill."

Jodie chuckled. He felt he was getting to know Nick by reading his philosophy planted here and there on the walls of his shop. He wondered who had stitched these pieces. He didn't know much about women's sewing, but he recognized quality work. Jodie had a thought; maybe Nick had sewed them himself. Anyone who could be so enamored with lumber might also enjoy sewing. Jodie hoped not. His dad would never understand a man who did feminine work. "Girly Work," he would call it. Jodie would remember to ask Nick who had stitched the wall hangings. He really hoped it had not been Nick.

Jodie nosed around the shop. He didn't mean to snoop, but he opened the desk drawers, thinking perhaps there might be money lying around. No luck there. He opened the cabinet doors but found nothing of interest there either. Nick's appointment book was open on the desk, and every day was penciled in with various jobs. Nick was a master craftsman and a perfectionist to boot. Because merchants lined up to hire him, Nick had built many of the structures in Bodie. But Jodie did not know this, and he was getting bored now. He wished Nick had left Cindy with him for company.

And then Jodie got himself into trouble again. He had meant to stay at the shop and had promised Nick he would put the wood away. But it was a bright, crisp, sunny day, and he heard boys outside. School had ended for the day, and they were throwing a baseball around. Jodie stuck his head out of the shop door and watched for a while. Finally, one of the kids noticed him.

"Wanna play?"

Jodie was thrilled. Few things excited him as much as baseball. "You bet," he hollered back. Without another thought, he left the shop and went off with his new friends. He was not around when the wood arrived. He did not hear the Chinese man knock and call out Nick's name.

It was nearly six o'clock when Nick returned to the shop and realized that neither Jodie nor the wood was there. He waited around for a few minutes, thinking Jodie might show up. Finally, he locked up and walked home. Supper was always served on time. Mary Kay had boarders to feed, dishes to wash, and pasties to bake for lunches the following day. So, the rule was "Be There" if you planned to eat.

Nick had no idea where Jodie was. After their talk this morning, he doubted he had left town. Nick knew that Jodie didn't have enough money for the stage. No stages were leaving this afternoon anyway. He figured that Jodie knew where the Manor was, and he would show up when he was hungry. This would not sit well with Mary Kay though. Nick sighed in exasperation. He needed that supply of wood and had planned to use it in the morning. Now he would have to wait.

The supper table was full. Thornton and Wiley sat in their usual places. Coosie, a former cowboy who now worked at the livery stables, had returned from Aurora where he had visited with friends the day before. He had taken his seat next to Tristan who was now eight-years old. Mary Kay's daughter Nessie sat next to Wiley who helped her cut up her meat and who teased her throughout the meal. She and Wiley were best pals. Nick took his place at the head of the table while Mary Kay sat at the opposite end near the kitchen. A place was set for Jodie who was late.

The lively chatter subsided as they filled their plates. Mary Kay's cooking was legendary, and her boarders and family were happy to be there. They were still passing bowls around when Jodie came in and sat in the empty seat. He did not say anything but was reaching for a bowl of collard greens when Nick spoke up.

"So, Jodie, would you be saying good evening to your hostess?" He nodded toward Mary Kay.

Jodie took the hint. "Hello, Ma'am." He nodded toward the others. He looked surprised when he noticed Coosie. He had never met a Negro and had certainly not expected to see one sitting at the supper table.

"Where have you been, Lad?" Nick asked.

Jodie couldn't wait to tell him. "Baseball, Nick. A bunch of fellows were playing ball down by the stables, and they asked me to play. We had a great time."

"Which boys were those?" Thornton asked.

"I didn't catch all of their names, but one was called Marty. Another was Stevie. A fellow named Walter was there too. Big guy. We had a great time."

"Better be careful of those kids," Wiley said. "They are often in trouble around here. They don't care much about following the rules."

"Bunch of troublemakers," Thornton added.

Jodie looked at them but said nothing. He was not used to so many people telling him what to do. He wondered that strangers could have such a say in his life.

Nick also had plenty to say but wisely waited until after supper to say it. He took Jodie outside, so the others couldn't hear. "Let's take a walk." They walked down the dirt road in the dark. "So, you were playing baseball, were you?"

Jodie brightened. "Sure was. It was fun, and they were great guys."

Nick shook his head. "Did you hear what Wiley and Thornton said to you? Those kids are not great guys. They are a bunch of hoodlums. The town folk complain about them all the time."

"Well, I liked them."

"That's not even the point. I brought you out here to talk about the wood delivery. I asked you to stay until it was delivered. Why didn't you do as I asked?"

Jodie hung his head. "I forgot. When I heard the boys outside, I just wanted to go with them. I didn't think."

"Well, the wood wasn't delivered. I needed it for work tomorrow. Now I'll be behind a day. By you breaking your word, I find that I will be breaking mine." Nick shook his head. "Now the job won't be completed for an extra day. I had promised to have the bar ready."

"Stop yelling at me."

"I'm not yelling at you. I'm just telling you what's what."

"My dad never yells at me. He thinks everything I do is swell." Jodie paused because he knew this wasn't true. His dad was often disappointed in him. But Jodie now came in for a strong finish.

"You are nothing like my dad."

Nick refrained from saying, "Good. I wouldn't want to be anything like your dad." He bit his tongue instead and tried to reason with the young boy.

"Jodie, you promised to stay. A promise is a commitment."

"A promise is no big deal." Jodie scowled at Nick. "Leave me alone and quit preaching to me." Jodie backed up, distancing himself from Nick. "I can't stand you. You're so cranky." And with that, Jodie ran back toward the boarding house.

Nick stood and studied the stars overhead for a long time before he too headed back to the Manor. Perhaps he had bitten off more than he could chew when it came to Jodie.

* * * * * * * * * *

That night in bed, Jodie thought back over his first full day in Bodie. He had never heard of the Chisholm Trail until that evening at supper. He had never met a Negro either, but there one sat at Mary Kay's supper table. He wasn't serving the meal as Jodie thought Blacks were supposed to do. No, he sat there as though he were a guest. Jodie wondered that a Black man would be invited, and then it dawned on him that this man wasn't a guest at all. He was one of Mary Kay's boarders. This seemed wrong to Jodie. The Blacks he had read about did not share the supper table with White folks. His dad would have been appalled. Dad had little patience with people who did not look like him.

This man, Coosie, did not seem to know his place. Instead of sitting quietly, he regaled the others with stories of his time as a cowboy. Despite himself, Jodie was fascinated. He had never met a real cowboy. Coosie had spent a few years on the cattle trail as a cook, preparing meals from a chuckwagon. This was an important job with a lot of responsibility. So much could go wrong on the trail, and according to Coosie, it often did.

"Every year, the boss would hire on a couple of greenhorns, young fellows who knew nothing but thought they knew it all." Coosie chuckled as he thought back. "These youngsters would try to tell us how to do our jobs. I remember one young cuss who thought he was the tall hog at the trough. Wouldn't listen to instruction but would blather on. He was small potatoes in my book, and I didn't have the time nor the patience to deal with him. Finally, I told him to quit his yammering— that only a fool argues with a mule, a skunk, or a cook."

Everyone at the table laughed, and Jodie was drawn to this jovial, entertaining man. But then he shook himself. What was he thinking? This was just a Negro, after all. His dad would definitely not approve.

Jodie was learning a lot here in Bodie. The last year at home with his mother had been depressing. This was only his second day at this dynamic boarding house, and it was the most fun he had had in a while. He almost hoped that his Aunt Tess wouldn't return soon. Now, if he could just get Nick to lighten up a bit. Nick took his new job as Jodie's guardian much too seriously. Jodie knew that he and Nick would have another confrontation in the morning when Nick remembered to ask for the money intended for the purchase of the wood.

Jodie did not consider himself a thief. He had never had to steal because all of his needs and most of his wants had been satisfied by his parents. But he fingered the coins in his pocket and realized that he would not only lie to Nick, but he would steal from him as well. He would tell Nick that he had lost the money. Jodie had decided to keep it and to add to it when possible. He was determined to go back to San Diego and needed money to get there. He expected his dad to return. In the meantime, he was sure Ian's mother would take him in after all. She wouldn't leave him to sleep on the streets. But he had to get there, and that cost money. Tomorrow he intended to stop by the stagecoach office and find out how much the fare cost.

The next morning, things went just as Jodie expected them to. Nick asked for the money, and Jodie went through the pretense of going through his pockets looking for the coins and coming up empty.

"Sorry, Nick, but the money isn't here. I must have lost it out at the field. We ran around a lot, and it must have fallen out when I slid into second base. I don't know what to tell you, but I will get a job and make it up to you. I'll have to skip school though."

"You are not skipping school. I told you that. Five weeks until summer vacation, and you will go every day because education is important."

"You didn't get much education if you're just a carpenter," Jodie challenged him.

"I got enough. I finished high school, and you will too. You can pay back the money by working around the shop."

Jodie shrugged like it was no big deal, but now he had money squirreled away toward going home.

Jodie had liked going to school in San Diego. An intelligent student, he enjoyed learning. He didn't know why he had given Nick a hard time about it— just to get his goat perhaps. The next morning Nick walked him and Tristan over to the school just as the bell began to ring. Tristan went into the schoolroom while Nick introduced

Jodie to the young woman teacher, Belle Moore. Nick asked about her family, and Jodie decided that Nick did indeed know a lot of people in Bodie. Nick checked that Jodie had his lunch tin, and then he left. Miss Moore showed Jodie to an empty desk in the middle of the room. At recess, Jodie knew a couple of the boys from the ball game the day before, and they introduced him around to the other fellows. More girls were in the classroom than boys, but Jodie didn't give them any attention. He didn't care about girls and had always found them to be bothersome, whiney creatures.

The pleasant teacher knew how to teach and how to keep the students in line. Jodie was interested when she discussed Gregor Mendel who had published his scientific laws just twelve years before. Jodie thought he might like to learn more about heredity. Miss Moore assigned arithmetic homework, and Jodie knew he would have to ask Nick for some help with that. Miss Moore asked Jodie to read to her, and then she gave him a McGuffey Reader on his appropriate reading level. The day passed routinely as school days do. Nick had told Jodie that he would attend school for five weeks, but Jodie planned to be enroute home long before that.

CHAPTER 7

"Maybe Jodie is right. Maybe you do preach too much. And I'll vouch for the fact that you're cranky." Coosie smiled at Nick.

Nick often talked things out with Coosie because he considered his wisdom unmatched. Coosie was older than anyone else at the Manor. Having had several unrelated jobs, he had learned how to get along with others. Now with most of his years behind him, he thought he had people figured out. "Try preaching with your actions rather than your words," he suggested now.

"I only want what's best for the boy. You know he has nowhere else to go." Nick had already explained to Coosie about Jodie and his family and that Jodie's mother and Tess were sisters. Coosie knew Tess. He too had been in Bodie a while.

"I've known men like Jodie's dad," Coosie mused. "A loser! He thinks he owns the world, and everyone else is here just to do his bidding. Lordy, anyone who deserts his wife is worthless in my opinion!"

"Yeah, yeah, I agree, but he has his son hoodwinked. Jodie idolizes him. Sticks up for him every chance he gets. Loyal."

"Loyalty ain't a bad thing. All I'm saying is you feel fatherly toward this boy," Coosie said.

"Nah, that's not it."

"Hush now and let me finish. You do feel fatherly. At least you've taken on a dad's responsibility. So, show him how to be a man. Show him how to treat women folk, and how to be someone others can rely on." Coosie gave Nick a hard look. "Jodie needs to grow up. You don't want him to turn out like his father, do you? Just be glad the dad is gone and has no influence anymore."

"I wish I could get my hands on his dad. I'd teach him a thing or two."

"Well, he's not here. So, teach his boy instead."

"Yes, Sir." Nick smiled now. He liked and trusted Coosie. They often stayed up late at night talking and drinking tea. Mary Kay did not allow liquor in the house.

Coosie had much advice to give but never gave it unsolicited. He had lived every one of his forty-five years. Born a slave on a large plantation, he had toiled in cotton fields until 1863, when Lincoln had issued the Emancipation Proclamation. This Executive Order freeing the slaves meant nothing to slave owners who considered it a worthless piece of paper. These Southerners had already left the Union. They had disowned Lincoln as their President and had instead chosen Jefferson Davis. Lincoln had no hold over them, they thought, and certainly no authority to free their slaves. The slaves felt differently, of course, and many of them ran off the first chance they got. Coosie was one of them. Shot at and hounded, he had made his way north. There, Union soldiers had enticed him and other run-away slaves to join their army. By the time Coosie had entered the war, only a year remained of fighting; but he had done his part, grateful to President Lincoln who had given him his freedom. He still mourned this great leader who saw value in all men.

The war, gruesome as it was, had benefited Coosie in a couple of ways. First, he hadn't known he was a natural equestrian. In the North, he spent hours on horses and discovered he had both talent and horse sense. He spent his time in the army tending to the steeds of White officers. Prickly as some of the officers were, he learned to anticipate their needs and learned to get along with them. After his days in the cotton fields, working alongside Caucasians was a unique experience for him. But they were White, and he was a lowly Black man; he never forgot his place.

Coosie had also benefited from the war because he learned to read. This was something he had long desired but had had no opportunity to pursue. One of the less prickly officers had taken a shine to him, and during some of their long lag times, he had ventured to teach the eager young Negro. Coosie was intelligent and had picked it up readily. He spent hours practicing the alphabet and reading the rudimentary books at hand. He also learned to write some, but not much. The war ended before he become proficient. Also, he regretted having no time to learn about numbers. But Coosie had not been discouraged. He would learn writing and arithmetic as soon as he could. He hoped that someone would come along to help him, and he placed his trust In the Lord. The Lord took good care of him.

He had not always been called Coosie. That name came later in his life. On the South Carolina plantation, his owner had named him Joe. This name later reminded him of Stephen Foster's song "Old Black Joe." The name, of course, was a reminder that he was a slave, someone also referred to as "Boy." Someone to do back-breaking work for no pay and no dignity. No, he preferred the name Coosie. Both names had been given to him by White men. The first implied servitude. The second represented work done willingly as a free man. On the cow trail, the cook was often nicknamed "Coosie," so that became his new name as he took on the role of chuckwagon master.

Sundays were quiet affairs at the Manor. Mary Kay did her best to provide a serene, prayerful atmosphere for herself and her children. Nick spent Sundays at his shop, cleaning his tools and preparing for the following week. He and Cindy often took an afternoon walk, so they could think, he said.

Nick had given Jodie the choice— he could either attend the Methodist service with Mary Kay, or the Catholic Mass with Susanne.

"Why do I have to go to services? You don't go. Why can't I stay with you?"

"That's not going to happen," Nick retorted. "You need religion, or your mother will be unhappy with me. I'm certainly not going to chance your mother's displeasure. So, which is it, the Catholics or the Methodists?"

"I'd rather go with Susanne. I'm a Catholic. Besides, Mary Kay doesn't like me much."

"Okay. The Catholic service it is. I'll tell Susanne to meet you there."

And so, Jodie began spending Sundays with Susanne. After Mass, they would return to her apartment above the photo studio, and for an hour before dinner, she would help Jodie write a weekly letter to his mother. Jeannie knew from his letters that Jodie was faithful in his weekly Mass attendance. This brought her comfort.

Jeannie wrote to Jodie often too. Her letters were warm and encouraging. She talked of the other patients she knew and of the beauty of the hospital grounds where she spent time outdoors in the warm sun. She said she prayed for Jodie daily and hoped he was being a good boy. She wrote to her son faithfully, but not once did she say her condition was improving, and not once did she mention Jodie's dad. He had disappeared from their lives.

Nick and Susanne had talked it over and had decided that the truth was their best course of action. Jodie was not living with Tess, and it was best not to lie about it. So, Nick and Susanne had Jodie tell his mother that Aunt Tess was out of town, but that he was being well taken care of by a couple he had met on the stage who happened to be friends of Tess's. Nick had Tess write to her as well and tell her Jodie was with good friends, and that she planned to return to Bodie soon. Nick and Susanne did not want Jeannie to worry about Jodie's well-being, and so they had taken every precaution.

The boarders did not work on Sundays, and they too spent quiet time to themselves. They visited friends, picked up their clothes down on King Street where the Chinese laundries were located, and ran other errands. In the afternoon, they often sat back with a smoke and a good book. The work week was taxing, and men needed time to rejuvenate. Sometimes they walked down to one of the saloons and socialized with their friends, but Mary Kay would never hear it from them that they were drinking on a Sunday. They respected her too much and did not want to disappoint her.

Most Sundays, the boarders would help themselves to leftovers or sandwiches in the kitchen in the late afternoon. They had already eaten a hearty meal at noon and didn't expect Mary Kay to cook again. When the kitchen was again cleaned up, Mary Kay would get out her guitar, Nick would find his harmonica, and they would play songs for the group. Both she and Nick sang beautifully. They had grown up in Grass Valley where singing was part of their everyday lives. Every Cornish family had musical talent, it seemed.

Coosie also sang, and he knew several Gospel songs. He knew drinking songs as well. His friends at the Manor had learned from him that part of his job as a cowboy on the Chisholm Trail had been to ride around on his horse at night and sing to the restless cows.

"Well, I'll tell you, we cowhands couldn't afford to let them cattle get stirred up in fear they would stampede." Coosie shook his head as he remembered back.

"No, that would have been a very bad thing. So, we took two-hour shifts, riding our horses around the rim of them cows, singing soothing songs to keep the cattle calm."

He looked at Tristan then. "I bet you never sang to a cow, did you, Tristan? Son, you don't know what you've been missing!" This elicited a smile from the young boy who was known for his reticence. Yes, Coosie knew many songs, but not all of them were suitable for singing on a Sunday evening.

Jodie had not known that he could sing, but encouraged by the others, he gave it a try. He discovered that he loved singing. He also enjoyed listening to the others sing ballads; he liked the stories these songs told. He was intrigued that Mary Kay played the guitar because he would have thought it too masculine for a woman. He got a kick out of watching Nick play lively tunes on the harmonica. Nick was a natural showman. No, Jodie would not have missed these Sunday sing-a-longs, and he looked forward to them all week.

One would have thought that Mary Kay would have permitted only religious songs on a Sunday, but that was not the case. She enjoyed secular songs as well. She encouraged the three children to learn folk songs, telling them that these songs were the stitches that held the fabric of the new nation together. Her parents had come from Cornwall, England, but she had been born here and was immeasurably proud to be an American. She wanted her children to realize their good fortune and to know the history of their land. So, on Sunday evenings, all types of music filled the parlor. Mary Kay did begin with religious songs, of course. She had her favorites and always began with them. Soon, however, Nessie would be making requests.

"I want Coosie to sing the song about the sweet cherries. Please sing that one, Coosie," she would plead. The adults always smiled at this.

Coosie would stand and with a deep bass voice, he would sing the old Negro spiritual "Swing Low, Sweet Chariot." Later he invariably sang "Rock My Soul in the Bosom of Abraham." But after Jodie came to live with them, he never again sang his favorite song "Sometimes I Feel Like a Motherless Child." This mournful song seemed too close to home to sing in front of the boy. He knew Jodie missed his mother terribly.

Later, after everyone had eaten pie and had refilled their coffee cups, the more boisterous songs would be introduced. "The Arkansas Traveler" was always requested and also "The Yellow Rose of Texas" although Coosie was the only one in the group to have been anywhere near the Lone Star State. Mary Kay's favorite composer Stephen Foster had created the gold rush song "Oh Susanna." They all sang this with gusto and dedicated it to Susanne. Nick liked to sing an old folk ballad "Down by the River Lived a Maiden" even though he knew that neither Mary Kay nor Susanne approved of the words. In later years, this song would be known as "Clementine."

"It's belittling to the poor woman," Susanne would tell him. "We shouldn't make fun of an overweight woman."

"Or any woman," Mary Kay would add, looking Nick in the eye. He did like to tease her.

"No, it's all in good fun," he would retort. And so, it too was a standard. "Camp Town Races" was requested, and the whole group sang it as they tapped their toes on the hardwood floor.

Wiley had the least musical ability in the group and did not sing, but he always asked Susanne to sing an old song long known to his family, "Shenandoah." A year or so before, he had told his friends that his dad had been a French-Canadian fur trapper, and this had been his favorite song. Nessie would climb up on Wiley's lap and pat his hand while they listened to this soulful song.

A week after Jodie's arrival, Coosie confided in his friends the details of his early life as a slave. Until then, only Nick had known his story. Mary Kay had announced that she would like to end that evening's music with more songs by Stephen Foster. Coosie was filled with emotion when his friends sang "Old Black Joe" and "Old Folks at Home." These songs were both prewar songs that brought him back to another life — that of a slave on a plantation way down in South Carolina. That night Coosie told the others the sadness he felt when he heard these songs.

"I'm thinking back on all my kinfolk that I won't ever see again. I've got no idea where my people ended up after the war. You know, I wasn't married when I ran off, and I left no children. But I often think about my mother working in the fields, day in and day out. My sisters had all been sold off long before, so I left my Mammy all alone when I ran. I surely do regret leaving her." Coosie smiled ruefully. Then he looked his friends squarely in the eye. "I had no choice. If I hadn't escaped when I did, I would be a dead man for sure." He shook his head. "But that don't make me feel any better." He got up from his chair. "Time for me to hit the sack."

Mary Kay stood up and put her hand on Coosie's arm to stop him from leaving.

"Coosie, before you go to bed, please allow me to apologize. Forgive me please for my insensitivity. We won't sing these slave songs again."

"No, Ma'am. That's not it. I want to hear these songs. I want to remember my family and look back on that time of my life. I don't want to bury it. I lived on that Charleston plantation for the first thirty years of my life. It's part of my very fiber. It helped form me into the man I am today, wretched soul that I am!" Coosie smiled at Mary Kay. "Let's finish with 'Beautiful Dreamer.' Now that's another fine Foster song." And so, they all sang this last song together. And every Sunday after, they never neglected to sing Stephen Foster songs, even the ones that made Coosie sad.

CHAPTER 8

Nick found Jodie in the library at the Manor where he was reading in a chair in the back corner.

"Are you hiding?" Nick asked.

"Maybe."

"Why?"

Jodie looked up. "I'm just trying to stay out of Mary Kay's way. She scares me."

"Good idea. She scares me too." Nick grinned.

Jodie sat up straighter. "I picked up the mail at the post office. You have a letter."

Nick rifled through the stack of envelopes on the table until he found one addressed to him.

"Ah, it's a letter from my old friend Alf Dolten, the best writer I know."

"I thought Twain was your favorite author," Jodie said.

"I misspoke. I should have said 'the most prolific writer I know.' Alf keeps a diary and has for almost thirty years. He started writing it when he sailed to the gold fields in '49."

"I thought only girls wrote diaries," Jodie said.

"You thought wrong, Lad. Someday, Alf's diary will be valuable because he writes about everything he sees; he is recording a social history of the West. Like Susanne is doing with her photos."

"Have you read it?" Jodie wanted to know.

"No. Alf hasn't shared it with others yet. But aren't you glad I encouraged you to keep a journal when you first got here?" Nick had given Jodie a leather-bound book to write in.

"'Encouraged' is not the correct word," Jodie said. "Try 'manipulated' or 'coerced.'"

"Ah Lad, you give me too much credit." Nick smiled.

"Just because you keep a journal, doesn't mean I want to keep one. It's girly work."

"Nonsense. Someday you will thank me. You are in a new town, experiencing new things. You have met people you would not have known before. I hope you are recording it all. I also hope you will meet Alf one day. You would like both him and his wife Mary. Mary also keeps a diary."

"Do you know them from Grass Valley or from Virginia City?"

"Virginia City. Mary has an Aunt Lucy who is an old friend of my mother's. When Mary came to Virginia City to stay with Lucy, my mother asked Ed and me to look her up. I escorted her to Piper's Opera House a couple of times, and Mary Kay had her to dinner. We were all pals.

"Then Mary married Alfred Doten, a drinking buddy of mine. We all went to their wedding. You will laugh, but they were married on a steamboat in the middle of Lake Tahoe. Many people attended the wedding. Several small boats, filled with strangers, pulled up alongside the steamboat to watch the ceremony. We all had a great time."

"So, you are good friends with Mr. Doten?"

"Yes, good friends, even though Alf is twenty years older than I. Mary is closer to my age. Mary and Mary Kay are good friends too. They are both interested in voting rights for women."

"Suffragists? Is that the correct word?"

"Yes."

Nick silently read his letter. "Alf wants to see me in Virginia City. Says he needs to talk with me."

Jodie asked," Why doesn't he come here?"

"He can't leave Virginia City because he is the editor of the *Gold Hill Daily News* and needs to get the newspaper out every day. I'll go to him. I can ride over and get there in a day."

"I'll go with you," Jodie offered excitedly. "Please say I can go."

"Sorry, you need to be in school, but I'll tell you what; I will get Alf's autograph for you. I expect him to be famous one day. Years ago, he worked with Twain on *the Territorial Enterprise Newspaper* in Virginia City. Twain gave him personal copies of some of his works: the short story 'The Jumping Frog of Calaveras County,' and the book *Roughing It,* for sure. Some other books too."

"Wow! I would sure like to see those. Are you sure I can't go with you?"

"I'm sorry, Jodie. I will take you another time. School is important. I won't be gone but for a couple of days because I have commitments here. But I owe Alf. He certainly helped us when my brother Ed died. Alf has always been there for me, so if he wants me, I will go."

"What if Mary Kay kicks me out while you are gone? She could, you know! I better go with you."

"Yeah, yeah. Just mind your P's and Q's, and you will be fine. But now, it's supper time. Why don't you go wash up and then ask Mary Kay if you can help her?"

"No, I'd rather just stay out of her way. She wouldn't want any help from me."

"I suggest you go in the kitchen and ask her. It couldn't hurt."

Without another word, Jodie left the library. He came into the dining room a few minutes later carrying a bowl of asparagus. Nick had been right. Mary Kay had smiled at him and offered him the vegetables to carry in. Jodie often regretted that he had gotten off to a bad start with her. Maybe he would try harder. He loved her cooking and looked forward to supper every night. But it wasn't only the food that drew him to the table. It was the comradery of the boardinghouse residents: Nick, Mary Kay, her children, the three boarders, and most often Susanne. They gathered around the large oak table promptly at 6:00 o'clock. Coozie always led them in prayer— blessing the food and the cook, and remembering the less fortunate who went without that night. Then the food would be passed around, and they helped themselves. Chatter and good-natured teasing ensued with everyone talking at once, some with their mouths full.

"Great meal, Mary Kay,"

"You outdid yourself this time," another would add.

Even Nessie, the youngest, had a say as each took a turn going around the table recounting his day. The considerate boarders would lean forward and give Nessie their full attention.

Jodie had never seen anything like it. In his old world, children were considered unimportant and were mostly overlooked. At home, he had often felt like a nuisance. But at Mary Kay's table, he was made to feel important, and he too was asked about his day. He liked to tell the others that his baseball skills were improving. Nick was coaching him, and Jodie's love of the game was evident.

Jodie still played with the rowdy boys whom the adults disapproved of, but he was part of a larger group of boys so could not conveniently stay away from "the bad apples." Nick and the others wanted him to be happy. School kept him occupied, and he thrived in the fresh air and companionship of children his own age. Not all the boys were wild, and Nick kept his eye on Marty and Stevie the best he could.

If it wasn't whist night, all would linger at the table— some of the men smoking cigars, most drinking hot coffee. This was Jodie's favorite part of the day because he had discovered that he loved history. All the adults here knew history and enjoyed discussing current events and arguing about politics. At first, Jodie had no idea what they were talking about. He didn't know a Democrat from a Republican. He hadn't realized that a presidential election had taken place just two years before and that a man named Rutherford Hayes was now in office. At first, Jodie had just listened. He certainly had no opinions to contribute, but now he knew more about the world than he had ever imagined. He was being educated, and he loved it. In the process, he was also learning about geography. He must be learning grammar as well because at times Mary Kay corrected his speech. However, Mary Kay actually thought Jodie was well-spoken, and she gave his mother credit for his large vocabulary as well.

Teasing Mary Kay was a pastime of Nick's. As he started in on her now after dinner, Jodie sat up straighter in order to listen better. He enjoyed watching Nick get the better of her most times.

"So," Nick began, "how's our boy Hayes doing in the White House? From what I hear, his wife Lucy is even more devout a Methodist than you are."

"Not possible," Wiley muttered under his breath. The others heard him and laughed.

Mary Kay looked at Nick. "Lucy Hayes is indeed religious, a fine woman, and educated. No other First Lady has had a college degree."

"How about Rutherford? Is he educated?" Thornton asked.

"Harvard," Mary Kay told him.

"I hear that his wife won't permit him to serve liquor in the White House," Nick offered.

"I am certain he can serve anything he likes," Mary Kay snapped.

"I hope that's true," Nick said. "I would like to go to the White House and have a beer with old Rutherford. What do you say, Thornton? Want to go to Washington and have a beer with the President?"

Thornton chuckled. "Sure, Nick. Let's do that. I'm sure he would serve us a cold one. Say, why don't we take Coosie with us? Coosie, shall we go drink beer with the President?"

Coosie chortled. "That'll be the day when a Black man gets invited to the White House. These politicians want my vote but would never consider inviting me in for a beer. Or anything else," he added.

Mary Kay bristled, as Nick knew she would. "At least you get to vote," she declared. "As a woman, I don't have that privilege."

Jodie spoke up, "Why can't women vote, Mary Kay? My mother never cared about elections or voting, but I didn't know she wasn't allowed to."

Mary Kay sighed. "No, Jodie, she isn't allowed to by law. It's a privilege granted only to men. We women worked diligently to help the Blacks, first with emancipation and then with the Fifteenth Amendment granting them the right to vote. But we women still aren't allowed to cast our votes."

"Most of the members of the weaker sex don't care about elections," Nick suggested.

"What do you mean weaker sex?" Mary Kay was riled up now. "Who are you calling weak?"

"Well, if you women were strong, you would not only want to vote, but you would put forth a capable female candidate," Nick said.

"No woman has ever been president, right Nick?" Jodie asked.

"That's right. Too weak."

"We haven't had a woman president," Mary Kay practically spit the words at him, "but not because we haven't tried. Just four years ago, we women put Victoria Woodhull on the ballot for president."

"Ah, yes." Nick couldn't believe his good luck. He enjoyed ribbing his sister-in-law, and she was always in a temper when he teased her about Woodhull. He smiled at her now and said, "You're correct, of course. Victoria Woodhull ran in '72 with the Equal Rights Party."

"She was a very able candidate," Mary Kay said. "She owned a newspaper and so knew what was going on in the world."

"That newspaper folded two years ago," Nick put in.

"She and her sister also owned a brokerage firm on Wall Street in New York City," Mary Kay said. "They were the first women to do so."

Wiley spoke up now, "Cornelius Vanderbilt financed it for them. Talk about crazy!"

"What do you mean?" Mary Kay asked. "Why crazy?"

"I don't know if you remember the story," Wiley continued. "Vanderbilt's wife had recently died, and he was overwhelmed with grief. He was obsessed with contacting his dead wife, so Victoria Woodhull became his personal medium and held a séance trying to help him reach her. The entire story was bizarre. This occurred before she ran for president."

"I still say she would have made a capable president," Mary Kay said and then added, "She was a millionaire by the age of thirty-one. Very smart woman."

"Speaking of age, that was one of her problems. She was too young to be president. She wouldn't have been the required age of thirty-five even on election day." Nick knew all about her.

"That's what you think!" Mary Kay glared at him.

"Hey, I didn't write the Constitution. I'm just telling you what it says."

"Children, Children," Coosie soothed.

"Did she get many votes?" Jodie asked.

"No," Nick told him and grinned. "And guess where she spent election night?"

"Where?"

"In jail. She, her husband, and her nutty sister all spent a month in jail for publishing a scandalous article in their newspaper. Arrested for obscenity! So, the next time you ladies want to put forth a woman candidate, you better find one a bit more qualified." Nick was finished now.

"Oh, you men are truly hateful!" Mary Kay said and stood up.

"Yeah, yeah, I know. Come on, Suffragette, I'll help you with the dishes." Nick put his arm around her and walked her toward the kitchen. "But I get to wash."

Now Jodie was worried. He hoped his Aunt Tess would stay away for a long time because he liked these people, even Mary Kay. He wanted to stay with them. He would definitely keep out of trouble while Nick was away because he couldn't afford to get kicked out. He would be very careful not to get in trouble.

* * * * * * * * * *

But Jodie was not careful. Nick had barely left town when Jodie played tag with his friends after school. The boys ran wildly through people's yards— upsetting wood piles, buckets, chamber pots, and anything else in their path. Mary Kay's cotton bed sheets were hanging on the clothesline when the boys ran through them and knocked them to the dirt.

Mary Kay did not witness this, but her hired girl did. Chinoa, a Pauite Indian woman, worked for Mary Kay four days a week. Mary Kay had linen to change on eight beds, and she had insufficient time to change them. Chinoa needed a job to keep her family from starving, so this symbiotic arrangement worked well. Chinoa washed four sets of sheets on Mondays and Tuesdays, using a wash board and water she hauled from the well. Backbreaking work, but the Paiutes were used to laboring. She then ironed the sheets and pillowcases on an ironing table while all the pillows aired out on the clothesline. Finally, she carried the bedding up the stairs and made up the four beds, a tiring task. On Wednesdays and Thursdays, she changed the other four beds.

The Paiutes, a nomadic tribe, had long followed the animal migrations. The women also gathered pinyon nuts, a valuable food source. All this changed for these Native Americans when thousands of miners invaded their lands and drove away the animals they hunted for food. The men had no choice but to find work on ranches or in the mines. The women gave up gathering grass seeds and roots and hired themselves out as domestics.

Mary Kay was pleased with Chinoa's work. On Mondays, she packed food she had prepared for Chinoa's family and sent it home with her. The two women had a good relationship, and then Jodie and his pals upset their routine. Chinoa, usually submissive, was enraged by the boys' behavior. Now she would have extra work rewashing the sheets. She spoke sharply to Jodie who brushed her aside, intent on tagging Stevie. She called to him again, and he answered her rudely. Chinoa had no choice but to speak to Mary Kay.

Mary Kay, of course, was furious. She grabbed Jodie and sat him down on the porch steps.

"What do you think you're doing, Mister?"

"Sorry, Mary Kay. I wasn't thinking. We were playing tag, and I didn't pay attention to my surroundings. I apologize."

"You will apologize, but not to me. You owe Chinoa the apology for dirtying the sheets. And did I hear that you spoke rudely to her?"

"Yeah, I guess I did, but she's just an Indian woman. She doesn't matter."

"Matter? Of course, she matters! She is a person. Do you think she is unimportant because she is an Indian or because she is a woman? Oh, never mind! You are too selfish to understand."

Jodie started to get up, but Mary Kay sat him back down. "Don't move," she told him. "I am going to fetch Chinoa, and you are going to apologize. No more nonsense."

So, even though Nick thought school was important and had left Jodie in town to attend to his studies, Mary Kay had another view. She did not kick Jodie out, but she also did not send him to school for two days. Instead of leaning over his books, Jodie found himself leaning over the wash board, rewashing the dirty bed linen. When he finished his work, his hands were blistered and sore. This was nothing compared to the tongue lashing he knew he would get from Nick when he returned. Jodie almost wished Mary Kay had kicked him out.

CHAPTER 9

No one went hungry in Bodie because the town had an abundance of eateries. Many of the saloons also served food. Some offered a "Free Lunch" which consisted of cold cuts, cheeses, beans, and bread. At times, a celery stalk or two would be put forward. All food and drink had to be hauled into this desolate place, so fruits and vegetables were not always readily available. Saloon owners knew to also serve salty foods such as pretzels or even smoked herring— foods that increased a customer's thirst. They provided these free meals to build up their patronage of loyal customers and to keep the men in the bars. A shot of whiskey cost twelve cents, but only a cheapskate would buy just one drink. So, a two-bit coin was the usual payment. A wise barkeep kept the customers drinking.

The more discriminate diners had a choice of fine restaurants. Ladies of good breeding often lunched together at one of the hotel restaurants. A gentleman could invite his lady friend to dine on oysters or salmon at a corner table at one of Bodie's better lunchrooms.

Other more modest restaurants catered to the locals and business owners who then had to get back to their busy day. It was to one of these cafes on Main Street that Susanne invited Jodie to have lunch with her. He hurried into the restaurant and tumbled into his seat.

"I'm famished," he reported.

"You're always famished." Susanne smiled at him. She shared Nick's protectiveness of Jodie. Because she had spent the many hours in the coach with Jodie on his journey to Bodie two months earlier, she cared about the young boy. She, Jodie, and Nick had a special bond. She spent Sundays with Jodie, and because she and Mary Kay were close friends, she saw him almost daily at the boardinghouse.

Jodie regarded her as a friend and often showed up at her photography studio. Sometimes he went out in the field with her when she photographed outdoor shots. He liked to carry her equipment and be "Her Right-Hand Man." The boys in town thought of Susanne as "One Fine Lady," as they termed it. A couple of them, Jodie's friend Stevie in particular, had offered to help her out if she ever needed them. Smitten with her, Stevie had taken to hanging out in front of her studio, hoping to see her as she came or went. Susanne was flattered by the attention but finally had to tell him directly that she needed no help. She told the boy that she had trained Jodie in photography and had no time to train anyone else.

As part of her project to photograph "The Denizens of Bodie," Susanne had made it a point to capture the likenesses of the children in town. At the school, Belle Moore had graciously allowed her to photograph the schoolroom itself and the children at their desks. Susanne had done this work back in April when just a few children attended school. Now Bodie's population had surged, and Susanne knew that in September she would need to return. School was now out for the summer, and Susanne planned to photograph the children at play. Both boys and girls played dodgeball or crack the whip out in the open fields. The town children were also kept busy helping their overworked parents. Susanne had captured photos of daughters helping their mothers hang out clothes on backyard clothes lines. The wicked wind would whip through and sometimes tear the sheets right out of their hands. Susanne had gotten pictures of both boys and girls carrying buckets of water from the town well.

Susanne enjoyed the children and had gotten to know many of them by name. She often found an extra ribbon in her drawer to tie in a young girl's hair.

But it was Jodie who was her special pet. She knew his circumstances and mothered him as best she could. At Sunday Mass, he sat with her, and they shared a hymn book. She introduced Jodie to Father Cassin, the priest, and he often asked Jodie to serve as an altar boy, a job Jodie had learned back home. Jodie liked the priest who was much younger and more fun than the pastor he had known in San Diego. After Mass and a letter writing session, Susanne and Jodie would walk back to the Manor for the noontime dinner. There, Jodie liked to tease Nick about being a heathen.

"You know, Nick, anyone who skips Sunday services is sure to go straight to Hell."

"Yeah, yeah!" Nick would respond, "but Hell is for other miscreants as well. I'll see you there."

Nick took the good-natured ribbing in stride. It seemed that if Mary Kay wasn't nagging him about religion, Jodie was. Nick had then asked Jodie, "You know what Twain said about the afterlife, don't you?"

"What?"

"People go to Heaven for the climate, Hell for the company." Nick had laughed and tousled Jodie's hair.

Now in the café, after the waiter had taken their orders, Jodie said,

"Since school is out for the summer, I've been helping Nick. He's building a fancy staircase."

"Is he teaching you a lot?"

"Yes, he sure is. But don't tell him I said that. I wouldn't want him to think I like him." He grinned. "Carpentry is pretty interesting.

He shows me techniques and shortcuts, and he explains why he does things a certain way." Jodie smiled at Susanne and then happily added, "Nick lets me use his tools too."

"Do you still owe him money?"

"Yeah. My debt is almost paid off, but I plan to continue working with him. I like his company. He tells interesting stories as we work. Dumb jokes too. Really dumb! And he sings corny songs that make me laugh. But don't tell him I said that either."

Susanne smiled. "I think you actually like Nick. Why don't you want him to know?"

"Nick has been very decent to me, and yeah, I do like him. But we don't have that kind of relationship where we say nice things to each other. That would be too weird, so we joke around instead. Sometimes I wish he would let up on me a bit. He's always telling me what to do. He's pretty bossy."

"Do you like living at the Manor?" Susanne asked.

"Yeah, I sure do. I messed up that first night with Mary Kay. I don't think she likes me much, but to give her credit, she treats me okay. And I like her kids. The men who live there are decent to me too."

"You've got some great role models there, Jodie. Respected men, all."

"I know."

"I hear you did well in your studies. Your report card was very good, so I guess you liked school."

"I did like it and am glad Nick made me go. But don't tell him I said that either." Jodie grinned.

"How about your friends? Will you see them now that school is out?"

"Oh sure. We play baseball. But nobody at the boarding house likes them. They say they're rowdy."

"I've heard."

"You know that Nick, Tristan, and I play ball sometimes after supper. Nick is teaching me how to pitch."

Jodie looked around the crowded restaurant.

"This place is much nicer than Wagner's," he said casually.

"When did you ever go into Wagner's Saloon?" Susanne looked at him.

"Nick and I were in there just last Saturday," he said.

"Oh, now you're just being a Tall Poppy," she said.

"What's that?"

"A 'Tall Poppy' is someone who tries to make himself look important, to stand out. But in order to be a Tall Poppy, you must phrase your boasting correctly. You must begin your sentence with these words: 'The last time.' So, you would say, 'The last time I was in Wagner's, I had lunch.' This suggests that you have been to Wagner's before. You must act like going to Wagner's is a common, everyday occurrence. Like if I said, 'The last time I was in Paris. . .' even though I have been to Paris only once."

Jodie laughed. "Yeah, I guess you're right. I was being a Tall Poppy. I was trying to impress you by telling you I had been in a saloon. Most kids my age never get to go in there. It's a rowdy place."

"What were you doing in there?"

"Nick took me there for lunch. Did you know they serve food in some saloons?"

"Actually, I did. Along the right-hand wall is that chop stand, the short-order restaurant. I remember it had a lunch counter and stools. Is that where you ate with Nick?"

"Yes. But how do you know about the chop stand?" Jodie asked.

"I too have been in Wagner's," Susanne told him.

"You? But you're a lady! Ladies don't drink in saloons."

"I wasn't drinking. I was taking photos. John Wagner let me photograph anything I wanted. It certainly is a huge room, almost like a barn. The bar is long and to the left as you go through the swinging doors. Right?"

"Right," Jodie agreed.

"I remember the expensive mirror behind the bar. A beauty! Luckily, it hasn't been destroyed in the many fights there. And the back bar made of mahogany is really quite splendid."

"Did you see the gambling tables in the back?" Jodie asked.

"I did. Both the poker and the faro tables were busy, and I noticed how watchful the dealers were. They had thousands of dollars stacked on their tables."

"And guns at the ready in case of trouble," Jodie said.

"Trouble rarely takes a day off. But weapons make me uncomfortable." Susanne shuddered. "Someone invariably gets hurt."

"Do you know Mr. Wagner?" Jodie asked.

"I do. Actually, I know his wife better. She's a doctor in town. Lovely lady. Always helping the poor miners. She took me to her husband's saloon one morning, so I could take pictures for my project."

"Speaking of poor miners, Nick sure was upset last week when Alex Nixon got killed."

"You're right," Susanne said. "Nick was standing close to Alex in the Shamrock Saloon when Alex was shot by Tom McDonald. Nick said he was only five feet away. I guess Alex and Tom got into a tiff over a dollar, certainly not enough money to die for."

"It was the biggest funeral I ever saw," Jodie said, "what with all those miners marching up to the cemetery."

"Alex was president of the Miner's Union, so yes, the funeral was a major event. The Union most certainly paid for the funeral. The Union even has its own section of the cemetery, set aside for its members. Miners take care of their own, "Susanne told him.

The waiter came now and brought their food: soup and a salad for Susanne, and goulash for Jodie.

"Gosh, this looks good. I really am famished."

In many ways, Jodie reminded Susanne of her brother back home. They both had high spirits and were good company. She was certain Tom and Jodie would like each other.

But the one she had been thinking about lately was her old friend and mentor Mathew Brady. He had offered her advice, and as always, he had been right. He had given her the idea of photographing miners. Brady was too old to go West; he had told her. His wife would never consider moving. And frankly, he was tired, or he would jump at the chance. But opportunities out West were plentiful. History was being made, and someone needed to record it. Brady had suggested she compile photos of miners and publish a photo-journal book. Susanne had liked the idea immediately but thought she would take it a step further.

What if she did not limit her photos only to miners? Towns had sprung up around the mines. She could take photos of the miners' wives and sweethearts, of the merchants, the blacksmiths, the teamsters and all their support animals. She knew she would find country doctors and school marms— just ordinary people doing a day's work. Susanne would look at it as a project about people.

She had never been west of St. Louis, and the thought of travel excited her too. Her sisters had gone out West with their husbands; one to Leadville, Colorado and one to San Francisco, California. Perhaps she could visit them while she was out there.

She was excited too at the prospect of owning her own business and being her own boss. She and Brady considered the possible places she could go. Virginia City, Nevada was still booming because silver continued to pour out of the mines at an enormous pace. A town with such a large population would provide many subjects for her book. Her plan changed as she read the newspapers and learned of a town called Bodie. Miners were beginning to flock there because gold had been discovered. It was a new find. Why not invest her time in a nascent strike and watch it grow from its beginning?

With mixed feelings, she had said goodbye to Julia and Mathew. They had been so good to her. Mathew had taught her everything she knew about photography. Now she was eager to go apply that knowledge. She was sad to say goodbye to these good friends because she realized she would probably never see them again. Both were in their fifties. Their lives on the East Coast were almost a continent away from her new destination. She cried as she bid them goodbye and thanked them for their hospitality and friendship.

Susanne had perked up once she was settled on the train. She was going west to a new life, one of her own making. She would make new friends and see unique sights. She would indeed create a photobook about mining. However, it would be so much more than the life of a miner. She would look at it from a sociologist's point of view.

She stopped first in St. Louis to see her family. Her parents were excited to see her but displeased that she intended to move on again so quickly. Her younger brother Tom was away at school, but he wrote that he supported her decision and wished he could tag along. Someday he would visit her, he promised. So, eventually Susanne again found herself saying goodbye to people she cared about. Her mother was gracious. She had already surrendered two daughters to the West. Perhaps she would visit, she said. Susanne had smiled, knowing her mother would never leave home without her husband. Gerald, however, was always too busy with his horses to consider a vacation. Susanne had assured her mother she would come home soon. At the time, she had meant it. But then she had gotten to the West and had met Liam, and she knew she wasn't going anywhere soon. For the first time in her life, she was in love.

These thoughts ran through Susanne's mind as she watched Jodie eat. He did have a big appetite. He was constantly on the move, running here and there, and so he was always hungry. He and Mary Kay had not become friends as Susanne and Nick had hoped, but Jodie did appreciate Mary Kay's fine cooking. He showed up on time for every meal with hands washed and hair combed.

Now Jodie looked up from his apple pie and glanced out the window. Something out in the wide, dusty street had attracted his attention. He stood up and without a word to Susanne, he bolted for the door. Susanne watched as he ran across the street to where a man had just climbed down from his horse. Jodie flung himself at the man and hugged him fiercely. The man wrapped his arms around Jodie and hugged him back. Then, he walked Jodie around the corner, and they disappeared from view.

Susanne realized that this must be Jodie's father, the long-lost dad who Nick was certain had deserted his family. Susanne sat still, stunned. She knew the man whom Jodie had clutched so tightly. And while she was overjoyed for Jodie, she could not conceive of her own future right now because the man whom Jodie had run to was Liam. And although Susanne had chosen a career over marriage, she had recently considered marrying Liam. However, if Liam were indeed Jodie's father, then he was already married. Jodie had a mother. Tears rolled down Susanne's cheeks.

CHAPTER 10

Billy steered Jodie around the corner and off Main Street. "My God, Jodie, what are you doing here?"

"What do you mean?"

"What are you doing in Bodie of all places?"

"What do you mean? Aren't you glad to see me?"

"Just answer the question, damn it. Why are you here? Where's your mother? For God's sake, tell me she's not here too!"

"No, Mom's still in San Diego. She got sick and had to go to a hospital for a few months." She sent me to stay with Aunt Tess."

"Your Aunt Tess is here?"

"No. She was gone when I got here."

"Where the hell are you staying then?"

"I'm staying with a friend I met on the stagecoach on my way here. His name is Nick, and he owns a boarding house. I'm living with him and his sister-in-law. They don't live far from here. Do you want to meet them?"

"No, not today. How long have you been here?"

"About two months. I came in April. But now that you're here, we can go back to San Diego. I've been trying to save up money to get home. I knew you would go back there. Why are you here in Bodie anyway, Dad?"

"I've got business here. But it's going to take me a while. In the meantime, you can't stay here. I'm sending you back to San Diego."

"What do you mean? Why can't I stay here?"

"Don't be dense, Jodie. This is no place for you. You're going home."

"But who will I stay with? That's why Mom sent me here; I had no one to live with there. At first, I thought I could stay with Ian, but that didn't work out. You know how his dad is! And his mom didn't think it was a good idea either."

"Quit your damn blathering. You talk too much. And no, you can't stay here."

"But why can't I live here with you?"

"You can't, that's all. I have business that takes me out of town, so I'm not here much. I've been gone a couple of months and am just now getting into town."

"Aren't you mining? Isn't that what you left home to do? If you're a miner, why do you leave Bodie where all the mines are?"

"Quit asking me stupid questions. Shut up, and let me think for a minute."

Jodie stood quietly while his dad paced back and forth in the empty lot, but then he couldn't wait.

"Aren't you going to ask about Mom? I told you she was sick."

"Yeah? What's the matter with her?"

"She has tuberculosis. Doc made her go to the sanitarium. She'll be there for a couple more months. That's why I can't go home. When will you be able to go back to San Diego? We can go there together and wait for her to get better."

Billy began to pace again. What to do with a son he did not want? And a sick wife? He had no intention of ever returning to San Diego. But hell, having Jodie here would gum up his plans. His friends in Bodie knew nothing of a wife or child because he had presented himself as a bachelor. He intended to leave it that way. What a predicament! He couldn't send Jodie back to an empty house, and he certainly couldn't take him in here. When in town, he stayed at the hotel. Sometimes he stayed with Susanne but not often because she worried about her reputation. A good Catholic girl, she never felt right sneaking around. What would she do if she found out he was married? He knew the answer. She would dump him immediately. Damn Jodie for showing up here! He stopped his pacing and grabbed Jodie by the arm.

"Here's what we're going to do," he said. "You're going to go back to the boarding house and stay with your friends for a couple of months. I will finish my work, and then we will go home together. Give me a couple of months, will you, Pal?"

"Why can't I live with you, Dad?" Jodie was on the verge of tears.

"Sweet Jesus! Aren't you listening? I told you that I'm in and out of town on business. When I'm here, I have a hotel room. So no, you can't stay with me. If you mention it one more time, I swear I will beat you."

Jodie choked back tears. He didn't know how to please his dad.

"Do you want to meet Nick? Maybe you already know him. He's a carpenter in town."

Billy shook his head. Another complication because he did know Nick. And he knew that Nick knew Susanne. He must be careful now, or the life he had created for himself here would spiral downward.

"Listen, Pal." He put his arm around Jodie. "I don't know your friend. I'm not in town often. But my business is private, and I'm not ready to talk about it yet. So, for this to work, you must not tell anyone you saw me. That way, I can go about my pursuits. When I'm finished, we'll go home to San Diego. Your mother will be well in a couple of months, and then we will be a family again. I promise.

But this will only work if you stay at the boarding house, keep quiet, and let me finish my business."

Jodie looked at his dad. "You want me to stay at the boarding house and not tell anyone that you are here?"

"Exactly right. If your friend Nick knew I was here, he wouldn't be so accommodating. He would expect you to move out and live with me, and I've explained why that won't work."

"Maybe you could pay Nick to let me stay there. Then it wouldn't have to be a secret. I wouldn't have to pretend I don't know you. Would that work?"

"No damn it! That won't work. For reasons I can't tell you now, it won't work. You will have to trust me on that." Billy tightened his grip on Jodie's shoulders. "So, listen up. You are to tell no one you saw me or know me. NO ONE! Just let me get my work done, will you?"

Jodie nodded his head. "Okay, Dad. But in a couple months we'll go home, right? You promise?"

"Yes. I promise. So, don't come looking for me. I'll find you. If you run into me on the street, act like you don't know me. That will be better for everyone. In a couple of months, I'll tell you all about my business, and we'll go home. In the meantime, do you need any money?"

"No. I have some, but thanks." Jodie thought of the money he had stolen from Nick. He no longer needed it to get back to San Diego.

"Okay. Go along now. I have things to do."

Jodie turned and dejectedly walked away. He knew his dad was watching him and that made him nervous. Pretending not to know his dad would be difficult. What if he messed up and spoke to his dad on the street without thinking? His dad would certainly take his belt to him for that. Jodie shuddered as he remembered the pain his dad's belt had inflicted in the past.

Jodie wondered how he was going to explain his rude behavior to Susanne whom he had left sitting alone in the restaurant. He would have to bluff and pretend that nothing was wrong. So, he took a deep breath, ran back into the café as quickly as he had run out, and settled himself once again in the chair opposite Susanne.

"Where did you go?" Susanne asked innocently.

"I saw someone from home, a friend of my dad's."

"What's his name?"

"Who?" Jodie looked at her.

"Your dad's friend. What's his name?"

Jodie thought for a minute and figured it wouldn't hurt to tell Susanne his father's name. That wasn't the same as telling her he had actually seen him. "His name is Billy."

Susanne put down her glass of iced tea. "Your dad's friend is from San Diego?" she asked.

"Yes."

Susanne wondered why Jodie was lying. The man had obviously been his dad. She could tell by the eager way Jodie had rushed to him. Why would Jodie come back now and deny seeing him? Jodie had told her several times that he needed to get back to San Diego because his dad would go there. So, why deny seeing him now?

Then, Susanne thought of something else. She not only knew the man whom Jodie had hugged, but she knew him well. She was romantically involved with Liam. But Jodie had called him Billy. Why the name change? Then, she almost smiled as she realized that both Liam and Billy were the same name. Both were derivatives of William. Liam was merely the Irish version.

Susanne picked up her iced tea glass and began to fiddle with it while she thought things through. Then she asked, "So, does your dad's friend, Billy, live here in Bodie now?"

"No, he said he is here on business and then plans to leave again."

"Does he know where your dad is?"

"I asked him, but he said he doesn't know."

"Well, I am glad you were able to see someone from home, even if it was for just a few minutes." Susanne smiled at Jodie. "Here's a thought— since he is your dad's friend, I am sure your dad would be most grateful to him if he looked out for you now. Did you explain to him that you are living with a group of strangers?"

Jodie nodded. "I did. I told him about the boarding house, and he said I should stay there."

Susanne sat back in her chair and looked at Jodie. Her tea was forgotten. She had several questions. First, why had Billy changed his name to Liam when he came to Bodie? Second, why hadn't he returned to San Diego to his family or been in contact with them? Third, why wouldn't he take charge of his only son now that he knew he was here? Why send him back to live with Nick?

Nick and Liam knew each other. She had introduced them herself. She knew that Nick did not care much for Liam. Mary Kay had told her that. Mary Kay had also told her that Nick did not think Liam was good enough for her. Maybe Nick was right. Maybe the man she fancied she loved wasn't much of a man after all.

Why had he come to Bodie in the first place and pretended he wasn't married? Susanne had known him for almost a year, and he had never once mentioned a wife or a child. Instead, he had told Susanne that he loved her and had never loved another woman until he met her. He hadn't proposed marriage but had recently told her he wanted to someday spend his life with her. Why would a married man commit himself to another woman? Jodie thought his dad was a miner. Susanne knew him as a professional gambler. He had been gone for a couple of months on the gambling circuit. Now, Susanne realized, Liam had been out of town for the same two months that Jodie had been here. No wonder they hadn't run into each other before now.

Susanne did not know what to do. Both a man and his son had lied to her. She expected Liam to stay in town for a couple of weeks now as he always did when he returned from a trip. Bodie was part of his gambling circuit, and he enjoyed playing cards here. Liam would expect to be with her while he was here. They were a couple. Susanne sighed. How could she possibly be with him intimately, knowing he was a phony?

As she and Jodie left the restaurant, she decided to play dumb and pretend she knew nothing of Jodie's relationship to Liam. She would wait and watch. She was determined to figure out exactly what Liam's game was. In the meantime, she would tell no one what she knew.

* * * * * * * * * *

Liam was waiting for Susanne outside her studio when she arrived a few minutes later, and she was glad she had sent Jodie off to play ball. Unexpectedly, she was pleased to see Liam and her resolve to send him away faltered. She did not protest when he gathered her in his arms and kissed her.

"I didn't expect you until Wednesday," she told him.

"I missed you, so I decided to come on home. I had a run of good luck so didn't feel the need to stay longer. I really fleeced some of those fellows in Denver. It was all good. So, I checked into the hotel and came straight here. How late are you working?"

"A couple of hours. I have three appointments. Later you can take me to dinner. No, that won't work. I forgot that I am going to Mary Kay's for dinner, but I know she won't mind if I bring you. Let's go there instead." Susanne waited to hear his excuse. She knew now that he would not go to dinner at Mary Kay's.

"No, not tonight, Love. I don't want to share you with any-one tonight." Liam hugged her tighter. He could go nowhere near the boardinghouse because Jodie was living there. And with Nick! The worst possible luck! And to make matters worse, Liam realized he couldn't stay in town because he would run into both Nick and Jodie. No, he would have to leave again and stay gone until Jodie's mother sent for him. Jodie would certainly tell his mother that he had seen his dad in Bodie, but chances were good that she wouldn't come looking for him. Even Jeannie had too much pride to chase after a man who didn't want her.

Perhaps I should leave Bodie and just move on and forget Susanne, Liam thought now. *It would simplify things, now that Jodie is in the picture.* But Liam didn't want to do that. When he had left San Diego the year before, he hadn't intended to settle in Bodie. He was just passing through, playing poker for a few days. Nor had he been looking for romance when he unexpectedly met Susanne in the nearby town of Aurora. He had fallen hard for her even though he knew she was out of his league. She came from money and had family connections. She had told him nothing of her means, of course, but he had asked around and learned about her. Now he thought he loved her. He certainly loved her wealth. So, he had been thinking he would marry her. He was a gambler and would gamble that no one would ever find out he was already married. If he never returned to San Diego, no one would be the wiser. But damn Tess! And damn Jodie too! One indiscreet word from Jodie, and the persona Liam had invented for himself would dissolve. Would Jodie keep his mouth closed? This was the real gamble.

Susanne had not been specifically invited to Mary Kay's for dinner although she had a standing invitation. A place would always be set for her, and Susanne had been there just the evening before. She had fibbed about tonight's invitation just to see what Liam would say. He had gone to dinner with her at the Manor twice before and so knew the Pratts. He and Nick could often be found downtown at the same saloons, although Nick did not gamble. Nick said he worked too hard to squander away his money. He and Liam weren't friends but were friendly when they ran into each other. Many evenings when Nick went into the Commercial Saloon or into Wagner's for an after-shifter, Liam was already there.

Nick wouldn't have chosen Liam for Susanne but figured her love life was her own business, so he stayed out of it. At present, Nick had no love life of his own and preferred it that way. He was not one to meddle in other people's affairs, and he didn't want anyone interfering in his. He already had Mary Kay who knew no boundaries when it came to him. She was constantly telling him what to do and asking him personal questions. She was just like his sisters back home, irritating; but she also added immense quality to his life. She was his best friend, and he enjoyed living with her and being an uncle to her children.

CHAPTER 11

"Listen, you eejit! Someday you will be in love, and I will personally make your life miserable. I will taunt you and tease you," Nick barked.

Jodie smiled. He liked to tease Nick, and he liked to be teased by Nick in return. But now he asked, "Do you think you'll still know me when I'm old enough to be in love?"

"Yeah, yeah, you can count on it. I plan to be part of your life from now on."

Jodie felt reassured. Sometimes he asked questions like this just to hear Nick's response. He still felt the need to test Nick. If his own dad wouldn't take him, how could he expect a man like Nick to want him?

Jodie was feeling anxious. It had been a month since he had run into his dad, and he replayed the encounter over and over in his head. His dad had obviously been unhappy to see him. Maybe his dad had just been surprised. After all, he certainly had not expected to run into his son on a street in Bodie. But Jodie felt that it was more than just surprise on his dad's part. His dad had seemed almost hostile. He had been impatient, as though it was Jodie's fault for inconveniencing him. Yes, that was the word, Jodie decided. Jodie was an inconvenience to his dad. Jodie felt deeply wounded. How could a son be an inconvenience? Didn't most men want a son? Weren't children supposed to be loved and cherished? That's not what Jodie was feeling.

At times, he had felt neglected back home too. At times, he knew his dad hadn't wanted him around. For instance, Jodie knew not to bother his dad when he was reading the newspaper. Or when he was drinking whiskey with a pal at the kitchen table. But this incident with his dad was different somehow. Jodie felt depressed every time he thought of his family. It hadn't been perfect because his parents fought often, mostly about money. But they had been a family, and it bothered Jodie that they were now scattered in three different places.

He thought again of his dad's antagonism toward him and was ashamed for being disloyal. What was he thinking? Of course, his dad loved him and wanted only the best for him and his mother. That was why his dad had gone away. He needed to support his family and had fully expected to strike it rich at the mines. Then he would buy the house his wife wanted and get Jodie the dog he had long promised him. *So, no more disloyal thoughts*, Jodie told himself. He had to trust that his dad knew what he was doing. It wouldn't be long, and they would be a family again. His mom would get better, and they would return to San Diego. Jodie told himself to be patient and let the adults take care of things. After all, he was just a young boy.

But then it was the Fourth of July, and he saw his dad again. The day had started out pleasantly enough. Jodie had already been in town when the shooting started, but this time he hadn't been afraid because he knew the town wasn't under attack.

It had been different in May. He had been in Bodie for only three weeks, and the gunfire had brought him out of bed with a start. Running to the kitchen in his pajamas, he had found Nick calmly reading the newspaper with a cup of coffee in his hand. Mary Kay was stirring oatmeal on the stove. Neither had seemed upset when Jodie burst into the room asking, "Who's shooting? Who's shooting?"

Nick had looked up. "Today is Cinco de Mayo. The shooting will continue all day."

"Why?"

"Celebrating. It's an anniversary of sorts."

"What anniversary?"

Nick had closed his paper and had pointed to the chair next to him. Jodie sat down. Nick asked, "Do you remember that the United States fought a civil war?"

"Sure. It ended two years before I was born."

"Well," Nick had continued, "while the United States was occupied with our war, French forces came over here and invaded Mexico."

"Why would France want Mexico?"

"France didn't want Mexico, but it wanted a foothold in North America. It had lost its holdings when Napoleon sold the land to President Jefferson sixty years before," Nick explained.

"The Louisiana Purchase!" Jodie exclaimed. "We studied about it in school."

"You're right," Mary Kay said as she put a couple of hot biscuits and a glass of cold milk in front of him. Although it was only 6:00 o'clock, she was up, dressed, and had breakfast started. She said to Jodie, "Pretty sneaky of France, don't you think, to strike while the United States was preoccupied?"

Jodie nodded. "So, what happened? Did Mexico give in?"

"Certainly not. The French planned to capture Mexico City, the capital, but they were defeated before they could get there. The Mexicans stopped them at a town called Puebla. So, that's what we are celebrating today: Mexico's victory over France. It happened on the fifth of May. In Spanish, it's known as Cinco de Mayo."

Nick had been right about the guns. Men had fired them off all day. Later, when Jodie had gone to town, he had seen both American and Mexican flags displayed everywhere. That night, one of Bodie's fraternal organizations had held a masquerade ball, and townspeople had danced into the early hours of the morning. No one from the Pratt household had attended. If Mary Kay thought cardplaying was evil on Sundays, she definitely was not going to approve of dancing.

So, on the Fourth of July, the early morning gun fire had not frightened Jodie. He knew now that the patriotic citizens of Bodie would go all out to celebrate the country's birthday in style, beginning with a thirteen-gun salute at dawn. Two years before, the country had celebrated its Centennial. The population of Bodie had not yet exploded to the thousands it was at this time, but the day had certainly been celebrated as most of the men in town had spent the day in the saloons drinking to the country's health.

Now, with a town crowded with people, the town leaders had set the stage for a fun-filled day. Actually, it would be a three-day affair because most of the mines had closed after shift on July second. By the fifth of July, many in town would be nursing a hangover. Many would still be in the saloons hoping that the hair of the dog might help, when in truth, it would only delay the pain.

Community organizers had dressed the town in red, white, and blue bunting; and many American flags waved in the breeze. Some hardy souls had taken wagons out of town and had returned with branches and leaves of aspen and willow that they stuck up and down Main Street. The dust and dirt remained, but the greenery added to the festive mood.

So, the day had begun at dawn, and Nick and Jodie had been among the first to go to town. Nick hadn't been able to tempt Tristan from his bed at such an early hour to go along. Cindy had raced ahead as Nick and Jodie walked the length of Main Street, admiring the changed look. Nick clearly loved this town, and Jodie could see why. It bustled with activity even on days that were not holidays. Because Nick was acquainted with so many of the townspeople, Jodie now knew many of them as well. When Jodie went into stores or into the new post office, he was often greeted by name. This made him feel important. He liked being a friend of Nick's.

On this holiday, as the crowd converged, Nick had spied a certain woman and had taken refuge in his carpentry shop. He had not only closed the door but had locked it. He was in hiding. He had called Jodie an eejit because Jodie had teased him about having a sweetheart. Nick insisted that nothing was further from the truth, but he was indeed having woman problems. Jodie thought the situation was hilarious and teased Nick every chance he got. Now he stood up and put his hands on his hips and in a high-pitched voice said, "Oh, Sugar! Come here, Sugar."

"Stop your nonsense, Lad. There is no woman."

"Sure, there is. That's why you have us locked in here. Otherwise, Miss Alice could sweep in here any minute."

"Have you no mercy? You know I can't stand her, and every time she calls me 'Sugar' in that syrupy Southern drawl, I want to vomit."

"Why don't you just tell her to go away and not bother you?"

"I have told her. I can't get rid of her, and she embarrasses me. The other day, Casey, Lex, and I were in Wagner's when she swept in and called out, 'There you are, Sugar.' I'll never hear the end of it from my friends."

"I think she has marriage on her mind." Jodie grinned.

"Darn tooting, she does! And she's set her sights on me!"

"Maybe she can't resist your good looks, charming personality, and stable bank account."

"You calling me charming? And good looking? I didn't think you noticed my talents, Lad."

Jodie threw a rag at him. "Not me. I've noticed nothing of the sort. But the ladies have. 'Oh Sugar!'"

Nick tossed the rag back. "Alice is definitely pursuing me. Look at me, hiding in here like a scared rabbit."

Jodie had a question. "I know she and her mother moved in across the street from us a couple of weeks ago, but where did they come from?"

"Somewhere in the South, and I'm guessing that from her drawl. God, what an aggressive woman!"

"Why not tell her that you already have a lady friend? I'm sure Susanne would help you out and pretend to like you."

"Pretend? She wouldn't have to pretend. She likes me."

"Yes, but not romantically. You're just her good friend."

"True."

"People your age are too old for love anyway." Jodie smirked.

"I'm not old!" Nick was indignant.

"You're old enough to be on display in a museum somewhere." Jodie laughed at his own joke.

Nick grimaced. "Speaking of romance, I forgot to tell you that Susanne's beau is back in town. He's taking her to the ball tonight. I don't think he's good enough for her, but it's her life, so I don't interfere. Come on, let's go stake out a place to watch the parade, but keep an eye out for Alice, will you?"

"Yes, and then we get to watch the ball game. Are you sure you don't want to give me the Bodie team?" Jodie asked hopefully.

"Not a chance. That's my team. Yours is Red Cloud, and it's going to lose big time."

Just the month before, a meeting had been held at the Miner's Union Hall to organize a baseball club. Bodie residents were looking forward to today's game, but none were more enthused than Nick and Jodie.

So, on this Fourth of July, it was after the parade, after the picnic, after the baseball game, and after the tug of war that by chance, Jodie saw his dad in Bodie for the second time. This time Jodie did not run up and hug him. In fact, Jodie did not speak to him. Instead, he watched from across the street as his dad escorted a beautiful blonde toward the Miner's Union Hall. Jodie could hear a fiddle tuning up just as the lady turned around. It was Susanne! He watched his dad lean down and give her a quick kiss on the lips. Stunned, Jodie grabbed on to the wooden post next to him for support.

"Mother of God," he whispered.

After the Fourth of July, Jodie would have nothing to do with Susanne. He avoided her and spoke rudely to her when they met. She was both baffled and hurt by his behavior. She had no idea that Jodie had seen her with his dad and that Jodie blamed her for his dad's infidelity.

Jodie knew from his dad that women were weak and needed men to take care of them. Women, therefore, were always on the lookout for a man. His dad had instilled this philosophy in him. So, in Jodie's mind, Susanne had purposefully seduced his dad. She was beautiful and could have any man she wanted, and she wanted his dad. She had been elegantly dressed in a maroon silk gown when she had accompanied him to the ball. Jodie wondered if his dad had bought her the shiny diamond necklace she wore around her neck. Jodie could not remember his dad ever buying jewelry for his mother.

His dad always said there was no harm in a married man looking at other women as long as he didn't touch, and Jodie had seen his dad ogle waitresses right in front of his mother. His dad would laugh and say, "Looking is permitted because women go to all the trouble of dressing up just so they can catch the eye of us unsuspecting men. That's how your mother caught me." Then he would wink and laugh some more.

Jodie decided that this was the reason Susanne always dressed so fashionably.

Had he thought about it, Jodie would have realized that Susanne did not know Billy was his dad. Had she known, she certainly would have said, "Jodie, your dad is in town." But she hadn't said that and had said her beau's name was Liam. Jodie did not know why she didn't call him by his right name, but it didn't matter. She had set her sights on his dad, and so Jodie hated her.

Susanne couldn't get Jodie to tell her why he was acting so. She and the boy had been good friends. At the Sunday Sing-a-Longs, Jodie had always sat next to her on the sofa. Together, they would hum the songs they particularly liked.

He liked to ask her riddles. "Why is the library the tallest building in a city?" When she did not know the answer, he would gleefully tell her, "Because it has the most stories." She would laugh. He liked to make her laugh, so he looked for jokes to tell her. Nick's friend Casey had taught him some magic tricks, and Jodie liked to amuse Susanne with these as well.

But now, Jodie no longer sat with Susanne at Mass or walked home with her afterwards to write a letter. He did not come to her studio in the afternoons after he finished his chores. He did not meet her out in the field to carry her equipment. He wanted nothing to do with her.

Jodie did not place the blame where he should have, squarely on his dad. On July fifth, the day after the ball, Jodie had gone to town early and had stood outside the hotel where his dad stayed. He hoped to catch his dad as he exited. Instead, his dad had approached the inn, coming from the opposite direction. Jodie realized then that his dad had not slept at the hotel that night. He must have spent the night in Susanne's small apartment above the studio. Jodie wanted to cry.

Billy noticed Jodie yards away and wondered, *Now what? How does the boy know I'm in town?* He could feel himself getting angry.

"Hi, Dad," Jodie said softly. "I've been waiting for you. Where have you been?"

"Out for breakfast. What are you doing here?"

"Waiting for you. I saw you last night going into that fancy ball, so I knew you were back in town."

"Saw me, you say?"

"Yes, you were with a woman. I saw you kiss her."

"Kiss her? No. You are mistaken."

"On the lips. I saw you," Jodie was whispering now.

"No, I was just being friendly. I did kiss her, but it was just a peck on the cheek. She's an old friend of mine, my business partner's wife. He had to be out of town, so he asked me to take his wife to that dance. She insisted on going because it was the first social event in the new Miner's Union Hall. She was on some committee or other. So, I was doing her husband a favor."

Jodie had no words to contradict his dad. He knew he was lying about Susanne being someone's wife. Finally, he asked, "Dad, how long have you been in town?"

"Just since yesterday or I would have looked you up."

"Did you go see Mom in the hospital?"

"No. She needs rest if she's going to get better, so I thought it best to stay away."

"Will you go to see her? Will you take me? We really should visit her."

"No, we are not going to do that. Tuberculosis is contagious, so the hospital staff wouldn't let us in even if we went."

Jodie persisted. "Have you written to her?"

"No, not yet. You know I'm not much of a correspondent."

Jodie didn't know what to think about a dad who hadn't written even one letter. "Did you finish your business? Are you back in Bodie for good? Can I come stay with you now?"

Liam shook his head. "Not yet. I have a meeting in Reno. I came here only to take that lady to the dance. I have completed that obligation, and now I must leave."

"Will you take me with you? Please, Dad."

"No. Not now. I expect you are getting along fine at the Manor. You look well. I want you to stay there until your mother recovers. Then, you and I will go back home together. I promise."

"But Dad. . ."

"Damn it, Boy. Do not beg. Don't you ever beg. It's a sign of weakness."

Jodie began to cry. His dad took him by the shoulders and shook him. "Stop your damn whimpering, or I will give you something to cry about." How had he raised such a weak boy? Billy was disgusted.

Jodie took a deep breath and tried to stop crying. Everything had suddenly gone wrong.

Billy let go of his son and asked, "You haven't told anyone you've seen me, have you?"

Jodie shook his head no.

"Okay, I have to leave. Keep your damn mouth shut, do as you're told, and don't make a fuss. I'll be back to get you."

"When?"

"Jesus Christ! I'll be here when I get here. Stop your damn bellyaching." With that, Jodie's dad opened the hotel door, strolled through, and did not look back.

Jodie stood there and tried to catch his breath. He always seemed to make his dad angry. He put his hands in his pockets, his head down, and headed for home. He desperately wished he could talk to Nick about all this, but he had promised to keep quiet. He did have two questions though. First, why had Dad lied about Susanne? And second, how did his dad know they called the boardinghouse the Manor?

CHAPTER 12

Nick had not noticed Jodie standing across the street when he escorted Mary Kay into the dance at the Miner's Union Hall just minutes before Liam and Susanne arrived. He had been keeping a keen eye out for Alice though. Mary Kay leaned over and straightened his tie as she told him, "I promise to alert you the minute I see her. Then you can make your escape."

A few minutes later, Nick was not pleased to see Liam with his possessive arm around Susanne's shoulder. Nick just could not bring himself to like this man and did not understand how a woman as sophisticated as Susanne could fall for him.

Liam was a gambler, something else that Nick could not understand. Nick worked long hours producing quality work, so he did not understand a man who did no actual work. To have money and to gamble it away was beyond his ken. It showed laziness. It reeked of irresponsibility. Just thinking about it made Nick impatient with Susanne and her choices.

Nick spent a lot of time downtown at the bars. He liked his beer, but he also liked socializing with his friends. So, while he was with this group or that one, he and Liam often ended up in the same place. Liam didn't favor one gambling establishment over another—whichever ones offered poker or faro. Sometimes he could be found at the roulette table. He moved around, always on the lookout for unwitting miners who were eager to show off their gambling skills. Routinely, they lost. Their money would be gone before they had settled comfortably into the game. In Nick's mind, Liam was a vulture, preying on these young greenhorns.

"He's no good scum," he often remarked to Mary Kay. "Something about him is off, but I can't figure out what exactly." And yet, Nick said nothing to Susanne because she would certainly tell him to mind his own business. Liam had great card sense and traveled on the gambling circuit, competing against other card sharks of his caliber. He wasn't in Bodie often, so Nick did not often have to deal with him.

Liam had always had an eye out for the ladies. Although he considered them inferior to men, he wanted a beautiful woman on his arm to share his successes. He danced expertly and liked to show off his ballroom skills with young ladies equally adept. He relished the admiring looks he received from those less proficient. Women fawned over him and told him how amazing he was, but the more they flattered him, the less he respected them. And yes, he wanted women for their sexual favors. He used women to his advantage and felt nothing but distain for them all the while. They had no idea.

And so, even ladies of good breeding flocked to him. They were swayed by his handsome looks and his suave manners. He was gracious to all and a welcome house guest. Hostesses sought him out because he complemented every dinner table. He was in his element at dinner parties where he could speak eloquently and humorously on any topic. Men also liked him and thought he was a good sport. People would have been surprised to learn of his humble background, something he never shared with anyone. He had done his homework and had created the perfect but false pedigree for himself.

A year ago, he had gotten out of a bad marriage to a weak woman. He had simply walked away, changed his name from Billy to Liam, and resolved never to marry again. His marriage to Jeannie had been a mistake, but he had been young, and lust had gotten the better of him. He had desired Jeannie and desperately wanted to have sex with her, but the only path there was marriage. She came from a wholesome family with an attentive father who would have shot anyone who looked at his daughter indecently. Billy had no choice but to walk down the aisle with her. Now after twelve years, he had found marriage too confining. He promised himself that he would never be tied down or accountable to anyone again.

And yet, he was now considering marriage to Susanne. He loved her. She was nothing like the ladies he had courted or bedded before and certainly nothing like his wife. Susanne had confidence. Her welcoming manner and gift of small talk instantly put others at ease. She was well read and could intelligently discuss both world events and the world of sports. He appreciated that she was well connected and had friends in high places. This would be to his advantage someday. She was quite proper in public but warm and affectionate when the lights were turned down low, and they were alone together. Yes, Liam knew he would eventually marry Susanne. It had taken him months to get her into his bed, and she was not going to carry on illicitly for long without a commitment from him. She had too much class for that. He knew she loved him; she would never have put herself in such a compromising position otherwise.

Liam was not concerned about Nick's presence in Susanne's life. She had explained it to him. "We're just platonic friends. Nick is almost like a brother to me."

Liam had never had a platonic relationship; he preferred a girl who would cuddle with him in the barn. He wanted sex, not friendship. But he believed Susanne about Nick. He knew she spent evenings at the boarding house when he was away, and that pleased him. It was better that she spent time with Nick and Mary Kay, away from the eligible bachelors in town. He couldn't afford for her to fall for someone else.

Liam wasn't sure just why Susanne had chosen rough and tumble Bodie to photograph, and he wasn't certain she would stay long when her book was finished. But in the meantime, she owned her own studio and was self-sufficient. He wanted her.

Billy had broken several hopeful hearts when he did not return to Georgia at the end of the war. Instead, he and a fellow soldier decided to try their luck out West. He had seen enough brutality and needed a change of scenery. He had wanted to travel west with his best friend from school days, Drue Bailey, but Drue's cousin Mike Julian disapproved of Billy. He had taken a disliking to him the first time they had met as teenagers in Georgia. Mike was older than both Drue and Billy by five years. He had cautioned Drue that there was something off about his new friend.

"Just look at the guy, Drue. Billy is a pretty boy who thinks highly of himself. He is committed only to himself and his own interests. If you ever needed him, I don't think he would be there for you."

Drue looked up to Mike and usually listened to him, but he would not listen about Billy. He had found a pal who shared the same interests he did. "Yeah, but he's fun, Mike. He's always up for anything. I know I can't count on him; he's not that kind of friend. But we have fun together."

Drue had been born in Raleigh but had grown up in Gainsville, Georgia. He had met Billy the first afternoon he moved to town. On a warm, summer afternoon, they had encountered each other at the creek north of town. Each had a fishing pole in hand. Normally, Billy would have challenged the interloper to stay away from what he considered his creek, his territory. But Drue had won him over with a well-timed wise crack. Billy had laughed, and a friendship was born. School started a few weeks later, and they shared jokes about the new teacher as well as several of their fellow students, although Drue was always kinder than Billy. Also, as a teen, he was not the ladies' man that Billy was, but he enjoyed watching his friend juggle girlfriends with apparent ease.

The Civil War began, and Mike Julian and two of his brothers joined up, eager to fight for the Confederacy. Mike was captured by Union forces and spent almost two years in a prisoner-of-war camp. Later, he would recount horrific stories of his time there.

"I don't know which was worse— the stench of gangrene or the screams of dying men. We sat in our own filth and couldn't sleep because of the rats crawling over us. The food had maggots in it and was too rancid to eat. Scurvy was prevalent and caused all kinds of health problems. We would know we had contracted Scurvy because our teeth would fall out. We sat in that hellhole for nearly two years."

Billy and Drue fared better. When they were old enough, they signed up and joined the cavalry where they each received a signing bonus for supplying their own horses. Both were adept horsemen and spent the war fighting under General Joseph Wheeler's command. Another general named Sherman marched across their state and destroyed everything in his path including the Julian family plantation. The Julian and Bailey cousins had no home to return to, so they turned their vision westward and went off to prospect for gold. Billy was not invited to go, and he always resented Mike for that.

"Damn Mike," he told Drue. "What an adventure we could have prospecting for gold! I don't know why Mike doesn't want me to go. You and I have been together for years, and I hate for you to go off without me."

"Yeah, I get it, Billy. I feel the same way. But you know Mike. He's in charge of this outfit, and we have to do things his way. You and I will stay in touch though, and I'll let you know where we end up. Maybe you can join up with us later."

So, Billy and his buddy Wallace headed West. They traveled the northern route toward Pike's Peak, Colorado where they mined for a few months. They made money, lost it, and regained it. They gambled and drank their way, hooking up with some beautiful women and some not so beautiful.

Eventually they arrived in Montana, adding more gold dust to their savings. The mining town of Butte thrived as men made their fortunes. Here, Billy and Wallace decided to stay awhile. Wallace fell in love first. He met a young, sassy Irish gal who won his heart, and his carefree days ended when he decided to stay with her. Their marriage lasted fifty-four years, and they were blessed with six sons.

Billy also met a young Irish woman whom he would marry. Jeannie Mara was a dark-haired beauty whose family owned a popular bar in town. He liked her cheerful ways and her contagious laugh. He found her alluring and tried to kiss her and embrace her, but she would have none of it. She was a proper young lady, couldn't he see? The more she put off his advances, the more he desired her. Finally, he proposed and married her. Nine months later she gave birth to Jodie. Now both he and Wallace were the proud fathers of sons. They spent a week celebrating, and the mine foreman fired them. However, the mines were busy, and the men soon found other jobs.

At first, Billy had liked Jeannie's family. He liked that they owned a bar. He relished his mother-in-law's fine cooking and was glad Jeannie had learned to cook from her. But soon, he felt that his father-in-law kept too watchful an eye on him.

"Better slow your drinking down, Son," he would say. "You have a full day of work tomorrow, and you'll need to be steady on your feet. It's probably time you headed for home. Supper must be ready."

So, when Billy got off shift, he took to drinking in other bars farther down the street. Jeannie had dinner ready on time, and these meals often grew cold because Billy chose not to come home. Billy was proud to have a son, a display of his virility. But between his job and his drinking, he had little time to spend with his wife or his boy. Jeannie's sister, Tess, tried to warn him that the family thought he should stay home more often, but he wasn't about to take advice from a younger sister.

"Get the hell away from me," he told her. "My wife talks too much, or you wouldn't know our business. Go on home and leave me alone."

And then Billy decided to go south. He missed Drue and all the foolishness they used to get into. Wives were definitely not as much fun. Drue and the cousins had settled in a meadow town north of San Diego that they named for Mike— Julian. A former slave named Fred Coleman had discovered gold there, and Billy wanted in on the action. Jeannie was horrified when Billy told her he wanted to move south.

"South? What are you talking about? Didn't you tell me yourself that Butte was the place for you, and you planned to stay here?"

"Sure, Sweetheart. I know I said that. But that was before I heard from Drue. He's down south prospecting for gold, and he wants me to join him."

"You? He wants you to join him? What about me and Jodie? Would he also be wanting us to join him?"

"Sure, sure. He wants us all to go. He's in California where it's always sunny. We could get out of this bleak weather. Out of this cold."

"I thought you liked Butte. You told me your wandering days were over. You promised me that if I married you, you would stay put. I won't go and leave my family, and that settles it."

But it was not settled. Billy was determined to go and would not listen to her. Finally, her father took him aside and spoke to him. "I'm asking you man to man, Billy. Do not take me daughter and grandboy away. This is not what Jeannie thought she was getting into when she married you. This is not what her mother and I agreed to when you asked for our blessing."

"I get it, Raymond. I know I told you I planned to stay, but I've found a great opportunity in California, don't you see? Things have changed."

"What are you talking about, Boy? What's changed? You can mine here as well as in some God-forsaken place far from here. Please, I'm asking you. Don't take me family away. Jodie is only three years old. He won't even remember us. You would be breaking me wife's heart if you took Jeannie and Jodie away. Reconsider, won't you?"

"I'm going, Raymond. I've made up my mind. Now it's up to Jeannie. She can go with me, or she can stay here. It's her decision."

"You would leave your family behind? What kind of man are you?"

Billy showed him what kind of a man he was when he did not change his mind. The decision was Jeannie's. Would she watch Billy go off, chancing never to see him again, or would she go with him?

Tearfully, she gave in. She packed up her son and her belongings and traveled to Julian, California, so her husband could reunite with his best friend.

And now, this husband whom Jeannie had chosen over her family had deserted her because marriage no longer appealed to him. Jeannie and Jodie did not fit in with his plan anymore. Jeannie was ill, and so it was good that she did not know that Billy was presently considering marriage to someone else, even without proper divorce documents. Billy was not worried about the legal ramifications because he did not think there would be a problem. Legal papers were often lost or misplaced. He would claim that he had filed for divorce. A timely bribe to the proper clerk would help, if it came to that. Then, he would marry Susanne – and her fortune.

CHAPTER 13

Liam would have been surprised to know that Susanne was not as keen on marriage as he was. Marriage had never been a priority for her. Her parents had been happily married for many years, and yes, someday she hoped for a successful marriage like theirs. But not today. Not to Liam.

At age twenty-one, she had preferred a career. Of course, others wanted marriage for her— her father certainly. Young women were expected to go from a father's responsibility to that of a husband's. How else could a man retire successfully into old age if his children were not settled? So, her father was troubled when Susanne refused to marry. It wasn't that she was unmarriageable; everyone thought she was lovely. She had had several suitors but had never considered any of them seriously. Each was looking for a wife, a home, children. At age twenty-one, Susanne had wanted none of that.

Susanne was interested only in photography. Her father could not understand her. He had sent her to college but expected her to return home afterwards, marry, and give him grandchildren. It was what women did. It was her mother, Elizabeth, who understood her. Now in the latter part of the nineteenth century, opportunities existed for women that had not available when Elizabeth was young.

Life had changed since the war between the states. Turmoil prevailed now, and life was unsettled, especially in the South during this period of Reconstruction. What to do with the destroyed plantations and the four million newly freed people? Serious problems, certainly. On the other hand, the railroad had been built, and people were mobile. This was an opportune time for women. Women were not only looking for opportunities, they were creating them. Elizabeth understood that her daughter did not want a traditional lifestyle, and she cheered her on. "Go," she urged. "Do what makes you happy. You have only this one life. Go make the most of it."

Susanne resembled her mother in both appearance and temperament. Elizabeth, a traditional southern belle, brought elegance and charm to her home. She had settled into an appropriate marriage because it had been expected of her to bring two, old, established families together. Fortunately, she loved her husband, Gerald, and was devoted to him and to their family. They had married before the war when life was pleasant and bucolic. Gerald, an expert horse breeder, owned a majestic farm with many thoroughbreds. He traveled regularly on business, and so Elizabeth had brought up their four children often without him. Their girls were grown and gone now, two of them married and settled away from the family home in St. Louis. Susanne was living in Bodie, but her mother hoped that someday she would return home. St. Louis, a cosmopolitan city, had more to offer a young woman— even one who did not want to get married. The only son, Tom, attended a Jesuit college in another state. He would be expected to take over his father's business when his dad retired.

So, Susanne graduated from college and insisted on a career in photography. Perhaps it was her mother's fault that she was so independent. It was her mother who had introduced her to her childhood friend, Julia Brady. Julia's husband, the famous Civil War photographer Mathew Brady, was passionate about his work, and his enthusiasm had rubbed off on Susanne when she had met him as a young teen. After college, she had pleaded with her mother to allow her to go to Washington D.C. to study with him. Yes, Julia could arrange for a suite of rooms for Susanne at the National Hotel, Julia's and Mathew's own residence. Julia would welcome her best friend's daughter and look out for her. Brady was extremely busy; he had two galleries in two different cities. But, yes, Susanne would be welcome to come and study under him. She could follow him around, and he would teach her techniques as they worked. Without delay, she went.

Brady was every bit as busy as he told her he would be, but they got along well. A perfectionist, he spent long hours at his work. Susanne had been content to stay long hours too. She believed she was of some use to him: cataloguing negatives, mixing chemicals, and coating plates. And she learned. Photography, a fairly new art, had been invented by Frenchman Louis Daguerre less than forty years earlier. Brady explained Daguerre's technique to Susanne. Although Brady had never met Daguerre, his teacher Samuel Morse had. Brady knew much about Daguerre from Morse.

On one particularly hot afternoon in August, Brady removed his hat and wiped his brow. Julia was in the gallery at the time and liked to tease her husband.

"With your straw boater, you look like one of those French impressionists – Monet, perhaps."

"Or Degas," Susanne chimed in. She too enjoyed art.

Brady smiled as he removed his thick, blue-tinted eyeglasses and wiped the lens of those as well. His eyes had been weak all his life but were now failing. Most often now, his famous clients sat for one of his assistants in the studio. Brady was there, of course, but not behind the camera. Today he had been explaining the wet plate process of developing film to Susanne.

"I wish you could have known Alexander Gardner who taught this process to me. Although Gardner worked for me, he was an accomplished photographer in his own right. Because of my poor sight, I depended on him to take many photos when I could not. He and I were together at both Gettysburg and Antietam. We had what we called 'Whatizzit Wagons' with us. These horse-drawn wagons were mobile dark rooms. We photographed thousands of war scenes using this equipment."

Although somewhat reserved, Brady had the Irish blarney about him and told Susanne interesting stories as they worked. He had met many important people.

"You do have many famous faces displayed everywhere," Susanne said as she looked around his gallery. "Just on this wall alone, I can see portraits of Clara Barton, Walt Whitman, and even Tom Thumb."

"One of my proudest moments was when I photographed Jenny Lind, the Swedish soprano," Brady told her. "The circus man, P.T. Barnum had arranged for her United States tour. I wanted her to pose for me while she was in New York, but Barnum declined my offer. Said Jenny was too busy." Brady smiled now as he thought back. "I knew of an old school friend of hers who had emigrated to Chicago. Without Barnum's knowledge, I got this school chum to persuade her to pose for me in my studio. I expected Jenny to stay just a few minutes, but she stayed several hours looking at the photos on my walls and asking questions. She was enchanting company."

"Was Barnum angry?" Susanne asked.

"I don't know. I never heard from him again." Brady smiled. "Jenny Lind is one of the highest regarded singers of the century, and she spent time here. I was most honored. Here, look at these photos of her." Brady handed Susanne a portfolio.

Susanne looked at the photos of the beautiful young singer, "The Swedish Nightingale," as she was called. "I expected her to be blonde," Susanne said. "Aren't all Swedes blonde? But look at Jenny's beautiful dark hair. I have much to learn about both photography and life."

As much as Susanne wanted to see Civil War combat scenes, Brady refused. Nor would he talk of the grisly battles. He had spent the war years recording these horrific events, and they had stayed with him and had changed him. He would never talk to Susanne about them; they were not suitable stories for a young woman's ears.

"I will tell you one story about the war that I find mildly amusing," he told her one day. "Remember, no one expected the war to last long, so while he had the chance, New York Congressman Alfred Ely drove to Virginia to watch the first battle. Bull Run, it was called. The Union army was expected to trounce the Confederates, and Ely wanted to see that. So, with picnic basket in hand, he joined others to watch the festivities." Mathew chuckled. "I hope the congressman enjoyed his lunch because he was captured by Confederate forces that afternoon and spent the next six months as a prisoner-of-war."

With his story-teller's gift, Mathew offered Susanne glimpses of many of the renowned who had graced his studio: senators, cabinet members, and Indian leaders. President Lincoln had been there, once with his young son Tad.

Brady picked up the ivory-handled walking stick he always used. "This was a gift from the Prince of Wales, Queen Victoria's oldest son and the future King of England. The prince and his entourage had their photos taken here before the war.

"Speaking of British royalty, let me tell you about the first World's Fair, also known as the Great Exhibition. It was the project of Queen Victoria's husband, Albert. A magnificent Crystal Palace was built in 1851 in London for the occasion, and thousands of people attended. Fortunately, I too was able to go."

Mathew did not take out the display case housing the three gold medals he had won there for his daguerreotypes, the ones that had gained him international fame as a photographer. Mathew was not one to brag.

Although Brady had taken photos of most of the U.S. Presidents of his day, he liked to show a photo of a man who would never be president— the likeness of Robert E. Lee on his faithful horse, Traveler. After the war, the Confederate general became president of Washington College in Virginia, a far cry from his counterpart, General Ulysses S. Grant, who was elected President of something greater than any college. Brady knew and admired both men.

Brady regaled Susanne with stories as they worked. Susanne took it all in and learned from him. Others worked in the studio also, and she learned from them as well. It was a memorable time for her.

Susanne also spent time with Julia. They went to the theater, to luncheons, and to garden parties. Susanne enjoyed Julia's company and eagerly listened to the stories Julia told of her youth.

"Susanne, my dear, you look much like your mother did when she was young— when we were growing up together in Maryland. When we pulled off pranks at school, your mother was always the ringleader." Susanne laughed. She could believe that of her mother.

Julia described the beaus who had courted them after they, as debutantes, "had come out" into society. "It was a whirlwind of parties, dances, and concerts. We attended sporting events and horse races. With so many young men wanting to take us to these events, we could barely catch our breaths.

"It was at one of my garden parties that Elizabeth met your father. What a dashing young man Gerald was back in the day! He was interested in horses even back then. But he certainly could dance. He literally swept your mother off her feet."

Julia gave Susanne details of her parents' wedding— stories that Susanne had not heard before. Julia was Susanne's godmother, and Susanne found her delightful.

Julia shared unhappy news, as well. She told Susanne about financial troubles besetting her beloved husband. When Brady had decided to turn from a commercial photographer to "Pictorial War Correspondent" in 1861, Julia and some of his more conservative friends had tried to dissuade him. He had not listened to them and had spent $100,000 creating plates and photos to record the history of the war. He fully expected the U.S. government to buy these photographs, but after the war, government officials declined. They told him public interest was not there. People had been saturated with grim photos for years, and they wanted to move on. So, Brady had not recouped his losses and was now talking of bankruptcy. At the very least, he was going to have to sell his New York gallery.

To add to the burden, Julia confessed that her doctor suspected she might have a heart problem. No, she hadn't told Mathew. She did not want to bother him when he was so busy. Susanne realized that Julia must sometimes be lonesome because Brady spent so much time working. Who would want a lonely marriage like that, she wondered. Not she.

* * * * * * * * * *

That had been three years earlier, before Susanne had settled in Bodie. Today she was thinking about Liam and how much she loved him. Because she loved him and had wanted to please him, she had given herself to him intimately— more than once. She was thrilled when he whispered that he loved her beyond measure, that he wanted her in his life always. So, this was love! She had never experienced such a powerful emotion. She hated the times when he left town. She felt she couldn't breathe properly until he was home again, standing in her doorway.

"I'm home, Darling," he would say as he swept her up in his arms. He would then lead her upstairs to the darkened bedroom.

And then came the day when she had had lunch with Jodie. When Jodie had run out and hugged Liam, Susanne's idyllic world had stopped spinning. Liam was married. Not only was he a father, he was Jodie's father! He wasn't the unencumbered bachelor he had claimed to be. But then, Susanne reminded herself, she was not the good Catholic girl she pretended to be either. Not anymore. Her mother would be ashamed of her.

At lunch that fateful June day, Susanne had determined to end things with Liam that very afternoon. But when she saw him standing in her doorway, she couldn't muster up the words to tell him to go. She knew she had no claim on him; he belonged to another woman. But this was love, and she found herself powerless in its grip. Susanne's mother had raised her to be a strong woman. Susanne didn't feel strong now, and her mother would be ashamed of her. Her mother's words to her would have been, "Have you no self-respect?"

The answer was, "None," and she continued seeing Liam when he was in town. Oddly, Liam had been spending little time in Bodie recently.

Today, Susanne had unexpectedly found her life upended when she learned she was pregnant. Pregnant by a husband who was not her own! Because she had acted recklessly, her life would be forever altered. Her reputation in the community was in jeopardy as well. Her foolishness astounded her!

Liam had never spoken of marriage, and Susanne wondered if he would offer to marry her when she told him about the baby.

What am I thinking? she admonished herself. *I can't marry a man who is already married, and why would I want to? Liam has not been honest with me from the first day. I was taken in by his charm. I followed my heart instead of my head. Shame on me!*

Susanne made up her mind. Marriage to a liar was out of the question. She also had no intention of living the lonely life of a gambler's wife. She would find herself in the same boat as Julia, having a husband who was rarely home. She did not want to settle for that. She did not want to settle at all. She had no intention of allowing a man to take control of her, her decisions, or her finances. She would give up her independence for no one.

Susanne knew people would talk about her behind her back and call her a hussy. She couldn't help what people thought or said. She could account only for her own actions. She would hold her head up high, go about her business, and pray for a healthy baby. Her reputation in the community would be what it would be. Her dad had a maxim that he liked to bring out at appropriate times: "You made your bed. Now, you have to lie in it."

Susanne had indeed made her bed and must now suffer the consequences. At least she knew that Mary Kay and Nick would be there for her. Relief swept over her as she thought of these good friends. She knew she could count on them, come what may. Susanne sighed deeply, and then she put her head down in her hands and sobbed. Perhaps, she wasn't as strong as she thought she was.

CHAPTER 14

Jodie seemed out of sorts all summer. Susanne noticed the change in him and attributed his change in mood to his dad's rejection the day Jodie had met her for lunch. She couldn't blame Jodie; he must have been greatly disappointed that his dad had not taken him that day, leaving the responsibility of his care to Nick for a while longer.

Susanne had been surprised when Liam left town again the next day. He normally stayed in Bodie for a couple of weeks when he finished a gambling circuit, but not this time. He had returned to escort her to the Fourth of July dance as promised but had left immediately again. Susanne had no idea that Jodie had seen her with his dad and thought she was stealing him away from his mother. She had no idea this was the cause of Jodie's rudeness to her. Instead, she thought Jodie's moodiness stemmed from his dad's rejection.

Nick saw the change in the boy but had no idea why Jodie was so temperamental. Growing pains, he told himself. He did notice that Jodie had given up on the idea of returning to San Diego and did not mention it every chance he got. In fact, he didn't mention it at all. He did not sing his dad's praises anymore either. When he had first arrived, he had begun almost every sentence with the words, "My dad. . ." But no more. Nick thought Jodie was settling in and satisfied with his life in Bodie. So, he didn't dwell on Jodie's irascibility.

Jodie's bad mood pervaded the Manor as he snapped at anyone nearby. He angered Thornton one afternoon. The engineer knocked on the boys' bedroom door, intending to give Tristan a book he had ordered for him. Tristan was not there, but Jodie was, lying on the top bunk. When Thornton asked Tristan later why he had given up the choice bed to Jodie, Tristan replied that Jodie had demanded it, so they had switched. Tristan said it didn't matter to him, and perhaps it didn't; children are resilient, but it mattered to Thornton who despised a bully. He ordered Jodie to take the lower bunk again, and Jodie did so, shrugging like it was no big deal. Thornton kept a close eye on Jodie after that, so he wouldn't mistreat Tristan. These were Mary Kay's children, and no one was going to hurt them while Thornton and Wiley were in the house. Thornton did tell Nick about it, but Nick decided to ignore it.

Jodie found himself in trouble again one warm July day, this time with Nick. Coosie and Nick had invited Uncle Billy to visit, and the threesome were sitting on the veranda having a drink when Jodie arrived home. Jodie joined the group, uninvited. Popular with everyone in town, Uncle Billy had been in Bodie a long time and had had as many interesting adventures as Coosie. Although born in the South, he had never been a slave. He had worked as a steward for the captain of a cotton boat on the Mississippi River. When gold was discovered at Sutter's Mill in the late forties, he and Captain Ralston had headed for the gold fields. Nick had been asking Uncle Billy questions about this time in his life when Jodie joined the group.

"You didn't sail around the Horn, you said. You went to Panama instead?"

"That's right. Men going to California often took a short cut through the Isthmus there."

"What's an isthmus?" Jodie wanted to know.

"I'll explain it to you later," Nick told him.

"No, tell me now."

"Not now. We have company. Don't you have somewhere to be? Some studying, perhaps?"

"Nope. It's summer, remember? No school," Jodie told him.

"Well, why don't you run along and let us gentlemen drink our drinks?" Nick encouraged.

"No, thanks. I want to stay with you."

Nick looked frustrated but did not want to make a scene in front of their guest, so he picked up the conversation where Jodie had interrupted them.

"What happened after you and William Ralston reached California? Did you head for the mines?"

"Ralston and I parted company then after being together for many years. He sailed back to Panama and went into business with some old friends there. Later, he returned and founded the Bank of California. He was always successful in everything he did. Heck of a nice fellow."

Uncle Billy then began to describe the placer mining he had attempted. "We were in Tuolumne County. . . " he began.

Jodie interrupted again. "I bet you're going to tell us you struck it rich and never had to work another day in your life!"

"Jodie, don't be rude to our guest," Nick said. "Apologize now."

Jodie flared up. "Apologize? What did I say? I don't even know who this man is." Jodie looked at Uncle Billy. "Are you a Bonanza King?"

Uncle Billy chuckled. "Nah, Son. No Bonanza King here. I was just about to tell you what a complete failure I was at mining."

Nick stood up. "Uncle Billy, please excuse my bad manners. I should have made introductions when Jodie first sat down." Nick looked at Jodie. "Jodie, I want to introduce you to Mr. O'Hara. He is a great friend of ours, and I expect you to treat him respectfully. Mr. O'Hara, this young lad is Jodie Burke. Jodie is staying with us for a few months while his mother recovers from an illness."

"Yep," Jodie said, "then they're going to kick me out. Send me back home where I belong. They're just counting the days until I leave."

Nick reached across the table to shake Uncle Billy's hand. "It was a pleasure seeing you again, and I enjoyed our visit. Please come any time. You know you are always welcome. Now, if you will excuse us." Nick grabbed Jodie by the shoulders, turned him around, and marched him down the steps and out on to the dirt road.

"Keep walking," he told Jodie. When they were out near the cemetery, Nick stopped and stared at the boy.

"What in the hell was that?" he demanded.

"What?" Jodie was defiant.

"Don't you pretend innocence with me. Why on earth would you be rude to our guest?"

"Who? That man? He's just a Negro. Since when do Negroes get to be guests?"

Nick stared at Jodie like he had never seen him before. "Surely, you don't mean that, Jodie?"

"My dad would never entertain a Negro. He's from the South where Negroes are never guests. Never!"

"What the hell are you talking about?"

"You don't understand about the South. White men there are far superior to the slaves. My dad is a Southern Gentleman. You are nothing like my dad."

Again, the comparison to Jodie's dad! Nick was sorely tempted to tell Jodie just what he thought of his absent father—Southern Gentleman or not. Again, he attempted to reason with the boy instead.

"There is no slavery anymore. Moral men saw the inhumanity of slavery and got rid of it."

Jodie glared at Nick. He had no comeback.

Nick asked, "Did you know Mr. O'Hara before today? Had he offended you in anyway?"

"No, I've never seen him before."

"Well, you certainly were rude to him, and it was uncalled for. We don't treat people like that. You will apologize to him."

Jodie looked at the ground and didn't commit to an apology.

Nick was not finished. "And what was all that about us kicking you out? Lately, you act like you want us to do just that. Is that what you want?"

"You're going to do what you want, just like every adult I've ever known. I have no say."

Nick stepped closer to Jodie, and the boy shrank back as though he were going to be slapped.

"I'm not going to hit you. What's the matter with you?" Nick was thoroughly baffled.

Jodie shook his head. "Please don't kick me out. I have nowhere else to go." Tears rolled down Jodie's cheeks, and then he began to sob.

Nick was flummoxed. He didn't understand Jodie or his mood swings. He grabbed Jodie now and hugged him tight. He stood there in the late afternoon sun and held the boy and let him cry. He didn't realize that Jodie had been testing him, wondering how far he could go before Nick would indeed kick him out. Because his dad had rejected him, he felt unloved and unwanted. Nick didn't owe him anything, not a home nor his friendship. Jodie was in a precarious situation. He knew that. What would it take for Nick to decide enough was enough?

But Jodie did not know Nick. Sure, Nick was often frustrated by Jodie's antics, but if Jodie had given Nick a chance, he would have found that Nick was in it for the duration. Nothing Jodie could do would get him kicked out. Nick couldn't speak for Mary Kay; she wasn't as tolerant. But Nick would never give up on this lonely little boy. So, he held him and let him cry. Finally, he let go of him and wiped away his tears. In a soft voice, he said, "Listen to me carefully, Jodie. I don't want to have to say this again, but I will say it again and again if I need to. I will repeat it until you get it. You are an exceptional young man. You are very special to me, and I am fortunate to have you in my life. You bring me joy every day. I care about you, and I will take care of you. There's nothing you can do to drive me away. Do you understand?"

Jodie nodded.

"Okay, that's settled then. You and I are good, right?"

Jodie smiled shyly at Nick. "Right. I want to stay with you."

"Now, I know something is bothering you. Will you tell me what it is?" Nick asked him.

Jodie desperately wanted to talk with Nick about seeing his dad in Bodie. He wanted to tell Nick that he felt bad because his dad had not wanted him. But Jodie knew he couldn't tell Nick any of these things. He had promised his dad to keep quiet, and he knew the wrath that would befall him if he told. He would get a beating for sure. Besides, Nick was always harping on him about keeping his promises, so for that reason also, he couldn't tell.

"I can't tell you, Nick. I promised not to tell," Jodie pleaded.

"Okay then. We'll leave it at that. Let's go home." They turned around and walked back toward the Manor.

* * * * * * * * *

"Just write the damn letter," Nick demanded. It was the next morning, and Nick was feeling less charitable.

"I don't know what to say. I've never had to write an apology letter before," Jodie told him.

"It won't be your last apology letter if you don't change your ways, Lad. Just tell Mr. O'Hara you are sorry for treating him so rudely."

"I'll say it, but I won't mean it."

"Why not?"

Jodie sighed. "I can't apologize to a Negro. My dad would be disappointed in me."

"Well, your dad's not here, and I am. I'm the one you don't want to be disappointing. You better think about that!"

Jodie rolled his eyes.

Nick asked, "Don't you like Coosie?"

"Sure. I like him a lot."

"Well, he's a Negro."

"Yeah, I know. It's just that my dad would take a switch to me if he thought I was associating with Negroes."

"What do you think about Negroes?"

Jodie sighed again. "I think they're okay. I never met one before I came here. But I do like Coosie."

"You would have liked Mr. O'Hara too if you had given him a chance." Nick stood up and put his hands in his pockets. "Why don't you ever think for yourself, Jodie? I don't know your dad, but I definitely disagree with his racial views. I think you may also disagree but are afraid to stand up to him."

"You're right. He'd kill me."

"Well, I just want you to consider the facts and make up your own mind. Not just about this matter but about everything in life. Think for yourself and have the courage to stand up for what you believe. That's part of growing up." Nick leaned across the table. "And another thing."

Jodie rolled his eyes again.

"Stop with the eye rolling. The other thing I want you to think about is Mary Kay."

"What about her?"

"You better not be rude to her. I won't kick you out, but she will. She won't put up with your nonsense for half a minute. She doesn't know you put Tristan out of his bed, and for your sake, I hope she doesn't find out. Just be careful; that's all I'm saying. And clean up your sour attitude."

"Mary Kay can't kick me out. It's your boarding house."

Nick smiled. "You think so?"

"Sure, women can't own property."

"You're wrong about that, Lad. The laws have changed, and women do own property."

"I thought you owned the boarding house, and Mary Kay ran it for you."

"No, Mary Kay owns it lock, stock, and barrel."

Jodie was confused. "But you built it."

"And a fine job I did!" Nick grinned. "But it's hers. I gave it to her."

"You're kidding!" Jodie couldn't believe Nick would give away an entire house.

"Sorry, no. I am not kidding, and so I am reminding you to mind your P's and Q's around Mary Kay before you get us both thrown out."

Jodie looked at Nick. "Do you really think women are smart enough to own property, and take care of money matters, and things like that? Shouldn't men do that kind of thing for them?"

"You would be surprised, Jodie. Women are plenty smart. Mary Kay is much smarter than I am, but I would never admit that to her."

Jodie giggled.

"Now write the damn letter!"

CHAPTER 15

A year after Mary Kay had settled in Bodie, she had been pleasantly surprised to learn that some old friends were moving to Bodie as well. Joel and Mary Rowe, both born in Cornwall, England, had been neighbors of the Pratt Family in Grass Valley. They came to Bodie, so Joel could take a position at the Syndicate Mine there. They had a son three years younger than Tristan. The Rowes were part of the Pratt's social circle in Bodie, and Mary Kay and Mary saw each other often. Today at lunch, Mary had told her she was expecting a baby. Mary Kay had happily shared the good news at dinner.

When it was Nick's turn to talk about his day, Nick told the others how busy he had been. Everyone wanted something built or repaired, and they wanted it done immediately.

"There's only seven days in a week, Nick. You can't work more than that," Coosie told him.

Tristan, who normally said little, spoke up now, "The Romans had a week with eight days in it."

"How do you know that?" Thornton asked him.

"I read." Tristan grinned at Nick who encouraged everyone to read.

"That you do, Lad." Nick mussed Tristan's hair. "You do me proud. I like a man who reads." Then he looked over at Jodie. "Why do you suppose we now have a seven-day week instead of an eight-day week?"

Jodie looked uncomfortable. "I don't know."

"Well, let's think about it," Nick prodded. "What institution would be so influential that it could change the number of days in a week from eight to seven?"

"The government?" Jodie asked.

"Yes, it would take the government to make it official. But who influenced the government?"

"I don't know," Jodie said.

Nick tried another approach. "Why don't we play cards on Sundays?"

Jodie looked at Nick. "What's that got to do with anything?"

"Answer the question."

"Mary Kay won't let us play cards on Sundays," Jodie responded.

"Right. So?" Nick sat up straighter. "Think about it. Who has influence over Mary Kay, so she won't allow cardplaying on Sundays?"

"I don't know." Jodie was getting angry.

"I don't want you to say, 'I don't know,'" Nick explained. "I want you to think."

"I know the answer," Tristan spoke up.

Nick's shoulders slumped. Jodie frustrated him with his apathetic responses. Now, he looked at his young nephew. "Okay, Tristan, tell us who influences your mother."

"It's the church. The Methodists say we can't play cards."

"Right you are, young man. So, why would the church decide a seven-day week would be better than an eight-day week?"

Tristan was excited to tell him, "Because in the Bible, it says that God made the world in six days, and on the seventh day He rested. So, that's why the church thinks seven is the right number."

"There you go! You are a good lad, Tristan."

"I read!" Tristan said triumphantly.

"Yes, you do. And you know how to think. Reading and thinking are important."

"I read," Jodie said.

"Yeah, yeah! I've seen you do that, but not often. I'd like you to read more. Remember, a person who does not read has no advantage over one who can't read."

"Is that a quotation from Abraham Lincoln?" Mary Kay wanted to know.

"No, not Lincoln," Nick answered. "Does anyone know?"

No one in the dining room answered him, so he said, "I'll tell you what; I'll give you three kids two days to come back and tell me the author of that quotation. Mary Kay has an excellent library here, and I'm reasonably certain she won't mind if you use her books. She has the encyclopedia, as well. And of course, we always have old newspapers and periodicals around here."

Mary Kay spoke up, "I also have the latest copy of *Bartlett's Familiar Quotations*. It would be useful."

"What do we get if we do this?" Jodie asked.

"Get? What do you get? You get the immense satisfaction of learning something you didn't know before. That's what you get!" Nick said. He was irritated.

Jodie rolled his eyes, but now Nick was wound up. "I'll tempt you further. As long as you're knee deep in reading material, I want each of you kids to come to supper on Thursday knowing not only the author of that quotation but also bringing an interesting fact that you found while you were researching. It can be on any subject of your choice."

Jodie again rolled his eyes. "Do we have to?"

"You don't have to. You get to," Nick responded.

Mary Kay spoke up, "I think it's such a good idea that I'll make an extra special dessert on Thursday. The child who brings the most interesting fact will get an extra portion. And I'll be the judge."

"I'm going to find something interesting about Christmas," Nessie piped up. "It's my favorite holiday."

"I thought your birthday was your favorite holiday," Coosie said to her.

"No, birthdays are different. They are not holidays." Nessie thought a minute and then said, "But maybe they should be holidays." She turned to look at Jodie. "Did you know that Wiley and I have the same birthday? January seventeenth."

"It's a big day around here," Wiley said. "Lots of festivities."

"I'm going to be six years old," Nessie proclaimed.

Jodie looked from her to Wiley. "How old are you going to be, old man?"

"Not old enough, Son," Wiley said with a smirk, "not nearly old enough."

"Okay," Nick said. "Supper is over. Let's clear the table. Somebody, deal the cards."

And so, the tradition of bringing interesting facts to the supper table on Thursdays began. In later years the children would fondly remember these times and always called them, "The Thursday Facts." Two of the children would continue the tradition with their own offspring.

It was on the third Thursday that Jodie annoyed Nick. The first two Thursdays went well. With her mother's help, Nessie contributed the fact that the Christmas tree originated in Germany. Her mother also told her that it was only when Queen Victoria put one in her own home that the idea of a decorative tree became popular in England. Nessie always thought kindly of the queen after that.

Tristan told the group that the piggy bank was so named because of the pygg mud that was used to make it. In the spirit of show and tell, he brought his own bank to the table and welcomed any and all contributions. Nick and the three boarders immediately reached in their pockets and dropped coins in his bank. Tristan decided that Thursday was his favorite day of the week. When it was Jodie's turn, and he supplied a baseball fact, no one was surprised. He told another fact about the game the second week. When he arrived at the table the third week with yet another tidbit about America's new pastime, Nick had had enough and put his foot down.

"No more baseball," he told Jodie. "I want you to branch out and learn new things."

"But I'm interested only in baseball," Jodie protested.

"Yeah, yeah, I know. But humor me. In fact, in the spirit of this endeavor, I insist. Next Thursday, surprise us with your ingenuity. I want to listen to your fact and say, 'Wow, I didn't know that.'"

"But you know everything already," Jodie protested. "At least you think you do."

Nick looked at Tristan, "Lad, will you explain to this young man how it is that I do indeed know everything."

Tristan looked solemnly at Nick, and then he grinned. "You read," he almost shouted his answer.

"I do indeed. So, what book are you currently reading, Jodie?"

Jodie was ready for him. He had been expecting the question and had prepared. Proudly, he exclaimed, "I'm reading *Tom Sawyer*."

"Excellent. We'll discuss it when you're finished. When will that be?"

Now Jodie was disgusted. "Do you mean that I have to prove to you that I read it? Like a book report?"

"No, not at all. We'll have a conversation about the book. You'll tell me what you think. I'll tell you what I think. It will be enlightening for both of us. We'll have great discourse."

Jodie rolled his eyes. He was not amused.

Mary Kay asked Jodie, "Why did you choose that particular book?"

"Well, when I discovered that it was Mark Twain and not President Lincoln who said that famous quotation about reading, I decided to try one of his books. I actually like the book."

"Did you know that Mark Twain once lived near here?" Coosie asked. "In Aurora which is only twelve miles away. He had a cabin there back in the early 60s when Uncle Billy lived in Aurora. This was when he was still known as Samuel Clements."

"No, I didn't know that." Jodie looked at Nick. "Now, that's an interesting fact," he said sarcastically.

"Glad to hear you like the book," Nick said. "Now, for next week, I want you three young researchers to tell us about Mrs. O'Leary's cow."

"You have got to be kidding!" Jodie made a face. "Who wants to read about a dumb old cow?"

"Mama, are cows dumb?" Nessie wanted to know.

"They certainly are," Mary Kay responded.

"That's okay. I still want to learn about them. I like cows. I'll do it, Uncle Nick." Nessie smiled at her uncle. She wanted to please him.

"Fortune did indeed smile on me when she gave me such a sweet little girl in my life." Nick winked at her. Nessie tried to wink back but just screwed up her face instead. Everyone at the table laughed.

Mary Kay would help Nessie and the boys research this new fact. By next Thursday, all three children would know about Mrs. O'Leary's cow who seven years earlier had set Chicago ablaze.

Jodie looked at Nick. "I was talking with Judge Bechtel this afternoon when I mailed a letter. Now, that's an interesting man! Quite intelligent. Educated."

Nick did not rise to the bait, so Jodie continued. "The judge told me this town was named after a tin smith from New York who left his wife and six children to come West to prospect for gold."

"Yes," Nick said, "his name was actually Bodey. The name of the town is spelled differently."

"The judge said he died before he could become rich."

"Yes, that was in '59. There was not much interest in this place for a few years after that. Both Virginia City and Aurora kept the miners busy there."

Thornton said, "Actually, a small group of prospectors stayed on here. Always thought they would find gold. Our friend Uncle Billy looked after the mining property and ran a boarding house. It was only because of a cave-in at the mine that gold was unearthed here."

"Yes," Wiley continued the story, "Bodie went from a town of about twenty people to what it is today. Thousands are here now and are still arriving daily."

"I came in the early '70s, right before the cave in," Nick said. "The stars must have been in alignment because I was here before the crowds descended, and I had my choice of properties. First, I built my shop, and then I began work on this place."

"I have a question," Jodie asked now. "Why do you all call this boarding house 'The Manor?'"

"Do you know what a manor is?" Mary Kay asked him.

"In school, we learned that it was an estate in the Middle Ages. I think the manor itself was actually a mansion."

"Correct," Mary Kay agreed. "So, does this boarding house look like a mansion to you?"

Jodie didn't want to get in trouble with her, but he felt that he had to be truthful. "No, not really," he said.

Everyone laughed. Mary Kay smiled and said, "It's a joke, Jodie. This is just a common house. Certainly not a mansion. Nothing special about it."

"Wait just a minute!" Nick jumped up. "I'm offended by your remarks. I built this house myself. All eight bedrooms and a library. Are you seriously going to say that this house is not special? You truly offend me. I am offended!"

"Be quiet for once and sit down," Mary Kay told him. "I'm explaining the joke to Jodie. "To the Manor born,' is a famous expression. . . "

Nick stood up and interrupted her again. "It's an expression all right. From Hamlet. Actually, it's about drinking."

Mary Kay folded her arms and looked at Nick. He sat down. She continued, "'To the Manor born' is a famous Shakespearean expression. It means to be born into a life of wealth. As an aristocrat would. Well, we certainly are not aristocrats here at the boarding house. We're just common people. So, we call this place 'The Manor' just to be funny. It sounds like we are putting on airs."

"Like a tall poppy?" Jodie chimed in.

"Yes, just like a tall poppy," Mary Kay agreed.

What she did not tell Jodie was that her late husband, Ed, had told her he would someday buy her a manor. He had teased her that she needed a manor to lord over. The memory was still too painful.

Jodie smiled. He loved these common people and thought this boarding house was special even if it wasn't a manor. He wanted to live nowhere else. But then he was suddenly filled with a pang of disloyalty as he thought of his dad and mom. His dad would return soon to get him, and together they would go home to San Diego to wait for his mother to get well. He already had a family.

CHAPTER 16

"You're out."

"No, I'm not. I tagged the base," Pete said.

"No, you didn't," Stevie yelled as he threw his glove down on the dirt.

Jodie wiped the sweat from his neck. "It's too hot to play anyway. I've had enough for today. I can't run another step." He walked over to the water bucket, cupped his hands, and took a long swig.

"Me too. It's a real scorcher, and there's not one tree for shade. I wonder if it's always this hot in August?" Marty asked as he too headed for the bucket.

The other boys helped themselves to the water. They were glad Jodie had thought to lug it out to the field earlier in the day. The Bodie boys, as the residents called them, liked Jodie. Even though most of the boys were a year or two older than he, they respected him. They thought he was a good athlete and a good sport.

"Let's go to Bonanza Street and look at the whores," Marty suggested.

"What's a whore?" Jodie asked.

"Damn, Boy! I forget how young you are. Let me tell you about it," Marty offered, and he proceeded to do so. The other boys all wanted it known that they too were worldly and didn't need anything explained to them, so they added bits and pieces of information. Some of the facts they supplied were inaccurate, but Marty didn't correct them. Maybe he wasn't as knowledgeable as he thought he was. And so, Jodie learned about prostitution.

But he had questions. "Prostitutes live here in Bodie?"

"And everywhere else in the world. But here in Bodie, you'll find them down by Chinatown, on Bonanza Street. Haven't you been down there?"

Jodie shook his head. "No, I don't know much about it. Are there a lot of those ladies down there?"

"Dozens," Marty said with authority.

"And men pay them?" Jodie asked.

Marty knew all about it. "Of course, they pay them. Ladies aren't going to give it away for free, are they?"

"I have no idea." Jodie shrugged his shoulders. "I thought you had sex once you got married. I've never given it much thought."

"Nah, men get lonely and want to snuggle up next to some pretty young thing. Marriage has nothing to do with it. There are always whores in mining camps. Lots of them willing to take a man's money. Some of them aren't all that young anymore, and after a while, whoring is all they're good for. Can't get a decent job. Can't get a man to marry them either. It's pretty funny seeing those old broads."

Jodie didn't think it was funny, and he said so.

"It must be awful to be old and have nobody want you anymore."

Marty wasn't so compassionate, and he didn't want to lose his place in the limelight. The other boys were watching, so he said," I bet your boardinghouse mama doesn't just give it away. I bet she makes Nick pay for it."

Jodie was appalled. He looked at Marty and couldn't think of a comeback. He didn't think Nick and Mary Kay liked each other that way. Nick always said she was a sister to him. But a few nights earlier, he had seen Nick put his arm around her after dinner. Also, Nick had taken her to the dance at the Miner's Union Hall on the

Fourth. Jodie would have to think about this. He had never known about whores before. If Nick were sleeping with Mary Kay, would that make her a whore too? Jodie realized he was learning a lot about life since he moved to Bodie. He had never thought about sex before. His mom and dad slept in the same bed, but that's what married people did. His dad hadn't talked to him about any of this, and Jodie had no younger brothers or sisters so had never wondered where babies came from.

Because Jodie still looked bewildered, Marty explicitly explained the facts of life to him out there in the field, where they had earlier played an innocent game of baseball. The other boys all seemed to know about this, so Jodie would have been surprised to know that several of them also learned about sex for the first time that afternoon. They had kept quiet, so no one would know of their ignorance, and they had gladly let Marty and Pete show off. Who knew how Marty and Pete were so knowledgeable at age thirteen?

"So, let's go look at the whores. Sometimes they don't wear many clothes when they are out back smoking cigarettes," Marty said.

"Are they pretty?' Jodie wanted to know.

"Some are. Some are old, like I told you—maybe as old as thirty even. They don't get paid as much."

"Where do they go to have sex?"

"There's a row of small houses called cribs behind Bonanza Street. They do it there. I'm surprised you haven't been down to Bonanza Street."

"Nick keeps me pretty busy when I'm not playing ball with you fellows. Besides, he told me not to go there because it was just a bunch of drunkards, and I didn't need to be seeing that."

"Your Nick seems to know a lot about it," Marty said, and the boys laughed. "So, let's go. Sometimes two or three whores show up about this time of day. Gotta be quiet when we get there though. We'll hide behind a stack of old furniture that's piled up there in the alley."

Jodie nodded and followed the others north toward the wrong side of town. He had much to think about because at age eleven, he had been innocent of such matters. He had seen fancy ladies come out of some of the saloons on Main Street. Once, he had gone looking for Nick at Wagner's Saloon, thinking Nick might be there with his friends for an after- shifter. Jodie had opened the swinging door and looked in but hadn't seen Nick. Before he could leave, an attractive blonde woman with many curls and a tight bodice approached him and asked him what he needed. She had been friendly enough, but since Jodie hadn't needed anything, he had quickly made his escape. He figured she probably worked there and hadn't given her another thought. Now he wondered if she could be one of those ladies. He hadn't told Nick about going to the bar looking for him, and now he didn't think he could ask him about her. Jodie had a sudden thought and wondered if Nick paid money to be with the ladies. Nick knew everyone in town, so maybe.

Jodie and three other boys walked over to Bonanza Street that afternoon. They jostled and rammed into each other as they walked along as boys do when fooling around. As they approached the stack of old furniture, Marty held his hand up to stop the boys. They stopped and were silent. Each stationed himself in a hiding place and waited. After all the talk of whores, Jodie hoped he would see one that afternoon.

After a short while, the back door of Sophie's Bordello opened, and two little girls walked out and sat on the back steps. They each carried hair ribbons.

"That little girl with the long dark hair and bangs lives there," Marty whispered to the others. "I see her around here often. Her mother is a whore."

Jodie felt uncomfortable. With his new-found education, he hadn't considered that children would be involved.

"Makes you wonder who her father is," Pete speculated. "I bet even she doesn't know. It could be any one of the dozens of men her mother has been with."

Jodie looked at the cute girls. Neither could have been more than four or five years old. He thought of Nessie who was about the same age. She didn't have a father anymore, but at least she knew who her dad had been. Ed's name was brought up often, and his photo hung on the wall of the kitchen, so Mary Kay and the children could see it. His photo was also in a frame on each of the children's night stands next to their beds. Mary Kay made sure her children knew who their father had been and how much he had loved them. His spirit was a real factor in their lives.

Jodie watched as the young girls tied ribbons in each other's hair. They laughed and giggled and seemed genuinely happy. Jodie wondered about this because being a whore's child seemed like an awful thing to be. Four o'clock turned into five o'clock, and when no fancy ladies with skimpy clothes came outside to smoke, the boys grew restless. Just as they were thinking of leaving, a pretty young woman came to the door and beckoned the girls in.

"Dinner time, Annabelle," she called. The girls ran inside, and the lady closed the back door after them.

"Gotta go," Jodie told the other boys, and he took off running down Main Street toward the boardinghouse. He didn't wait for the others, nor did he look back. All he could think of was the pretty woman and the name she had called her daughter: "Annabelle!" Jodie felt sick.

* * * * * * * * * *

"He's a liar." Jodie was crying so hard that he ran smack into Coosie as he rounded the corner. He could barely get the words out.

Coosie had never seen Jodie distressed. Usually, he had a smirk and an attitude. Coosie was an excellent judge of character and had seen through the young boy's bravado. He knew some of Jodie's story from Nick, and he knew that the child was hurting because he felt abandoned by a dad he revered. Add to that, a sick mother too far away to help. It was good that Jodie had Nick who played an immense role in Jodie's life here. But now with the word, "Liar," Coosie guessed correctly that the damnable word was uttered against Nick.

"Whoa, Son. Hold on a second." Coosie put his arm around Jodie and held him tightly for a minute. Then he let him go and said, "I was just on my way to see Rosie. Come along with me. You don't need to be going to the Manor just now. Seeing Rosie will do us both good."

Coosie walked Jodie over to the corral where Rosie munched hay. The roan-colored horse lifted her head as she heard them approach and gave a welcoming whinny. Coosie took a carrot from his pocket and presented it to his horse. "You're a good girl," he told her as he patted her head. "Look who's come to see you. Jodie's here."

Jodie nestled his head in the horse's neck. He had not been allowed to own a pet when he lived at home because his dad said they were too much of a bother. However, Dad had promised Jodie a dog when he returned from the mines, knowing he had no intention of returning. Jodie did not know this, of course. Here in Bodie, both Nick and Coosie had generously shared their animals with the boy. Jodie loved both Nick's dog and Coosie's horse.

"Let's take Rosie out for a ride. She needs the exercise. Why don't you saddle her up while I tell Mary Kay we won't be home for supper. I'll borrow Jasper's horse and meet you back here. You won't go away, will you?"

"No, I'll stay," Jodie said.

Coosie handed Jodie the rest of the carrots and walked off.

Coosie and Jodie rode horses for a couple of hours. It was a good way to ease the tension Jodie was feeling. Coosie wanted to talk with Jodie and hear what he had on his mind, but he waited for Jodie to be able to talk with him. He didn't know why Jodie had turned against Nick, but he would do what he could to help them both. Jodie depended on Nick for everything here in Bodie.

Nick loved the young boy, and Coosie could tell that Jodie felt the same way about Nick. Jodie most often gave Nick a hard time though and was flip with him. Jodie did not show him the love he felt because he had been hurt too often and was afraid of trusting one more adult with his affections. Adults he cared about eventually left him, one way or another. So, Jodie kept up a front and did not let Nick get too close. When Nick was out of earshot; however, Jodie spoke constantly about him. He began many sentences with "Nick says. . . "

"Ready to talk?" Coosie asked. They had dismounted and were leading the horses back to the stable where they would ready them for the night.

Jodie sighed. Coosie was only a Negro. Jodie could never get past that fact. But Jodie had learned to somewhat trust this older man, and the two had become friends. However, Jodie knew his dad would disapprove, and he hoped his dad would never see him with Coosie.

"Is Nick the liar?" Coosie asked.

"Yes. I thought I knew him pretty well, but now I find that he has been lying to me all along."

"Go on," Coosie said.

"Well, when I first came here, he told me that my aunt and cousin weren't in Bodie, that they had gone away for a few months. He said they would eventually return, but he didn't know when."

"So, that's how you ended up at the Manor?"

"Yes."

Coosie knew what was coming but asked the question any-way, "So, where does the lie come in?"

"Aunt Tess and Annabelle never left Bodie. They have been here all along, and Nick knew it. He lied to me."

"Why do you think Nick would do that?" Coosie asked.

"I don't know."

"Sure, you do. Why would Nick lie about your aunt?"

"I told you. I don't know."

"Come on, Jodie. I don't see Nick lying to you without a good reason. You know he would never deliberately hurt you, so why do you think he lied this time? Think about it for a minute."

Jodie remained quiet for a long time. When he spoke, the words were barely audible, "My aunt is a prostitute."

"Are you sure?"

"Yes, she lives on Bonanza Street."

"That don't necessarily make her a prostitute."

"I saw her come out of the bordello."

"Jodie, you're wrong. She doesn't . . . "

But Jodie was no longer listening. He looked Coosie in the eye and defiantly said, "No, I don't believe you. You are just defending Nick. I know what I saw."

Coosie realized that Jodie was too angry to listen to reason, so he said, "Okay, for the sake of this conversation, let's say she is a prostitute. How do you know about such things?"

"I learned this afternoon from my friends. Prostitutes are bad people. They're vulgar."

"Whoa! Let's think this out. Why are they vulgar?"

Jodie looked at him indignantly. "Don't you know? They sell their bodies for money. They get paid to sleep with men."

"I get paid for working at the stables. Nick gets paid for carpentry jobs."

"That's different."

"Maybe. But you sell what you have. What if your aunt has nothing to sell but herself? What if she has no marketable skills? It's one thing to starve on the streets yourself, but you say there is a young child involved. Your aunt might have taken any job she could get in order to feed her child. She's doing the best she can."

"But not that! She didn't have to be a prostitute."

"Jodie, you're young. Just like you learned about prostitutes today, there's a lot more to learn about this world. And sadly, I'm here to tell you, it ain't all good!"

Jodie started to argue, but Coosie held up his hand. "Let me finish. My understanding of people is that most folks do the best they can; that includes your aunt."

Jodie sighed. "But she's a prostitute," he protested.

"You don't know that for sure."

"I know what I saw, and I saw her in that bordello!" Jodie bristled.

"Again, for the sake of conversation, let's say she is. Do you suppose she likes being a prostitute? Do you think that's the life she chose for herself? Do you think as a child she dreamed that one day she could grow up and sell herself to any man who could afford her? Nonsense!"

"So, you don't think she does it because she likes it?"

Coosie shook his head. "Hell no! I've met a lot of ladies in my travels. Not one would have resorted to prostitution if she had been given the choice. Imagine having to go to bed with someone you don't even know? Think about it this way: most of the cowboys and roustabouts I know are sweaty and unwashed. Hell, they're filthy! They haven't changed their clothes in months, not even their underwear. Their hair is long and stringy and probably itchy with lice. These fellows have rotten teeth, bad breath, and body odor. Why in hell would a woman subject herself to that if she didn't have to?"

Jodie was crying again. "This is all new to me. I never thought of it that way."

"You're doing a lot of growing up here, aren't you?"

"You have no idea!" Jodie muttered.

"Well, you're pretty young to have all this dumped on you. But remember the lesson I taught you a minute ago."

"What?"

"That people do the best they can with whatever hand they're dealt."

"So, I shouldn't think bad about my aunt? I shouldn't judge her because maybe she's doing the best she can?"

"Exactly right. Your aunt must have fallen on hard times somewhere along the way. Until we know her story, we can't judge her. Hell, Jodie, we can't judge her even then! Who are we that we're so high and mighty that we get to judge others?"

Jodie stood quietly for a while, thinking things over. Finally, he spoke, "Coosie, you know everything. You sure understand about people."

"Look at the color of my skin, Jodie. I'm a colored man, no getting around that. This black color has gotten me into plenty of trouble at times. Nothing I could do about that. I was born a slave. Yes, plenty of trouble there too. But on the other hand, folks have helped me too. Along the way, people have been kind. And yes, I've met many different kinds of folks in many different places. Lord knows, I sure been a lot of places! But of the folks I've met, I'm telling you; most people are good. And I'm telling you; most people do the best they can."

"Okay, Coosie. I get it now."

"So, now back to the real question. Nick lied to you about your aunt. Why would he lie?"

Jodie remained silent for a minute before asking, "To protect me? To protect her?"

"Probably both. You obviously couldn't stay with her down on Bonanza Street when you got to town. Nick knew that and took you in."

"Coosie, how do you think Nick knows her – my aunt? Is he one of her customers?"

"Naw, Son. I don't know nothing about Nick's private life or what he does in his spare time. None of my business. None of your business either. But I do know that he and your aunt are good friends. Remember, Nick knows a lot of folks."

"Does he know Annabelle?"

"I ain't gonna tell you no lies, Jodie. Nick does know Annabelle. She loves him and calls him 'Uncle Nick.'"

"Could he be Annabelle's father?"

"No, not her father. That I know for certain. But he is her friend. He helps her and her mother when he can."

Jodie looked at the older man. "Coosie, does my mom know that her sister is a prostitute?"

"Don't know nothing about that neither, Son. I couldn't tell you. But let's think about it. Your mom wouldn't have sent you here to a prostitute, would she?"

"No, I guess not. So, that's how I ended up with Nick at the Manor! And he lied to me to protect me and to help my aunt. Maybe I'm not mad at him anymore, now that I know why he did it."

"Now you're thinking for yourself, which is something I want you to do more often. Find out the facts of a situation before you go off half-cocked."

Jodie nodded. "Nick was doing me a favor by taking me in, wasn't he?"

"That's what I've been trying to tell you. He's doing the best he can."

"Coosie, please don't tell Nick about my going to Bonanza Street and about our talk. Please."

"Yeah, okay. But I want you to tell him yourself. When the time is right, I expect you to tell him."

Jodie nodded. Then he said, "Coosie, I get that Nick is one of the good guys, but I think you're one of the good guys too. Thanks for today."

Coosie chuckled. "You're welcome, Jodie, I'm just doing the best I can."

CHAPTER 17

"Ah, you're all a bunch of knuckle heads," Nick protested.

"No, it's true, Uncle Nick," Tristan said.

"What's true?" Susanne asked as she walked into the dining room.

"About the Buffalo Soldiers," Tristan said. "We kids say they are soldiers who are in charge of the buffalo out on the Plains."

"They get to boss the buffalo around," Nessie explained. "Bossy like Uncle Nick is bossy."

"I am not bossy," Nick protested again.

The three children smiled at each other, conspirators all. Jodie had taught Tristan and Nessie how to roll their eyes, and all three did so now.

"You're the bossiest person I know," Jodie chimed in. "By far, the bossiest!"

"Yeah, yeah. Well, I wouldn't have to be bossy if you didn't make me. You bring out the worst in me at times."

"I don't think three young children have that capability," Mary Kay said. "You bring out the worst in yourself."

After Coosie blessed the food, and everyone had a chance to talk about his day, Nick looked at his nephew. "So, why were we discussing buffalo?"

"Not buffalo, Uncle Nick. We're discussing Buffalo Soldiers. I have to write a report for school about them but can't find anything in the encyclopedia. It's my summer assignment."

"I may be able to help you, Tristan," Coosie said. "I know a bit about them."

"How so?" Susanne asked.

"I was one," Coosie replied.

"You were a boss of the buffalo?" Nessie was impressed. "Gosh, Coosie!"

"No, Child. That's not what a Buffalo Soldier was. Is. We still have Buffalo Soldiers."

"Did they fight during the War Between the States?" Jodie asked.

"No, the war ended in '65. Buffalo Soldiers didn't exist until the next year." Coosie turned his attention toward Tristan. "The Congress authorized the creation of regiments of Black soldiers. Led by White officers, of course. Heaven forbid Negroes should be allowed to lead themselves!" Coosie sighed and then added, "Four groups were formed. "

"For what purpose?" Mary Kay asked.

"To fight Indians, I bet," Jodie said.

"Is that true? Buffalo Soldiers were created to fight Indians?" Mary Kay asked.

"Yes," Coosie said, "but that wasn't our only purpose."

"Maybe not," Wiley said, "but the Indians were creating havoc out on the plains, and who better to solve that problem than soldiers?"

"The government had all these highly trained veterans with no war to fight. Why not send them out to solve the Indian problem?" Thornton added.

"You're right," Wiley said. "After the war ended in '65, army generals were left with no command. Think of Sherman and Crook, and of course, Custer—experienced fighters and leaders. Let them earn their keep by either killing the Indians or getting them on to reservations."

"Is that why Custer was killed a couple of years ago? Was he trying to get Indians to go to the reservation?" Jodie asked.

"No," Thornton explained. "Custer was killed because he broke a major treaty with the Indians— the Fort Laramie Treaty. The treaty promised the Indians the land up in the Black Hills if the Indians pledged not to harass settlers as they passed through there on their way west. But Custer led an expedition there in '74 looking for gold. When he found it, he announced his findings to the world, and the world walked in, picks and shovels in hand.

"These men took the ore that rightfully belonged to the Indians. They even made permanent settlements on Indian land, a blatant violation of the treaty. That's when the Sioux went to war. Enough was enough! That's why the Indians attacked Custer."

"Our government has broken every treaty it has ever made with the Indians," Nick commented.

"The Indian attack was a real massacre," Wiley said. "The battle took place in Montana, at a place called Little Big Horn. Indians killed 220 men that day including four of Custer's family. "Two of Custer's younger brothers died."

Susanne shuddered. "Too much violence against our people," she said.

"No," Thornton told her. "We Whites have committed violent acts against the Indians as well. Neither side is innocent in these wars. For instance, about fifteen years ago, our soldiers led a massacre against a peaceful group of Cheyenne who were camped at Sand Creek. The chief, Black Kettle, flew both the American flag and a white flag from the top of his teepee. Soldiers attacked anyway and killed 123 Indians that day. Ninety- eight of them were women and children. So, both sides have blood on their hands, not just the Indians."

"How do you know all this?" Jodie wanted to know.

Thornton smiled at Jodie. "We read," he said. Tristan and Nessie both looked at Jodie and laughed.

Coosie spoke up, "Wait a minute. I agree that war veterans were sent out to fight Indians. No disagreement there. But that wasn't the primary job of the Buffalo Soldiers. We built roads, protected the railroads, and helped the settlers in many ways. Sometimes, we escorted the U.S. Mail. At times, we captured cattle rustlers and thieves." Coosie shook his head. "No, it wasn't all about killing Indians. As I told you, there were four groups formed. Two of those groups were cavalry soldiers. I was in the cavalry."

"What's a cavalry, Coosie?" Tristan asked.

"Soldiers who ride horses are in the cavalry," Coosie told him. "The other two groups were the infantry. "Soldiers in the infantry are foot soldiers— those who fight on the ground," he explained before Tristan could ask.

"We cavalry soldiers of the ninth and tenth regiments were all Black men. Most of us were former slaves, so we certainly knew how to work. But we also had to know our way around a horse. We were sent to Fort Leavenworth, Kansas for training in '66. There, we had a terrific leader, Colonel Grierson."

"How long were you a Buffalo Soldier?" Jodie asked.

"I had to enlist for five years. Infantry men signed up for only three."

"Did you get paid?" Jodie asked.

"Thirteen dollars a month. That was good pay for a Black man. Many Blacks joined up because it was more money than they could make otherwise. Gave us dignity too. Nothing was going on back home, wherever home was. The plantations and farms had all been destroyed."

Coosie looked at Jodie and added, "Of course, we didn't end up with thirteen dollars. We had to pay the laundresses a buck every month. And the company barber and tailor. Some money went to the sutler. That's the company store. So, I was left with about nine dollars a month. Kept hold of it too. Not everyone did."

Coosie leaned back in his chair and folded his arms. "A lot of the men gambled. Some soldiers squandered away their whole paycheck and then borrowed what they could for the next month. Someone was always willing to lend them money, but always at a high rate of interest. Some poor fools never learn."

"Why did you quit the army?" Jodie asked.

"I had a chance to go to Texas with another soldier to work on a cattle drive. My enlistment was up, so I left. Sometimes I get itchy feet and want to go try something new."

Nessie looked concerned. "I hope your feet don't itch while you live in Bodie," she said. "I want you to stay here."

Mary Kay looked at her young, naive daughter. Nessie took things so literally.

Coosie ruffled Nessie's hair. "Nah, Child. I ain't going nowhere for a while. This is the happiest home I've ever known."

Nick suddenly had a lump in his throat from hearing such honesty from his friend. To realize that Coosie was middle-aged before he found a happy home made him sad. Nick couldn't help but count his blessings.

He was glad the children could know Coosie, a true role model for them. Coosie worked hard every day and fulfilled his commitments. He was well liked by others for his common sense and calm disposition. Nick wanted the children to know that a real man was not necessarily the richest or most powerful man in town. No, a real man was like Coosie: a man who had values and was both confident and comfortable with himself.

Too often in Bodie, a loud mouthed braggard with a gun was mistaken for a real man. Many a gunslinger thought making a name for himself meant firing his weapon.

Nick's mind wandered now as he thought about Bodie. Although he loved this town, he recognized that it was a violent place, especially at night when the bars were in full swing. Saloon doors were often flung open and drunks thrown out on to the dusty or muddy street. Liquor promoted aggressiveness. Some men liked to fight with their fists, and the more they drank, the more damage they did. Others liked to beat up on women who were vulnerable and unable to fight back.

Gambling was prevalent, and that often meant desperate men trying to hold on to their bankroll or their reputation. Fists flew when a man's honor was at stake. Yes, Bodie could be a dangerous place, so Nick always walked Susanne home after supper to keep her safe. Too much hostility out there for a woman alone!

Now Nick brought himself back to the dinner conversation. Mary Kay was serving a peach cobbler, and Susanne was pouring coffee.

Jodie was asking, "Why were you called 'Buffalo Soldiers?'"

Coosie gave a big smile. "Now, that name really means something to those of us who are eligible to be called that. We were all expert horsemen, and we must have impressed the Indians because they gave us the name 'Buffalo Soldiers.' Our black, kinky hair reminded the Comanches of the black, wiry hair on the buffalo— an animal they considered noble. So, it was a compliment. At least, we took it that way."

"Did you like your job?" Jodie asked.

"I did and I didn't. We spent too much time drilling, in my opinion. The nights out on the Plains could be downright frigid, but I did like working for Colonel Grierson. His boss did not think 'Blackies,' as he called us, should serve in the army though. He made sure we had inferior food, equipment, and weapons."

"Were you angry, Coosie?"

"Nah, nothing to be angry about. We were used to it. However, it was there that I learned to write and to figure."

"Figure?"

"Numbers, Child. Each regiment was assigned a chaplain to provide us spiritual guidance. In addition to Godly advice, the chaplain provided more fundamental services like tutoring. I'll always be grateful for the education that man gave me. And I'll always be obliged to that officer who taught me to read during the war. Sometimes, I think back on these people who came into my life at just the right time. Seems like God placed them in my path just to give me a shove along when I needed it."

Nick agreed. Nothing random about that.

"The hardest part of leaving the army was having to give up my horse. The army assigned each of us our own horse, but when I moved on, the horse stayed. I loved that gal! Sometimes, I think about her and wonder if the next soldier took good care of her." Coosie sighed.

Nick looked at Mary Kay and couldn't help his next comment, "Too bad women weren't allowed. Women must not be good with horses." He winked at her.

Coosie held up his finger. "Wait just a minute, young fellow. We did actually have a woman who was a Buffalo Soldier."

"How could that be?" Mary Kay asked. "Women are not allowed to join the army."

Coosie laughed out loud. "She posed as a man. The medical exam for induction into the army must not have been very thorough because she was in the infantry for two years before she was found out. She went by the name of William Cathay."

Jodie had a question. "How was she found out? Did someone snitch on her?"

"Nah, she got sick with small pox and ended up in the infirmary. The doctor knew immediately that this was no man he was treating."

"What happened to her?"

"The army kicked her out."

"Yes," Susanne said, "I remember reading her story in the St. Louis newspaper. I was inspired by her daring. It takes courage to try to make it in a man's world."

"Yes, what some women will do to make a name for themselves!" Nick said.

"Be quiet," Mary Kay told him. "If women had equal opportunities, we wouldn't have to pose as men." She stared him down.

Coosie stood up. "Children, children, stop the bickering." He frowned at Mary Kay and Nick. "One more story and then I'll stop monopolizing the conversation."

"No, monopolize away, Coosie," Jodie said.

Nick kicked Jodie under the table. Jodie looked up, first at Nick and then at Coosie. "No, I meant it. I like to listen to Coosie's stories. Please, I meant no disrespect."

Coosie continued, "Do you children know about West Point?" The children all shook their heads.

"West Point is a military school. Men go there to learn how to be soldiers."

"Really? You have to learn how to fight?" Tristan asked.

"Certainly. Soldiers must learn to shoot a gun, to read a map, and to devise different battle plans. They are taught leadership skills. West Point is in New York. It's been around a long time."

"Here's an interesting fact," Wiley inserted. "Custer graduated from West Point, but he graduated last in his class. Not a good recommendation, but he went on to become the youngest general to serve in the Civil War. He is now buried on the grounds there at West Point."

"Do only men attend West Point?" Mary Kay asked.

"Sadly, yes," Coosie told her. "But your day will come. I do realize that we Negroes are faring better than you women. I was talking about West Point a minute ago because I read in the newspaper that Henry Flipper just graduated from there. He is West Point's first Black graduate. His dad was a slave, but Henry is now an officer in the United States Army. An officer! Imagine that! He presently commands my beloved tenth regiment."

Mary Kay stood up to serve more coffee. She truly was happy that the Negroes were making gains in society. She felt that White males had dominated the scene for far too long. She changed the subject. "So, you didn't actually fight any Indians then, did you, Coosie?"

He shook his head. "Wish I could tell you I didn't, but that would be a lie. We fought many Indians, but mostly we helped the settlers. Our presence kept the Indians in line, I suspect."

"Would you have killed an Indian if you had had the chance?" Jodie asked.

"No, not if I could help it, Jodie. I also didn't want any part of taking away Indian land. The settlers and gold seekers want the land, sure, but the Indians have lived on the land long before you Europeans arrived here."

"Aren't you a European, Coosie?" Tristan asked.

"No, Child. My family came from Western Africa. "

Thornton spoke up. I agree with you about the government. It certainly is handling the Indian problem badly. Seems that it could show a lot more humanity toward these people."

"You are right, Sir. And now I'll leave you with one last thought," Coosie said. "I grew up without any rights, so my sympathies lie with the Indians. Seems like we good Christian people are trying to take away their rights. The Constitution says that all men are created equal, but I don't see that being the case for the Indians. Why should they willingly give up their land and way of life to go live on a government reservation? The government has promised to 'take care of them.' The Indians are an independent people who certainly don't need to be taken care of. Okay, I've said enough. Tristan, go get paper and pen, and I'll help you with your report while the adults play cards."

Jodie looked at the former Buffalo Soldier. Coosie had again given him something to think about. In San Diego, Jodie had never given much thought to Indians. Certainly, he had never considered them to be real people with real feelings, and he knew about them only from his dad's disparaging remarks. Because he was from the South, Dad also despised the Blacks. He had always muttered hateful words about them and toward them. Could his dad be wrong about both Indians and Blacks?

This was a new world for Jodie, and he realized he did not know much. Men he now admired had a different view of the world from the one in which he had been brought up. Could his dad be wrong? Jodie tried to put this disloyal thought out of his mind, but then he looked at Nick and the other men sitting around the dining table. How could they all be wrong? He excused himself and went to his room. He had things to think about.

CHAPTER 18

"How exciting for the Rowe family!" Susanne said when Mary Kay told her that Mary had given birth to a healthy baby girl.

"Yes, and because she is the first child of a miner at the Syndicate Mine, Mary and Joel have named her Syndicate. They will call her Syndie. Joel's fellow miners got together and bought her an eighty-dollar baby buggy."

"Pricey!" Susanne said.

"Yes, but it was a token of respect. They all like Joel at the mine."

"I have news as well," Susanne announced. It was a Saturday morning, and she and Mary Kay were drinking coffee at the break-fast table. "I hear Alice is leaving town."

Nick and Jodie were just leaving for the shop, but when Nick heard this news, he threw his arms into the air and yelled, "Hot diggity."

"Your one chance at romance, and you're going to let her walk out of your life!" Jodie shook his head as if in dismay.

"Yes, I hope she walks far away. And I add… good riddance! And don't let the door hit her on her way out." Nick grinned back at Jodie.

"That's unfortunate because I don't see other women lined up at the door hoping to be courted by you," Jodie teased.

"Certainly, no one at this table," Mary Kay mused.

Susanne smiled sweetly and said, "You may have to broaden your horizons because I'm not interested either." What she really wanted to say was," I'm here, Nick. I need a husband, and you would do nicely. Look my way." But then she thought, *What am I doing? Stop it!*

"I'm not in the market for a wife," Nick said now.

Jodie interrupted him, "Who said anything about marriage? We were talking about romance."

"Don't be fooled, Lad. All women are looking for a husband."

"Not me," Mary Kay said. "I had a husband, the best of husbands. I don't think anyone could ever fill Ed's shoes. So, I'm not looking."

Nick thought of his friend Lex. "The minute you change your mind, I have just the man for you. A decent, hardworking guy. A nice guy who has wanted to meet you for a long time. Just tell me when you decide the time is right."

Mary Kay stood up and faced Nick. "Are you telling me that you would have me marry another man? Where is your loyalty to Ed?"

"My brother is dead, Mary Kay. My loyalty is to you. Ed would not expect you to stay single the rest of your life. He wouldn't want you to grow old by yourself. He would just want you to be happy. That's what I want for you too."

Mary Kay sat down again. "Truly, I have not thought of it. I have these young children to raise."

"Well, maybe your young ones would like to have another man in their lives, other than me."

"We have Thornton, Wiley, and Coosie. They are part of the children's lives."

"Yeah, yeah, I know. But I'm talking about a husband for you. None of those fellows fits the bill, I reckon. Thornton and Wiley are too old for you, and of course, you can't marry Coosie. Just think about marrying again, will you? That's all I'm saying," Nick said.

Mary Kay nodded but did not commit herself to what she considered a laughable request. Who would want her, a widow with two young children? Besides, she had a boarding house to run. But wouldn't it be fun to go dancing with a fellow? Someone other than Nick. Perhaps, she would think about it. Ed had been gone for more than four years.

"Nick, why haven't you ever married?" Jodie asked now.

"Jodie, take a good look at him." Mary Kay laughed, trying to lighten the mood. "Who would have him?"

"Alice would, but she's leaving," Jodie reminded her.

"Do I have to repeat my 'Hot Diggity' remark?" Nick asked.

Mary Kay smiled at him. "No. Seems like we've come full circle." She looked at Jodie.

"Jodie, if you have a couple of minutes to spare, would you run to the post office for me? I have a letter to mail to my old friend Ina Coolbrith."

"Sure, Mary Kay. Anything you want."

"Okay then. I could use a can of baking soda too if you have the time to go to the store."

"Yeah, yeah, go help Mary Kay. I will meet you at the shop when you get through," Nick said.

So, Jodie took off toward town, glad to run errands for Mary Kay. He was still trying to get in her good graces, but he couldn't tell if he was making any progress. Some days she seemed to like him. Other days she was short with him. It kept him off guard.

As Jodie walked toward Main Street, he was thinking about Nick and wondering why he had not married. Nick wasn't too bad looking, and he seemed to have charm that ladies liked. Maybe he liked going to the saloons and didn't want a wife to tell him he couldn't go. Jodie was actually happy that Nick didn't have a wife. This way Jodie didn't have to share him. A wife would have complicated things, and having Mark Kay around was bad enough. Jodie decided to get the baking soda first and then double back and pick up the mail.

Near Green Street, he ran into Walter and Marty who had a stray dog cornered in an alley. They were throwing rocks at the whimpering mutt. Jodie was irritated when the dog cried out in pain, and he grabbed Walter's arm to prevent him from hurling another rock.

Walter looked at Jodie, jerked his arm away, and demanded, "What the hell are you doing, Burke?"

"Quit hurting the dog," Jodie demanded.

"Make me," Walter grunted.

"I don't want to make you. Just stop torturing the damn dog. He's done nothing to you."

"So, you say! The dog's very existence annoys me." Walter threw another rock and hit the dog's ear. The dog yelped in pain.

"Stop it, I say," Jodie insisted.

"Don't tell me what to do. Don't even think about it," Walter yelled.

"I'm not telling you what to do, but why beat up on a defenseless dog?"

Walter turned and smiled at Marty. "Okay, Jodie, we'll beat up on you instead. We'll teach you a lesson about butting into our business. Is that what you want, Jodie, a lesson? Jodie is a stupid name, by the way. Jodie! Sounds girlish to me. Are you a girl, Jodie? Jodie Bodie! It sounds almost poetic. Are you a poet, Jodie? Let's see how poetic you are with your bones broken!"

Jodie turned to run. He wasn't looking for trouble.

Walter tackled him and threw him to the ground. Jodie landed face down in the dirt. He couldn't have been more surprised. These were supposed to be his friends.

"What the hell!" he yelled.

Marty walked over and kicked him hard in the ribs. He had no quarrel with Jodie, but because he wanted the older boy's approval, he would never help the younger one.

Jodie had no way of knowing that Walter's no good, drunken father had spent the morning beating up on him, and Walter was looking to repay the favor. Jodie was an easy target.

"If you don't think I should lay into the dog, then I'm going to lay into you instead," he said.

Jodie lay in the dirt where he had fallen. Walter jumped on him, preventing him from getting up. He twisted Jodie's arm back, and Jodie heard a pop. A sudden rush of pain filled him.

"So, what do you say? Should we kill the dog, or should we stick with you?" Walter demanded. Neither Walter nor Marty had seen the dog slink away.

"What's your problem?" Jodie was crying now.

"No problem. We just don't need you sticking your nose in our business. If we want to kill a dog, we don't need you telling us we can't."

"But he's defenseless. He was cowering in the corner when I showed up."

"Again, not your problem." Walter slammed Jodie's face into the dirt. Jodie cried out.

"Dammed cry baby," Marty muttered.

"So, now you gonna call Nick to come save you?" Walter sneered.

"Nah, Nick's too busy whoring to save anyone," Marty said. "I saw him again yesterday down on Bonanza Street talking up that pretty whore who lives down there. You can't tell me he ain't got something going on with her. They looked pretty chummy."

'Yeah, your Nick who you think is so special. Well, we aren't buying it," Walter said.

Marty continued. "Got something going on with that sister of his too. Damned unnatural." He snickered.

"No," Jodie whimpered. "It's not like that. She's not his sister."

Walter slammed Jodie's face back into the dirt. "She's who-ever we say she is, Boy."

Walter grabbed Jodie and picked him up. It was an easy job since Jodie was so much smaller than the older boy. "So, gonna tell Nick on us?" He raised his arm intending to slug Jodie.

Jodie whimpered. His arm hung at an odd angle, and he hurt terribly.

"I'll tell anyone I want," he said defiantly.

"Yeah?" Walter slammed his fist into Jodie's face, breaking his nose. "One word from you, and we'll come back and finish the job. In fact, one word from you to Nick, and we'll get acid and throw it in Nick's eyes. See what kind of a carpenter he'll be after that. He'll wander around with a white stick looking for his shop." And with that, he hit Jodie again and threw him down. Walter and Marty walked away, leaving Jodie crying where he lay. The boys were only sorry that the dog had sneaked away. Walter had murder on his mind, and he didn't need some snot-nosed brat telling him what to do. If Jodie told anyone about today, he would come back and do exactly what he told Jodie he would do.

Jodie lay in the dirt where he had fallen, too hurt to try to get up. An hour went by before Cal, the tailor, stepped outside his back door intending to throw garbage out. He saw the young boy lying in the dirt. Jodie had long since stopped crying, so Cal couldn't tell if he was dead or alive. He leaned down and turned the inert boy over to get a better look. Jodie cried out when the tailor touched his arm. Cal carefully picked Jodie up, carried him into his shop, and gently laid him down on the floor. He covered him with a blanket and then sent for the constable and the doctor.

Constable Kirgan knew Jodie and immediately sent for Nick who came on the run. When Jodie hadn't arrived at the shop within a reasonable time, Nick had wondered what trouble he had gotten himself into. Nick had not expected to see the child so badly beaten up.

"Tell Doc to find us at the boarding house," he told Kirgan. And with that, he gently picked Jodie up and carried him home. Mary Kay heard him as he stomped up the porch steps. She too had been concerned when Jodie had not come home. She hurried to open the door for Nick, and he took Jodie upstairs and laid him down on the bed in Nick's room.

The doctor arrived and confirmed that both Jodie's arm and nose were broken. Jodie hurt everywhere. He tried to be brave and not cry when the doctor set his arm, but he couldn't help himself. He was miserable.

Nick kept muttering, "Oh, my darling boy, oh my darling boy," over and over as he raked Jodie's hair off his face. He tried to get Jodie to talk to him, but Jodie was in too much pain to try. He had nothing to say anyway. He wasn't going to tell Nick who beat him up because he knew the boys would come after both of them. He knew he would fear those boys forever. He had never felt so vulnerable.

Finally, Mary Kay shooed Nick away. She sat on the edge of the bed and carefully wiped Jodie's bloody face with a warm, wet rag. She whispered soothing endearments as she looked at the small boy on the bed, "It's okay, Sweetheart. It's okay. You will be okay, Darling." Jodie closed his eyes, reassured by Mary Kay's gentle touch. After a while, he slept. He was in Nick's bed and would be there for the next few days until he recovered enough to again share a room with Tristan. In the meantime, Nick would bunk in with his nephew. He would even let Tristan keep the top bunk.

Kirgan's deputy constable, Teddy Brodigan, came by the house that afternoon asking questions. He wondered who had given Jodie such a beating, but Nick had no idea. The tailor had found him behind his shop in a heap, and no witnesses had come forward.

"I have no idea who beat him up," Nick told him. "Jodie is only a small lad. He looks so fragile lying on that bed. Anyone could have gotten to him, and he couldn't have defended himself. But for what purpose? I don't know that Jodie had any trouble with the kids around here. I thought he was well liked."

"Maybe it wasn't a kid," Brodigan speculated.

"Again, I have no idea."

"Do you think he will ever tell you who assaulted him?" Brodigan asked.

"I don't know." Nick shook his head. "I was supposed to protect the lad, but I sure fell down on the job. And now with a broken arm, he won't be able to play baseball for a while. That's the one thing he loves to do. I should have taken better care of him."

CHAPTER 19

Coosie blocked the doorway to the kitchen, so Mary Kay could not enter. "No, Ma'am! You might be queen for today, but the kitchen is mine. My domain! You are not allowed in there. It's your birthday, and you will not be working today. I suggest you go to lunch. Perhaps you could shop for something you don't need in one of those fancy stores downtown. Or even shop for something you do need. Makes no never mind to me. All I'm saying is dinner will be ready at 6:00 o'clock— same as it is every day, but today you won't be cooking it. And another thing— we don't want to see you back here at the Manor much before six." Coosie delivered his ultimatum and then grinned at Mary Kay. She grinned back. Mary Kay never took for granted her many blessings, and she always considered Coosie to be one of her greatest.

So, Mary Kay took him up on his offer and spent the day with Susanne. They hired a carriage and drove a few miles out of Bodie to get away from the incessant noise of the stamp mills. There, they set up a picnic and idled away the afternoon talking. Mary Kay wanted to know Susanne's thoughts on allowing Nick's friend to call on her. Susanne, like Nick, just wanted Mary Kay to be happy, so she gave Mary Kay her most frank advice: Sure, Mary Kay had young children to raise, but there was no reason she should do it alone. No one could replace Ed. No one would try, but Mary Kay had many years left, and wouldn't it be nice to have a partner to share both the burdens and the joys? However, with that said, no one was pushing

Mary Kay to move forward until she was ready. Only she could make that decision.

"I do have a question," Susanne said. "Have you ever considered the possibility that Nick will not marry and get on with his life until you are settled in yours?"

Mary Kay looked at her friend. "No," she said, "I never thought about it. Could Nick possibly be waiting for me? I certainly wouldn't want to hold him back. Oh, my!"

"I don't know what his thinking is. Perhaps, I am way off base, but it did occur to me. He is so protective of you and the children. I think his bossiness is an attempt to make everyone's life run smoothly, which of course, is impossible."

Mary Kay chuckled. "Nick is bossy, but he does go out of his way to take good care of us."

"I love to watch Nick interact with the children," Susanne said.

"I agree. He is a terrific uncle, and the children are crazy about him. He is a role model for them, hardworking and honest."

Susanne smiled. "Even if he likes his beer?"

"Yes, even then. Tristan will soon learn carpentry skills from him. Tristan is a smart young lad who will go to college one day, but it certainly wouldn't hurt him to know how to frame a house or to build a cabinet. He's nearly ten years old, just the right age."

"I'm glad Nick is teaching some of those skills to Jodie," Susanne said.

"Yes. You know, Jodie and I got off on the wrong foot that first day, but I was wrong about him. He's a sweet little boy. I think he was just nervous that day, knowing he was alone so far from home, so he tried a bit of bravado."

"I remember that he was rude."

"I was very worried about him when he got hurt, but he is recovering from his injuries." Mary Kay shook her head. "We still have no idea who beat him up, and he refuses to say. Nick is furious that someone would pick on a child. " Then she added, "And Nick is also annoyed at Jodie because he won't tell him who hurt him."

"Both Nick and Jodie are stubborn," Susanne agreed. "I think Jodie likes living at the Manor."

"Yes. He is a big help to me, running errands and such, but he is a lonely little boy who misses his mother. Do you have any recent news on her condition?"

Susanne sighed. "No, I don't. As I have told you, Jodie wants nothing to do with me. I don't know what I did to put him off. We used to be great pals, so I am sad but don't know what to do about it."

"Yes, I am sad for you because I know you were friends right from the beginning. He is tight lipped, so we'll probably never know what's bothering him."

Mary Kay shook her head. "It's a good thing he has Nick. I love to watch them banter. He gives Nick a run for his money."

Susanne laughed. "It's a love/hate relationship for sure. Nick will miss him when he goes home to his mother."

Mary Kay looked at her friend. "How are you? We talk about everyone but you. Is there anything going on in your life that you want to share?"

Susanne smoothed out the wrinkles in her skirt. Then she said, "No, not today. Not on your birthday. I do want to talk to you, but it can wait until another day."

Mary Kay put her hand on her friend's arm. "Susanne, we rarely get time to ourselves. We always have a house full of men to tend to, and we have no real time just to be together. This has been wonderful having leisure time alone with you today. Please tell me what's on your mind."

And so, Susanne did. "I am going to have a baby," she said quietly.

"Is it Liam's?"

"I'm afraid so."

Susanne continued, "I can't believe my irresponsibility! How could I have allowed this to happen? I knew better, but I spent several nights with him. I am nothing more than a harlot."

"Oh, stop!" Mary Kay told her. "You are no harlot! I know that you care for him, or you wouldn't have slept with him. Have you told him about the baby?"

"No, and I don't intend to. I have no intention of marrying him, so what would be the point?" Susanne couldn't bring herself to tell Mary Kay that Liam was already married. So, she said instead,

"Marriage to Liam would mean the lonely life of a gambler's wife. He would be out of town most of the time. That's not the life I want. And another thing— I have money that I wouldn't want a gambler to get his hands on. So, no, I have no intention of marrying Liam."

"Susanne," Mary Kay began, but then Susanne started to cry. Mary Kay put her arm around her shoulder and hugged her. "How can I help you? What do you need?"

"Just a friend. The town will look at me differently when I start to show. 'Look at her,' people will say, 'no husband, no father for the baby. What loose morals she has.' I will be an outcast."

"Nick and I will be in your corner. We will stand with you."

Susanne cried harder. "That's another thing. Nick will be so disappointed in me. I know he never liked Liam. He will never look at me the same way."

"Oh, Sweetie, Nick loves you. You are one of his closest friends. He will support you always."

"You're right." Susanne shrugged. "I don't give him enough credit. I know he will be there for me, but please, will you tell him about the baby? I just can't."

"Yes. If that's what you want. Now tell me— will you stay in Bodie or go home to St. Louis?"

"No, not home. Definitely not home! How can I tell my parents? I can't. Not yet! So, I'll stay here. Besides, I want to finish my photo project. The baby is not due until February."

"A winter baby, how wonderful!"

"Yes, I know I can have the baby any day except January seventeenth. Nessie and Wiley have that day locked up." Susanne gave a small smile.

Mary Kay laughed, and they talked for a while longer, and then Mary Kay suggested leaving.

"Coosie told us to be home in time for supper, and we must return the carriage first. Thank you, dear friend, for confiding in me. I will be there for you always. And thank you for spending my birthday with me."

* * * * * * * * *

Nick had been busy while Mary Kay was out of the house. He, Lex, and Casey had gone to his shop where a large crate had been delivered a few days before. Now they put the crate on a dolly and walked it up to the Manor. The crate was heavy, and Coosie left the kitchen long enough to help them get it up the porch steps and into a corner of the library where they pried the box open and removed the object inside. Nick attached a large blue bow to the top of it. He was excited about this gift because it was something that Mary Kay had long wanted. He enjoyed making her happy.

At promptly 6:00 o'clock, they were all seated around the table where Coosie had a roasted turkey and all the trimmings ready. It was a lively group, everyone filled with good spirits.

"Nick said, "Mary Kay, would you consider trading places with Coosie? You can work at the livery stables, and Coosie can stay here and roast a turkey for us every day. This food is marvelous, Coosie."

Mary Kay shook her head. "You would get tired of turkey if you ate it every day."

"One cannot live by bread alone," Nick retorted.

"Look at you – you of all people, quoting the Bible to me!"

Mary Kay looked across the table at Susanne. "Susanne, give Nick a good kick, will you? I want to enjoy this delicious dinner without having to listen to him talk all through it."

"Give Nick a kick! You made a rhyme, Mama." Nessie giggled.

After they had eaten, Coosie served coffee. He then brought in a large carrot cake on a tiered plate.

Jodie asked, "Coosie, do you always cook for Mary Kay on her birthday?"

Everyone broke into hilarious laughter and looked at Nick. Coosie spoke up, "No, Jodie, this is my first foray into the kitchen on Mary Kay's behalf. Last year, Nick cooked."

"And we all know how that turned out!" the group said in unison and then laughed some more.

"We'll explain it to you another time," Thornton promised Jodie.

"Mary Kay, it's gift-giving time," Coosie said.

Thornton disappeared and returned with several packages. The first gift was a pink parasol from Wiley. Mary Kay twirled it around and admired it. Thornton had sent for the new Wilkie Collins novel, which he knew Mary Kay wanted. Coosie gave her a yellow gingham apron. Mary Kay exclaimed over the gifts and thanked the men.

"Mama, we have presents too," Nessie told her.

"Indeed, they do. We have arranged a program for you," Thornton told Mary Kay. "Get comfortable." She settled back in her chair.

Tristan walked over and stood next to his mother. He looked at the script that Wiley and Thornton had prepared for him. He looked at his mother and cleared his throat. "Hear thee, hear thee," he said. "We know that you believe in women's issues: equality with men, the right to vote, and equal pay. We can't give you those things tonight, but we can gift you some important ladies and their accomplishments." Tristan looked at Thornton, and Thornton smiled encouragingly at him. "You are doing great, Lad."

Mary Kay looked at her son. "I hope you are going to tell me about Susan B. Anthony."

"No, Mama. You already know about her."

"Does she ever!" Nick piped in. Mary Kay ignored him.

We have chosen ladies you don't know about," Tristan continued.

"I am going to tell you about the paper bag lady." Nessie jumped up.

"Not now. It's not your turn," Tristan told his sister. Nessie sat back down.

Tristan read his script: "We shall begin with Mary Edwards Walker. She was the first female surgeon in the United States. She volunteered for the Union Army during the Civil War. President Johnson gave her the Congressional Medal of Honor after the war. She's the only woman to ever receive it." Tristan looked up. "That's why she is important, but I know some other interesting stuff about her. Do you want to hear it?"

"I certainly do," Mary Kay said.

"Okay, here goes. When she got married, she wouldn't allow the word, 'Obey' to be included in her wedding vows."

"Bad decision," Nick muttered. The others ignored him.

Tristan continued. "She wore men's breeches all the time, even to her own wedding. She got arrested several times for dressing like a man." Tristan was pleased when everyone laughed.

Mary Kay pulled him in for a hug. "Thank you, Honey, for such a lovely gift. I enjoyed hearing about her, but it seems to me that an intelligent person should be able to dress as she thinks best."

"Oh, here we go!" Nick said. The others ignored him.

"My turn." Nessie jumped up again. She had no script because she was not yet a proficient reader. Wiley and Thornton had helped her to memorize what she would say. "I am going to report on Margaret Knight. She is famous because she made machines safer." Nessie too looked at the engineers for assurance. They both nodded to her. "She invented a machine that makes brown paper bags with flat bottoms. Here's one for you, Mama." Nessie handed Mary Kay a bag.

"Why is that important, Nessie?" Wiley urged her.

"Because the bags make it easier to bring groceries home now. I call her 'The Paper Bag Lady,'" Nessie ended triumphantly.

Mary Kay held the bag up to her heart. "What a dandy invention. Anything to make a woman's work easier!"

"Men also shop," Nick said. The others ignored him.

"I shall keep this bag forever. Thank you, Sweetheart." Mary Kay gave Nessie a hug.

Mary Kay did keep the bag forever. A few days after her birthday, Nick encased the bag in a frame with a glass covering where it hung conspicuously on the kitchen wall. Everyone in the Manor thought the bag picture was one of the best things in the house because it was a special gift from a sweet child to her beloved mother.

Jodie stood up. "My turn, I guess. I thought you would like to know more about a woman author, so I chose Harriet Beecher Stowe. She was an abolitionist." He looked at Nessie and Tristan. "That's a person who was against slavery. She wrote a book called *Uncle Tom's Cabin* that showed the evils of slavery. President Lincoln even invited her to the White House. It is reported that when she walked in, Lincoln said, 'So, this is the little woman who brought on the big war.'" Jodie smiled at Mary Kay. "So, I thought she was important— Anyone who could start a war and all."

"Thank you, Jodie. You are right. She is a great writer, and she did help stop slavery."

"A very great lady," Coosie added his thoughts as a former slave.

Mary Kay reached out and gave Jodie a hug and said, "I did know about her because she is so famous. I even happen to know where she lives and who her closest neighbor is. Anyone know?" No one did, and for once Nick kept his mouth shut. So, Mary Kay continued, "She lives in Connecticut, and her neighbor is Mark Twain. Their properties are adjacent to each other."

Jodie looked up. He was interested because he considered Twain to be his favorite author. He was pleased that Mary Kay had liked his gift to her.

Mary Kay stood up. "Thank you, Children. Your gifts are a highlight of this birthday."

"Have a seat, Mary Kay, because I too have a woman to present to you." Nick stood up. "I give you a woman who made a huge difference in history. A Swedish scientist named Eva Ekeblad who made a discovery that had far-reaching consequences. She experimented and found that vodka could be made from potatoes." Nick gave a bow.

"What's vodka?" Nessie wanted to know.

"Nick!" Mary Kay warned, "I thought you were serious."

"I am serious. When you use potatoes to make liquor instead of using wheat or rye, it frees those grains up for bread making. Famine reduction, etc. Truly life changing! Unfortunately, there was a sharp increase in alcohol consumption in Sweden about the same time." Nick grinned.

"Sit down, Nick," Mary Kay ordered.

"What's vodka?" Nessie asked again.

"Never you mind, Child," Mary Kay told her.

"I have a gift," Susanne spoke up now. She handed Mary Kay a pretty box tied with a pink ribbon. Mary Kay opened it and discovered a sampler that Susanne had cross stitched for her. The words on the sampler read, "When male and female combine, all things achieve harmony." The author was Lao Tzu. Susanne smiled and said, "See, even an ancient Chinese scholar recognizes the importance of women." Mary Kay hugged her too. "Thank you for making this for me. I love it."

Nick spoke up now, "But we haven't sung "Happy Birthday" yet, and we need to do that. If you all don't mind, I think we should sing in the library. I'll go ahead. Please follow me."

Wiley offered Mary Kay his arm. "May I escort you to the library, Madam?" As she took his arm, the revelers could hear music coming from the library. They hurried in to find Nick playing "Happy Birthday" on a Steinway piano. A large blue ribbon sat on top of it. Mary Kay gasped. "A piano? Oh my! Just look at the beautiful ivory keys."

"Yes. For you, Sweetheart," Nick said. "We wish you the happiest of birthdays. I hope this makes up for last year's disastrous dinner." He laughed and gave her a hug.

CHAPTER 20

Nick habitually arose early before the rest of the household awoke. He was up and about even before Mary Kay began breakfast preparations for her boarders. He would dress quickly, and then he and Cindy would go for a walk.

Nick enjoyed people, but he also enjoyed being alone with his dog, and so they walked every morning. Nick often had things on his mind, and he found that tramping around in the early morning light and the brisk breeze brought clarity to his thoughts. Some of his most important decisions were made before coffee.

Jodie was often on his mind these days. He had been with Nick and his family since April, four months ago. No solution had been found to resolve Jodie's problem. His dad had not surfaced, nor had any word of him reached them. Nick had sent inquiries to friends in San Diego, but they had found no sign of him there. Billy Burke had simply vanished.

Nick found it odd that Jodie had stopped campaigning to return to San Diego. Also, when the young boy had first come to Bodie, most of his sentences had begun with, "My dad says," or "My dad thinks." Nick wondered why Jodie no longer mentioned his dad. Once, when he had asked him, Jodie had shrugged and turned away. He said he didn't want to talk about his dad.

Nick still had no idea who had attacked Jodie a few weeks before. The tailor had no additional information. Nick had examined the alley behind Cal's shop but had found no clues there. He had gone to the nearby businesses looking for a witness but was again disappointed. The constable had nothing to offer and had moved on. Bodie was a boisterous town; the lawman had bigger problems. Jodie refused to talk about it. He said he did not know who his attacker was and preferred that Nick leave it alone, but it was not Nick's nature to do that. He worried that the thug would someday go after Jodie again. He wished Jodie would trust him and tell him what had happened, but it was not to be, and Nick's hands were tied.

And then there was Jodie's mother. She continued to convalesce in the sanitarium but had shown no improvement according to Jodie. Jodie had given Nick her letters to read, and although she wrote optimistically, Nick could see that Jodie was worried. Jodie had confided in Nick that he had not always treated his mother decently, and he now regretted every sass he had given her. He wanted her to get better, so he could make it up to her. He planned to take good care of her for the rest of her life. Because Jodie was distressed, Nick considered ways to help him.

School was scheduled to begin its fall term soon, and Nick wondered if he should take Jodie to San Diego before then to visit his mother. He thought it would relieve some of Jodie's worry if he could actually see her. Nick wasn't sure they would be allowed into the sanitarium because of the contagiousness of the disease, and so he had sent a telegram to the doctor asking for advice. He wouldn't say anything to Jodie about the trip until he heard back from the doctor. He also needed to talk his plan over with Mary Kay to see if it would inconvenience her if he were away for several days. He had a couple of jobs to complete before he went anywhere. So, he had things to think about as he and Cindy walked along.

Today, however, it wasn't Jodie who was on Nick's mind but Susanne. He and Mary Kay had talked on the veranda last night after her birthday party. Coosie had again shooed her out of the kitchen, telling her he would clean up. If she was to be queen for the day, it would be for the entire day, he told her. So, she went out to the veranda, and it was there that she told Nick about Susanne's pregnancy.

"Susanne is worried that you will be disappointed in her and that this will ruin your friendship," Mary Kay told him.

Nick tapped his fingers on the arm of the oak chair and then abruptly got up and began to pace. He walked to the chimney and back several times. "Damn that Liam. I never liked him, and now he's got our girl in trouble. Where is he anyway? I haven't seen him around."

"Reno, I think. Gambling with his cronies. Susanne hasn't told him."

"And now she'll have to marry him, the no-good SOB!"

"No, I don't think so. She says not."

"No marriage? She can't have a baby alone," Nick said.

"She won't be alone. You and I will be with her."

"No, damn it! That's not the same. She needs a husband. But damn that Liam! I could string him up." Nick began to pace again. He and Mary Kay talked for a long time, and Nick assured her that this matter would not ruin the strong friendship he had with Susanne. He was worried about her reputation though. People could be cruel.

Mary Kay smiled ruefully and wondered aloud why it was always a woman's reputation that was at stake, never a man's. "In fact," she said, "Liam's buddies will probably congratulate him for having gotten Susanne in his bed. Another conquest, so to speak." But Nick was no longer listening to Mary Kay. He often tuned her out when she talked about women's issues.

That had been last night. Now, on his morning walk, Susanne's troubles had edged out Jodie's problems from Nick's mind. Cindy heard him mutter, "Damn that Liam," several times as they walked along.

* * * * * * * * * *

Then it was midmorning, and Nick stood in the doorway of Susanne's studio. Susanne was always happy to see him when he showed up unannounced. His job permitted him free time to drop by, and he often did.

"I have fresh coffee in the back. Interested?" Susanne asked.

"Yes, let's go in the back." Nick followed her through the curtain that led to her office. Susanne went to the side table to pour two mugs of coffee. She turned around to hand Nick his cup and was surprised to see him down on one knee.

"What in the world?" she gasped. "What are you doing?"

Nick had an engagement ring in his hand, which he now presented to her. He had taken it from his dresser drawer this morning, an heirloom of his grandmother's. She had given it to him four years before.

"What in the world?" Susanne repeated, clearly baffled. "What are you doing?"

"What do you think I am doing? I'm proposing! I'm obviously not good at it or you would recognize it." Nick got to his feet. He took the coffee mug from her and placed it on the desk. "But yes, Susanne Regina Connelly, I am proposing to you. I am asking you to marry me. I am presenting myself to you, abject failure of a man that I am— unsuited and flawed in every way. But yes, I am asking you to marry me."

Susanne stared at him. "You're a wonder," she said.

"Yes, I do have several good qualities. So, is that a yes? You will marry me?"

Susanne said nothing. She looked at Nick who then continued.

"One of my best qualities is that I am loyal. I would care for you and be faithful to you. You could depend on me to be there for you always. I would devote myself to your happiness. So, is that a yes?" Nick looked at Susanne earnestly, and she could tell that he meant every word. She was touched by his generosity and thought she might cry because he was so sweet.

"Do you love me?" she asked.

"Love?" Nick was surprised by the question. He hadn't thought about love.

"Yes, you didn't mention love when you asked me to marry you."

Nick looked uncomfortable. "You know I love you. You're one of my best friends."

Susanne looked at him for a moment and then said, "It's about the baby? Is that why you are talking about marriage?"

"Mary Kay told me you are expecting a baby in February and that you don't intend to marry Liam. Good decision, by the way!" Nick grinned. "So, I thought perhaps you would consider marriage to me instead. I would make an excellent husband and father. I am good with small children, and I even know how to change diapers, if it comes to that."

Susanne smiled at Nick. "What are you doing?" she asked.

"I am proposing to you, my sweet friend. I am asking you to marry me and give me the chance to claim your baby as my own. I want to be the father of this baby. I will love him as my own and do right by him."

"You said you will love this child?"

"Yes, of course. Certainly."

"But you don't love me, Nick, and I don't love you. Not romantically. Not in the way that matters. Frankly, not in the way I love Liam."

"Then, why don't you marry Liam?" Nick asked. "If he is the father, and you love him, why won't you marry him?" Nick was genuinely confused.

"Sit down, will you?" Susanne sat down in the nearest chair and nodded toward a second chair nearby. "I will try to explain it to you. I already love this baby more than anyone I have ever loved, and I feel protective of him or her. Fiercely protective! So protective that I want to keep the baby away from Liam at all costs."

"His own father?"

"Yes. I told you that I love Liam. Maybe it is only lust. I don't know. But I recognize that he is not a good man. Not honest and honorable. Not like you, Nick." She gave him a weak smile. "I do not intend to intertwine my life with his, and I would be a fool to tie myself to him legally. He is unreliable and self- absorbed. As a gambler, he is gone all the time, so it would be a lonely life. I want more from life than that for the baby and me. Does that make sense?" she asked.

Nick nodded thoughtfully. "I understand, and I admire you for being so strong. But that leaves you in a precarious situation. An unmarried woman with a baby – well, it is frowned on by society."

"Yes, I know," Susanne said. "Condemned by society, to be more accurate."

"So, that's why I am asking you to marry me, to protect you from the scorn of others. I couldn't stand it if you were mistreated."

"But, Nick, that's not a good reason to marry."

"No, perhaps not, but I am offering it. I understand that we don't love each other romantically, but we do love each other as good friends. Could that be enough for you?"

Susanne did not know what to say. She had never known anyone like Nick, sweet generous Nick. A man who was willing to give up his own dreams to help her salvage her reputation. Even though the residents at the Manor endlessly teased him, Susanne knew that Nick was the heart and soul of the place. He was the glue that kept it all together. Most onlookers would guess that Mary Kay was the center, but they would be wrong. It was Nick who was the gravitational force that kept everyone moving smoothly along the path. It was Nick whom everyone relied on. It was Nick whom the children adored. And here he was offering to marry her and be the father of her baby! How blessed she was to have Nick in her life.

When Susanne did not reply, Nick asked her, "Do you want to think about it? You don't have to answer me now. My offer stands. I will marry you anytime you say."

Susanne shook her head. "No, Nick. I don't need more time. I know my answer. You are truly the kindest man I have ever met. You take care of everyone, and now you are offering to take care of me— to help me out of a tough spot because I acted foolishly and irresponsibly."

Nick interrupted her. "No, it's more than that. We would be a family."

"Nick, I want you to have a family someday. A family of your choosing, not one thrust upon you by circumstances. Someday you will meet a woman, and I hope you fall hard for her. She will be the love of your life, your soul mate. You will ask her to marry you, and you will do so because you love her romantically and every other way. That's what I want for you. And when that woman shows up in your life, I want you to be available for her. That can never be if you are encumbered with me."

"Encumbered? I don't see it that way."

"Thank you, sweet Nick. Thank you for your unselfishness and your generous spirit. But no, I will not marry you. I want you in my life, and I want us to continue our friendship as before. I will need you to stand by me because I realize that tough times are coming. Yes, society can be unkind, but I will get through it. Just be there for me."

"So, instead of 'Daddy,' I will once again be 'Uncle Nick.'" Nick grinned at her. "Demoted! Story of my life!"

Susanne grinned back at him. "Someday, you will be 'Daddy' to a dozen children, and you will look back on this day with great relief that I said no. Go find the girl of your dreams and have a happy life."

Nick thought to himself that as usual, Susanne was right. A marriage of convenience wouldn't have fulfilled either of them. And worse, it might have ruined their friendship. What Susanne didn't know was that he had already found the girl of his dreams, the girl he did want to marry. However, this girl had never given him a second look, so he had no false illusions that he would be having a dozen children with her any time soon. *Too bad*, he thought. Now he switched his thoughts back to Susanne.

"I do treasure you, Susanne, and you can always count on me. Know that."

"Thank you, Nick. I treasure you too. I do have a huge favor to ask of you though. It's something I may need you to do for me." Susanne leaned forward and told Nick exactly what it was she was going to need.

Nick nodded. He thought it was a good plan, and he agreed to do it for her.

"Okay, I'm off. Work beckons." Nick smiled as he got to his feet. "Before I go though, I want you to know I will be adding another word to my vocabulary."

"What are you talking about?" Susan asked.

" Do you remember when I described myself as a 'flawed man' a few minutes ago?"

"Certainly. You also described yourself as an 'abject failure.'"

"Yes," Nick affirmed, "but now I have to add 'insecure' to the words that describe me."

"Why is that?"

"Because you rejected my marriage proposal. That's never happened before. It makes me feel insecure."

"How many other marriage proposals have you made?" Susanne asked.

"None. Yours was my first, but I still feel insecure." Nick shrugged his shoulders and looked dejectedly down at the floor. Then he looked up and grinned at her.

Susanne grinned back. "I'll see you at dinner."

"See you then." Nick closed the door behind him.

The joke Nick made about being insecure was a lame attempt to lighten the mood after such a serious morning. Both Nick and Susanne knew that. They both also realized that their friendship would never be the same. The bond was stronger now; it had deepened to a new level.

Nick thought back to his chat with Casey and Lex at the bar months before where they talked about the randomness of things. He definitely could see the hand of God here, putting Susanne in his life in this far-away desolate mining town. There was nothing random about it. For all his denial of religion, Nick felt a moment of spirituality as he walked back to his shop. Yes, Susanne and her baby would be fine.

CHAPTER 21

The children were right when they told Nick he was bossy. It was true that Nick liked to be in control. His personal habits spoke of his attention to detail. The orderliness of his carpenter's shop and his accurate, up-to-date ledgers suggested the hand of a perfectionist. If asked, a therapist might have given the opinion that this fastidiousness was a rebuttal to a chaotic childhood, one without structure. The therapist would have been wrong. Nick had grown up in a large, stable household presided over by good, loving parents.

So, why this need to be in control? Perhaps, Nick felt inadequate and worked that much harder for success. Perhaps, Nick was impatient and simply did not want to waste time looking for misplaced items. Perhaps, it was his brother Ed's death, which he hadn't been able to prevent, that kept him always on his toes. Whatever the reason, Nick liked to take charge and felt anxious when things went askew. So, he left nothing to chance and made his plans each morning as he walked with Cindy.

In Grass Valley, Nick had a large, extended family, and he was on good terms with all of them. He was Uncle Nick to the dozen or so young children there too. He made it a point to go home a couple of times a year, but he chose not to live there because it brought back too many painful memories of his brother.

The bedroom that they had shared, the hills they had climbed, and the swimming hole where they had idled away countless hours all reminded him of happy childhood days. Because he and Ed were close in age, they had shared many of the same friends. All of them reminded him of Ed, and so Nick had chosen to remove himself from the pain. Mary Kay was the only reminder he had taken with him to Bodie.

Nick always had a plan, and he had one now. He had decided that his friend Lex might be the perfect match for Mary Kay. Nick cared about Mary Kay's happiness and thought Lex might just be the one to provide it for her. Ed's untimely death had unnerved him. Nick realized that this could happen to him too, and then what would happen to Mary Kay and her children? Certainly, he was overreacting because Mary Kay had a family in Grass Valley who would help her. But Nick was not thinking of them, and so he was on a mission to get Mary Kay settled— just in case.

In Nick's opinion, Lex was a decent man, a solid man. He was a trustworthy friend who could be counted on. A miner with a big heart, Lex had long had his eye on Mary Kay. He liked her spunk and thought she was pretty. Once, he had described her as wholesome. Casey had laughed at that. Who would choose wholesome over sexy? Lex would.

Mary Kay had met Lex once at Boone's store. Nick had introduced them, but it had been a brief encounter, so they did not know each other. Nick often talked about both Casey and Lex, and Mary Kay knew that Nick spent a lot of time with them.

Mary Kay knew about mining, and so when Nick told her that Lex and Casey worked as a team hoisting the buckets of men and rock up and down the shafts, she realized this was a job that carried great responsibility. Casey's job was to detach the empty, down-coming buckets from the hoisting rope and hook the loaded buckets onto the rope to send it back up. Lex was the hoist man and worked the rope that was attached to the head frame that stood over the shaft. Lex and Casey had worked together for so long and were so efficient that Lex needed no signal from below to know when to hoist the rope. He could tell by the feel of the rope what was going on down the shaft. Their supervisor appreciated the precision of their work, and so when they asked for a Saturday afternoon off in early September, he willingly gave it to them.

They were going to Nick's, hoping his plan to get Mary Kay and Lex together would work. Nick had invited them to the Manor for a beer out on the veranda. The days were still hot, and the men settled themselves in the chairs around the table outside. Jodie sat on a bench behind the table near Nick— but not so near that Nick would notice him and send him away.

After his friends were seated and beer and pretzels were served, Nick excused himself and went to find Mary Kay. He knew to look in the library because he could hear the Stephen Foster songs she was playing on the piano.

"Hi, Mary Kay. Casey and Lex have stopped by. Come sit with us outside. Casey is going to tell us about a circus clown he met. He's a great storyteller."

"Sure, I can do that. Let me grab some vegetables. I can shuck the corn for dinner while I listen to the stories."

Mary Kay suspected that Nick might be playing match maker, but she didn't let on. She wasn't sure which of these friends he had planned for her because he hadn't shown his hand. Now she stepped outside and greeted Nick's friends. She thanked Nick for the iced tea he handed her. Then she said,

"I hope you don't mind if I shuck the corn and tend to the beans while we visit. I always have one more chore to do." She spread out a newspaper on a small side table as she spoke.

Lex stood up and said, "If you give me the knife, I'll shuck the corn for you."

"Goodness, a man who knows his way around the kitchen!" Mary Kay smiled at him. "Did your mama teach you?"

"She sure did. And I have four older sisters who made certain I learned too. If I wanted to eat, I had to pitch in and do my share." Lex took the knife from Mary Kay and turned to the corn. She sat down and began to snap the beans.

Lex said, "Men should know basic skills around the house. That was my mother's view. She told me to learn to be independent, and she was right."

"Wise woman," Mary Kay said.

Lex grinned. "Yes, I think she was afraid I'd come back home if I couldn't fend for myself."

"Are your sisters all married, Lex?" Mary Kay asked.

"All but one who is a schoolmarm. Teachers are most often not allowed to marry, you know. Sarah would like to have a husband and a bunch of kids." He shook his head. "Well, maybe someday. She will have to quit her job first though, and that's too bad because she loves teaching."

"Nonsense! I don't see why she can't do both," Mary Kay agreed.

Nick stepped in quickly before Mary Kay could go off on a tangent about women's rights.

"Casey comes from a large family too, don't you, Pal?"

"Sure do. You know us Irish! A new baby every year or so. We have eleven children in our family. I think my folks were glad when I left. One less mouth to feed."

"Don't let him fool you," Nick spoke up. "Casey sends money home every month to help his family."

Mary Kay decided that it must be Casey whom Nick had in mind for her since he jumped to his defense so quickly. Too bad!

She had been leaning toward the young guy with the four sisters. She was snapping beans into a large metal bowl when she heard a woman's voice.

"Hey, Y'all, am I glad I caught you!" exclaimed a large woman in a yellow, polka-dotted dress with sweat stains under her arms. She was climbing up the porch steps and fanning herself with a paper fan as she climbed. "Hotter than blue blazes, ain't it!" She continued to fan herself. "I'm tickled I found you all at home."

Nick was not tickled. This was Alice's mother, and he wanted nothing to do with Alice or anyone related to her. He remembered his manners, however, and stood up; Casey took his cue from him. Lex was already standing over the corn. It was he who greeted her, "Ma'am."

"Good afternoon, Beverly," Mary Kay said and introduced her to Lex and Casey.

Beverly looked at the young men. "Sit down, gents. Take a load off. I find myself with a little problem, and I'm fixin' to ask for your help."

Nick looked at her warily. He did not like Alice, and he did not care for her brash mother either. He would have described her as a '"pushy broad." Mary Kay showed her neighbor to an empty chair and poured her a glass of sweet tea. Mary Kay's manners never failed her. Nick watched Beverly as she took a telegram from her dress pocket and waved it over her head.

"This here telegram is about my Alice," Beverly began.

"I thought she was gone," Nick interrupted.

"Oh, she is gone. She surely is! And that's why I'm here. She has gotten herself in a passel of trouble." Beverly let out a huge sigh.

"Go on," Mary Kay encouraged her.

"I'm hesitant to tell you this, but she got herself mixed up with a man she corresponded with in the newspaper. She was hoping to get married; you know."

Nick nodded. He knew.

Mary Kay asked, "A mail-order bride?"

"Yes, Ma'am."

"So, a man advertised in the newspaper for a wife, and Alice answered his ad. Is that correct?"

Beverly shook her head. "Not exactly. It was the other way around. Men usually do the advertising, but Alice didn't want to wait. So, she put an ad in the newspaper herself, asking for eligible bachelors to contact her." Beverly drained her glass of tea before adding, "A miner in Aurora answered her. Said he was eager for marriage and sent her the money for the stage ride."

Nick was interested now. "So, what's the problem?"

"Well, they weren't together ten minutes when this miner started backtracking. Said he didn't think the two of them were compatible after all. Then he got in his carriage and drove off. Just left her standing in front of the stage depot. What a snake in the grass!" Beverly fanned herself more vigorously. "Alice had just enough money to send me this telegraph. She needs someone to come get her and bring her back."

"You don't have any relatives or friends to help you?" Mary Kay asked the woman.

"No, it's just Alice and me. My husband skipped out years ago. Alice doesn't have any money, and I need to get her home. I thought maybe Nick would be willing to go fetch her." Beverly looked hopefully at Nick.

"No, sorry. I am unavailable," Nick responded.

"But you must go! Alice has no money. She always thought so highly of you, so I thought you would want to come to her rescue."

"Why don't you hire a carriage and go after her yourself?" Nick asked. "It's only twelve miles."

"I wouldn't know where to start. I am a helpless woman begging you for your help, Sir."

Helpless my eye! Nick thought. He folded his arms and shook his head. "No, sorry." He had no intention of getting involved with either Alice or her mother.

Then another voice spoke up. "I'll go. I'll be glad to help you." Lex put down the knife. "Aurora, you said? I can go and be back this same evening."

"Oh, you lovely man! Bless your pea pickin' heart." Beverly beamed at Lex and almost tripped in her eagerness to hug him.

Nick looked at Lex. What was he thinking getting involved with these people? Nick had complained to both Lex and Casey about Alice and her romantic fantasies. Surely, Lex had to know what he was getting himself into.

Lex took the telegram from Beverly and read the details. Then, he picked up the knife and again began shucking the corn.

"What are you doing?" Beverly demanded. "You said you would go. You promised."

"I will go," Lex said, "but I have corn to shuck first. One promise at a time. Give me twenty minutes, and then we'll go hire a carriage. Why don't you meet me at the livery stables?"

Beverly looked relieved but still had a pout on her face as she left the veranda. She didn't look back nor thank Mary Kay for her hospitality. Nick congratulated himself on not getting involved with two crazy women. He certainly hoped Lex knew what he was doing.

Casey stood up. "Lex, I think you are absolutely nuts, but I'll go with you. Somebody needs to keep you out of trouble, and I can tell that both those women are trouble. It would be unwise for a man to be alone with the two of them. No telling what they could claim happened. So, I'll go with you. Anytime you're ready."

"Oh, Hell!" Nick stood up and looked at his friends. "Never mind, I'll go! Alice is my neighbor. She's not your responsibility. You stay here with Mary Kay, and I'll go with Beverly."

"No. I say we all go," Casey said. "That way we'll keep each other out of trouble."

"Yes, you all go. That's a good idea," Mary Kay said, "but swing back by here on your way out of town, and I will have a picnic basket filled with sandwiches for you."

Lex spoke up, "Mary Kay, why don't I stay and help you make the sandwiches while these two lugs get the carriage?"

" Yes, I would like that."

No one had remembered that Jodie was sitting nearby until he spoke up now, "Mary Kay, I'll be glad to help you too. Just tell me what to do."

Mary Kay smiled at him. "Thank you, Jodie. Get out the bread and slice it, please."

After Nick and Casey headed for town and the livery stable, Lex gathered up the shucked corn and followed Mary Kay into the house. While they made cold chicken sandwiches, and they bagged peanut butter cookies, Mary Kay asked Lex how he knew Nick.

"A couple of years ago, I wanted to send my niece a hope chest for her twelfth birthday. Nick had the reputation as a fine carpenter, so I met him, and I asked him to make the chest. Nick agreed to take on the job, and then soon after, we met for a beer after my shift. For the last two years, we have shared much more than a beer. We have discussed everything under the sun."

Mary Kay laughed. "Yes, Nick does like to talk."

Jodie spoke up, "What's a hope chest?"

"I have one upstairs in my bedroom," Mary Kay told him. Mine is made of cedar, so we call it a cedar chest instead. I prepared for my marriage by filling it with linens and quilts I made for my new home."

"I could be flip and say that it's a box a woman fills with goods in hope that she will someday marry," Lex said, "but I know better."

"Actually, you are not inaccurate," Mary Kay said. "Even today, women are expected to bring something of value into a marriage: money or property. It's called a 'dowry.'"

Lex said, "I find a dowry demeaning. It suggests that women are property to be exchanged."

Mary Kay looked at him. Could this man with his modern views really be a friend of Nick's?

"I wonder what the Bible says about such things?" Mary Kay mused.

Surprisingly, Lex knew the answer. "When Abraham's son Isaac married Rebekah, Abraham brought gifts to the bride's family—just the opposite of a dowry."

Again, Mary Kay wondered what Nick and Lex could possibly have in common. Lex was so much more enlightened. And he knew the Bible!

Jodie had a question. "Lex, why did you offer to help those hateful women when you don't even know them?"

"Ah Jodie, that's a good question. Sometimes people make bad decisions. I know I have. So, I was thinking about my sisters.

If one of them had made a poor choice and was in trouble, I would hope someone would help her. That's why I offered to help."

Jodie had always liked Lex, and he liked him even more now. Helping others made perfect sense when Lex explained it that way. Mary Kay was also starting to like Lex.

As they filled the picnic basket, Lex showed them that he also had a playful side. He grinned and said, "As my mama would have said, 'With her sweaty dress and soiled shoes, Beverly certainly is no slave to fashion, bless her heart.'"

Mary Kay burst out laughing. Jodie thought about the words, and then he laughed too.

Lex continued, "I am from the South, and down there we know we can make a derogatory remark about a person if we just add, 'Bless her heart.' So, we could say, 'If Alice thinks Nick is going to marry her, she is barking up the wrong tree, bless her heart.'"

Both Mary Kay and Jodie laughed again. "My turn," Mary Kay exclaimed. "As my daddy used to say, 'Alice looks like she would be ten miles of bad road, bless her heart.'"

"By golly, you've got it," Lex said.

"These are all Southern expressions?" Mary Kay asked.

Lex nodded, and in an exaggerated Southern drawl, he said, "Some of our finest witticisms from down yonder, Ma'am." Mary Kay smiled at him. She felt like she had known him a long time.

"My turn but I don't know what to say." Jodie looked at Lex. "How would I say that Nick would like to get Alice out of his life?"

"You would say, 'If Nick could get rid of Alice, he would be happier than a pig soaked in hot mud, Bless his heart.'" They all laughed.

It was not Mary Kay's habit to gossip or to speak unkindly about anyone, but she thought these amusing sayings were delightful. She hadn't laughed so much in a long time. Lex promised to give both her and Jodie lessons in the correct phraseology. All three decided that these "Witticisms," as they would call them, would be their secret, and they would incorporate them into their conversations whenever possible. In the days ahead, whenever one of the three added, "Bless her heart," to the end of a sentence, the other two would smile knowingly.

And so, a young Christian woman, a Kentucky miner, and a displaced boy conspired, made sandwiches, and bonded. Friendships are made in unexpected places.

Nick would later think about it. Because a miner had a sister who had a young daughter who desired a hope chest, the miner would meet a carpenter who had a widowed sister who would become the love of his life. Random? Nick thought not.

CHAPTER 22

Nick stood at the bar in his usual spot at Wagner's Saloon. Next to him were Casey and Lex. All had finished work for the day and were now debating the merits of one of baseball's pitchers.

"Nah, he isn't going far. His arm won't hold out, and then he'll be finished," Lex told the others. "I don't expect him to last the season."

"Yeah, yeah, you're right," Nick acknowledged. "He ain't no Pud Galvin. That's for sure."

"I wish we could have seen the matchup last month between Galvin and McCormick," Casey said. "Now, that was some game!"

Lex agreed, "McCormick has some curve ball! It would have been great to see him."

"I wish we could actually watch those fellows pitch and not just read about them in the newspapers," Nick groused.

"Maybe someday we should plan a trip east and take in a few games. We could start in Cincinnati. Then, before we headed to New York and Boston, we could go to your part of the country, Lex, and watch the Louisville Grays. What do you think?" Casey looked at the others for encouragement.

"Not a chance, Casey," Nick told him. Then he reached out and socked Lex in the arm. "Not a chance now that Lex here is in love. Love I say!" Nick did a quick jig right there at the bar. Other customers looked on in amusement. They were used to Nick and enjoyed his antics. Nick stopped dancing and picked up his beer.

"Yes, our pal here is in love. He even got up his nerve and asked Mary Kay to the dance next week."

Lex laughed. "Yep, life is pretty good right now. I was scared to ask her— afraid she would consider me forward and turn me down. But she said, 'Yes.'"

Nick spoke up, "She not only said, 'Yes,' but she said, 'Hell yes.'"

Lex frowned at Nick. "She would never say, 'Hell,' would she?"

"No, of course not. She would never utter a swear word, even on a bad day. But she did something even better. She claimed you."

Lex looked at Nick, unsure he had heard him correctly. "What are you talking about?"

"Alice showed up at the Manor yesterday morning and asked me if I would go to the dance with her. Can you imagine?" Nick made a gesture as if to strangle himself. "I told her that I was already committed. So, then she said to Mary Kay, 'That's okay. I will ask that handsome, young fellow who fetched me from Aurora last week. Mama told me how eager he was to come to my rescue.'"

Nick continued, "Before I could tell her that you also were taken, Mary Kay spoke up. So sweetly, she told Alice that you were her beau and therefore unavailable. She actually used those words, 'My beau.'"

Lex took a big swig of his beer. How had he gotten so lucky, he wondered? He had wanted to be Mary Kay's beau since he had first met her. Now, it was all coming together, and he was both nervous and happy. *"I hope I don't mess this up,"* he thought to himself.

Nick looked up just as Tess and Annabelle walked in the door, and his eyes lit up when he saw them. He came forward and with a sweeping gesture toward the little girl, he exclaimed, "She walks in beauty like the night."

Annabelle giggled and then recited the next line just as Nick had taught her, "Of cloudless climes and starry skies." She then ran to Nick and hugged him tightly.

"That's a lot of words for such a little girl," Lex told her.

Annabelle giggled again. "Hello, Mr. Lex." She didn't know Casey as well and was shy around him but knew she should speak to him too. "Hello," she spoke softly. Casey tipped his hat and smiled at the winsome child.

Tess spoke up now, "Lex, please watch Annabelle for a minute, will you?" She turned to Nick. "Let's go outside. I need to talk with you."

Nick could see that she had been crying. He followed her out the back door to the alley. Tess handed him a telegram. He unfolded it and read, "Your sister gravely ill. Lungs failing. Come now." It was signed by Jeannie's doctor.

Tess began to cry. "My poor Jeannie."

Nick wrapped his arms around her and let her sob. Finally, he pulled away. "What do you want to do?"

"I'm not sure," Tess answered.

Nick sighed. "Let's go figure it out. Annabelle doesn't need to be at the bar. Wait here while I grab her and tell my buddies I have to go."

Minutes later, Nick and Tess sat at the table in Nick's shop. Annabelle sat on the floor nearby, petting and talking to Cindy.

"We have a couple of options here," Nick said. "You, Annabelle, and Jodie can go. Or you and Jodie can go. Or I can take Jodie and go."

"Well, Jodie has to go. He needs to say goodbye to his mother."

Tess started to cry again. "And no word from his dad? Excuse me, of course not. Billy doesn't know Jodie is here." Tess blew her nose and continued to cry.

Nick shook his head. "It's odd though. For the first couple of months, Jodie was determined to go home, and then suddenly, he wasn't. He hasn't mentioned his dad or San Diego in a while. I don't know what to make of that, but Jodie won't talk about it." Nick looked at Tess now. "So, what do you want to do? The stage leaves in just over an hour. You have to make up your mind."

"I can't go, Nick. It's a money issue. If I spend the money going to San Diego, I will never get away from Sophie's. Is that selfish? I haven't seen my sister in eight years." Tess shook her head. "But Jodie needs to go. I have the money to send him."

"I'll give you the money. Money shouldn't be the determining factor if you want to see your sister one last time. Why don't you and Jodie go? I'll keep Annabelle at the Manor with me. It's too long a trip for such a young child, and Mary Kay won't mind if she stays. Annabelle can play with Nessie." Nick thought to himself, *God, I hope Mary Kay agrees to this!*

"How will we explain my being here in Bodie?" Tess asked now. "Jodie thinks I am still away, right?"

"Right. We can tell him you returned just in time to receive the telegram. But you know what? I think we should just tell him the truth. There have been enough lies." If Nick only knew!

"Okay, I'll go pack. I'll finally get to see my nephew. I have wanted to for a long time."

"It's a long trip; you'll get to know him well. Pack a bag for Annabelle, so she can stay with us. I'll buy the tickets, get Jodie ready, and meet you at the stage."

"Thanks, Nick. Annabelle, come with me quickly, and I will tell you about your staying at the Manor with your Uncle Nick." A quick peck on Nick's cheek from both of them, and then they were gone.

Oh boy! Nick thought. *I hope Mary Kay takes this well. I hope she wants another little girl in her life. It didn't work out so well when I brought a little boy home. And how am I going to explain who Annabelle is? But I can't worry about that now; I've got to find Jodie. This won't be easy for either of us."*

Nick hurried home and found Jodie playing cribbage with Wiley. Cribbage was his new favorite game. His arm was out of the cast now, but he couldn't play baseball yet, so he spent a lot of his free time playing cards.

"Fifteen -two, fifteen-four," Jodie was counting his hand when Nick walked into the room.

"Sorry, Wiley," Nick said, "game's over for Jodie. I need him."

Jodie got up and followed Nick out to the front porch steps, where they both sat down. Nick put his arm around Jodie's shoulder and gave him a quick hug. "I need you to buck up and be brave, Jodie."

Jodie nodded, not knowing what was coming but knowing it wasn't going to be good. "Okay, Nick."

"Your Aunt Tess is here in town," Nick began. Jodie noticed that Nick did not say that she had just returned to town, so this wasn't a lie. Nick continued, "She just received a telegram telling her that your mother's condition is worse. Her lungs are failing. I'm sorry, Jodie, but your mother is dying."

Jodie nodded that he understood, but despair rushed over him. He didn't know what to say.

Nick hugged Jodie tighter. "You need to go home to be with your mother now. I hope you don't mind, but I have made arrangements for you. The stage leaves in less than an hour. You'll travel with your aunt to San Diego. We need to get you packed, so you can meet Tess at the stage in a few minutes. I hope you will get home in time to say goodbye to your mother, Jodie."

Mary Kay stepped out onto the porch. "Sorry, Nick, but I overheard your conversation with Jodie just now." She went over to Jodie, leaned down, and kissed the top of his head. "I am so sorry about your mother, Sweetheart. Yes, you need to go home." Mary Kay then looked at Nick. "And you need to go with him. Jodie will need you now."

Nick looked at his sister-in-law. "I can't go. I told Jodie's aunt that I would keep her daughter Annabelle here, so she could go with Jodie. I hope you don't mind. Annabelle is a good little girl."

"I'll take care of Annabelle. You go with Jodie and the aunt. You know they will both need a man along to help them."

Nick was surprised that Mary Kay would freely admit that a man was needed.

Mary Kay continued, "Go pack. I'll get Jodie ready." She looked at the young boy. "Come with me, Honey." Jodie followed her into the house.

So, Mary Kay went to the stage office with Nick and Jodie, and there she met Tess. Mary Kay took Tess's hands in hers.

"I am glad to finally meet you, Tess, but I feel terrible that it is under these circumstances. I can't imagine how painful this is for you. Nick has decided to go with you and Jodie, so if it is all right with you, I will keep Annabelle here with me. Please trust that I will take good care of her. Is this agreeable with you?"

"Yes, of course. How kind of you."

"Mama, am I going to stay with Uncle Nick?" Annabelle was near tears because she had just heard that Nick was leaving town.

Nick knelt down and gently explained that she too needed to buck up, so he could take her mother to a hospital, and that little girls were not allowed in hospitals. Nick told Annabelle he needed her to stay with his sister who was a very nice lady and an expert cookie maker. Would Annabelle do that for him as a special favor? Annabelle hesitated and then nodded.

Tess introduced herself to Jodie and smiled at him. He shyly smiled back not knowing what to expect. He thought she was even prettier than the first time he had seen her. However, he was relieved that Nick was going to be along because he didn't know what to say to her. *What does one say to a prostitute, even if you are related to her?* he wondered. Then he remembered Coosie's words about women sometimes having no choices in their lives, and his heart softened. He would try to get to know her.

And then it was time to go. Tess, Jodie, and Nick climbed onto the stage. Mary Kay and Annabelle watched as the stage headed west into the sunset. Then, Mary Kay took Annabelle by the hand, and together they walked home to the Manor, chatting like two old friends.

Susanne and Coosie had supper going when Mary Kay and Annabelle arrived home. Mary Kay could smell spaghetti sauce as she and her young charge stepped through the door. Again, she felt grateful for the good friends in her life. Supper would be late, but it would soon be on the table.

Thornton and Wiley had gone to tell Nick's customers that because of a death in the family, Nick had gone out of town, and his work would be delayed. They offered to fill in for Nick, but the customers thanked them and told them not to worry. The jobs could wait. Family came first.

Mary Kay introduced Annabelle to Susanne. She was surprised that Coosie and Annabelle already knew each other. Then she found Tristan and Nessie in the library and introduced Annabelle to them. She told the three children that Nick had asked them to care for Cindy while he was out of town. Who wanted to feed Cindy first? Tristan and Nessie didn't find it unusual that Annabelle knew Cindy, but they wondered how she knew Nick.

"Why do you call him Uncle Nick?" Tristan asked. "I thought he was our uncle."

Mary Kay jumped in. "He is your uncle, indeed. But Annabelle is Jodie's cousin, so she gets to call him Uncle Nick too." That settled it. The children readily accepted their new cousin, and Nessie took Annabelle to see the bedroom they would share.

CHAPTER 23

When Mary Kay met Tess, she saw the anguish on her face and appreciated that the next few weeks would be a horrific ordeal for her. Mary Kay knew about grief and was saddened that both Tess and Jodie would have to experience the enormity of it.

Mary Kay had liked Tess immediately. Although somewhat quiet and reserved, Tess also possessed a charisma that drew others to her. She was modestly dressed, and her long brown hair was pulled back in a bun, away from her face. Annabelle was also clean, and her hair was washed and brushed. The little girl wore cornflower blue hair ribbons that matched her plaid dress. Mary Kay concluded that Tess must be a good, caring mother; and yet she wondered about her because Mary Kay had seen her before and knew where she lived.

Mary Kay was not as naïve as Nick thought she was, and she recognized Tess as one of the Ladies who lived on Bonanza Street. Doc Wagner had taken Mary Kay to the rough areas of town, as the two women did what they could for the less fortunate. So, Mary Kay had been to Bonanza Street. Prior to that, she had been to the less desirable neighborhoods of Virginia City when she had helped her church there. So yes, Mary Kay knew what went on in mining towns. However, because she was a lady, she did not speak of unseemly things to Nick or the other men in her life. Nick would have been surprised to know just how worldly she was.

Mary Kay had no idea why Tess would have turned to prostitution but knew that many women fell on hard times. Women did the best they could; but sometimes, life was unkind and threw insur-mountable hardships at them. Not everyone had a brother-in-law to look out for her. Not everyone had a best friend named Nick.

Because Mary Kay remembered seeing Tess down on Bonanza Street, she now understood how Jodie had ended up at the Manor. Tess must have been in town all this time but couldn't have Jodie live with her. No wonder Nick had taken him in! Had Nick planned all along to take care of Jodie until his mother regained her health? Probably so, knowing soft-hearted Nick. Again, Mary Kay felt blessed to have such caring family and friends.

Another thought struck Mary Kay; *How does Nick know Tess? And how well? He must know her well or he wouldn't have been so quick to offer Jodie a home. Does Nick frequent brothels?* Mary Kay sat in silence as she considered the possibility. *No,* she decided. She knew Nick, and she knew that particular lifestyle was not for him. He was not a ladies' man. However, now, she had more questions than answers.

It was Mary Kay's nature to fix things, and she wondered how she could possibly help Tess. Jodie would need his aunt now and would not have access to her if she remained on Bonanza Street. Mary Kay had no idea what to do. Finally, she asked Coosie to bring Lex to the Manor. Lex came, of course. Mary Kay offered him a kitchen chair and a hot cup of tea, and then she got right to the point.

"Why is Tess a prostitute?" she asked bluntly.

Lex Looked at her, surprised that she knew such a term. However, he did know Tess's story, and he now conveyed it to Mary Kay.

Tess was born in Butte, Montana. She was a good Catholic girl from a respected, Irish family who owned a popular bar in town. Her father had figured out early that in mining towns, liquor was the real money maker. He had never hunted for gold himself but was always there to give a good pour to those who did. Tess's parents had come to America during the time of the potato famine in the '40s and had joined others from County Cork who had also found their way to Montana. There, they practiced their religion the best they could. This was difficult because no Catholic churches or parochial schools had yet been built. Prayer services were held in their homes, and it was considered a blessing when a traveling priest happened by, so they could receive the Holy Host.

Tess's parents considered education important, so they paid a local woman to teach their daughters in her home. Tess had enjoyed learning and had been a credit to her family. She then attended the local high school; and after graduation, her parents sent her to classes in downtown Butte to learn accounting skills, at which she excelled. Eventually, Tess had gotten a good job working as a bookkeeper at the new fancy hotel in town.

It was at the hotel that she met Darcy, another local Irish girl, but one who lacked the discipline or morals that Tess had. The two girls had not known each other as children even though they had both grown up in Butte. Tess's friends had been young, proper Catholic girls. Her mother, Grace, had seen to that. Darcy was a Catholic, but in name only. She slept in on Sunday mornings rather than attend Mass. She hadn't confessed her sins in years and thought nothing of breaking the commandments. Tess made it a point to tell her mother as little as possible about her new friend because she knew her mother disapproved. Tess had brought Darcy home once, and that had been a mistake. Later, her mother had described Darcy as "Cheeky."

Tess was a bit dazzled by her new friend. She had never known a girl who was so carefree and wild. Darcy was the life of any party.

She talked the most, laughed the loudest, and could out-dance any girl on the floor. Tess, of course, knew the Irish jig and danced it well. She had taken lessons and had belonged to a club where they competed against other dancers. Her closet still housed the special dresses that had been a requirement of the competitions. Darcy, on the other hand, knew little about the Irish jig or folk dances. Boy crazy, she was never happier than in the arms of a young man waltzing around the floor. She was adept at both the quadrille and the new two-step. She taught these to Tess who was eager to learn.

After work, the girls would get themselves "gussied up," as Darcy called it and head to one of the bars where bands played, and everyone hurried to the dance floor. There, they met both local men and miners from distant places, and they danced the night away. Tess often spent the night at Darcy's home, so she could stay out late. Even though Tess was out of school and had a good job, she still lived at home, and that meant a curfew. Darcy had no such restrictions. She had no dad at home, and her mother was content to let the girls do as they pleased. She wasn't home much herself— something else Tess neglected to tell her mother.

Tess had been seventeen when her sister Jeannie had moved away with her husband and son Jodie. She had listened to her mother cry and had experienced the heartache that both parents felt at losing their beloved daughter and grandson. Tess determined never to hurt her parents that way. But then as young girls will do, she did exactly that.

Tess had been working at the hotel for two years when Darcy suggested they quit their jobs and go see the world.

"Let's go to California," she suggested. "I've always wanted to visit San Francisco."

"What are you talking about?" Tess was shocked. She had never considered leaving home. "I can't leave. What would my parents think? And we have good jobs here."

But Darcy was persuasive. She had thought things through and wanted a companion to share her adventure. She talked big, but she did not want to go alone. It would be so much more fun with a companion. Safer too. Unlike Tess, she felt no allegiance to home or work.

"Don't you want to experience big city life? We can dip our toes in the Pacific Ocean and watch the golden sunsets on the beach there. We can drink champagne for breakfast if we want to because no parents will be there to tell us we can't. Just imagine the men there! Sophisticated men who wear nice clothing and don't smell of sulfur from the mines. Men with clean fingernails. You and I will get interesting jobs and buy glamorous clothes. We will experience life. How can you say no to that?"

Listening to Darcy describe San Francisco made Tess suddenly eager to go there. Yes, of course, she wanted to experience life. She just had never considered experiencing it outside of Montana. But Darcy painted a convincing picture, and Tess wavered. She had money saved from her job that she could use. The fact that Darcy had asked her to go off on this adventure pleased Tess. She was flattered to be chosen by such a popular girl. But then, Darcy told her she was going with her or without her, and Tess needed to make up her mind. Tess did not want to disappoint her parents, but she did not want Darcy to go off without her. She agreed to go.

Tess got up her nerve finally and told her parents her plans. Her father looked at her and at first was too stunned to protest. At no time had he ever heard her express the desire to dip her toes in the Pacific Ocean. What was she thinking? Finally, he said,

"If you want water, we have water here. There's plenty of water in Montana. Go dip your toes in one of our many streams."

Her mother sat down heavily on the sofa and began to cry. "I know girls like to go try new things," she told Tess. "I understand that. But you are making a mistake going away with that girl. She's not like us. She has no moral compass. She's a tramp."

"No, Mama. You don't know her like I do."

"Believe me, I know her! I see women like her all the time in the bar. She's not a faithful friend. She's a user, and she will use you. Oh, Tess, please listen to me."

But Tess would not be dissuaded. She and Darcy gave the hotel their notices and enjoyed a few bon voyage parties in their honor, and then they were off. Tess promised her parents that after she had had her fill of the bright lights, she would return to Butte, settle down, and take care of them in their old age. This was a promise she intended to keep.

San Francisco was indeed a thriving city. It was the city on the bay, and one of the first things the girls did was to run down to the water and throw themselves in. They marveled at the blueness of the water but screamed at the frigidity. Their skin immediately produced goose bumps, their teeth chattered, and both girls shivered in their wet clothes. This would be one of their often-told stories: just how cold the water was in San Francisco Bay in March. San Francisco was a far cry from Butte which had many mines and a dirty atmosphere. Everything here seemed to sparkle. They engaged rooms at an inexpensive but respectable boarding house and settled in.

They quickly found work at a high-class hotel. No jobs were available in the accounting department, so Tess found herself working with Darcy in the dining room where Darcy taught her how to wait tables. Tess found waitressing to be harder work than figuring numbers because she was on her feet all day, and that took some getting used to. She did find it rewarding to meet such interesting customers, and she wrote many letters home telling her parents of her adventures. She hoped they were happy for her.

In San Francisco, men greatly outnumbered women. Darcy had one beau after another but did not stay with anyone for long. Frankly, she did not want to be any one's wife or mother. She just wanted to have a good time. Tess went out with a couple of men, but like Darcy, she did not want to settle down.

That changed the day Connor Sullivan walked into the hotel dining room and sat down at her table. It was early for the lunch crowd, and Tess was not busy yet. She turned around, and he was there.

"Oh my," she exclaimed when she saw him. He was the most handsome man she had ever seen with his dark hair and ready smile. He laughed at her reaction and said,

"Perhaps, I should also say, 'Oh my' because you are a beauty. I can't take my eyes off you."

Two men then joined him, and the three filled the dining room with talk and laughter. Darcy noticed them and couldn't stay away. She practically pushed Tess out of the way as she offered the men fresh water, hot coffee, clean linen. But the men seemed to have eyes only for Tess, and so Darcy had given up and had gone back to her own station.

"I may come here for lunch every day if I can count on seeing you," the first man told Tess. "My name is Connor, and I work at the bank across the street. Tell me that you work every day."

"Yes, every day except Monday."

He smiled at her and said, "Excellent. Then you must be free in the evenings. Would you consider having dinner with me on Saturday evening?"

Yes, she would consider it, and it was settled. And yes, inviting her friend Darcy would be a good idea. Connor would invite one of his friends to accompany her. Both of his luncheon companions offered to be Darcy's escort. Connor chose the unmarried one.

On Saturday evening, the girls met the gentlemen at Maxwell's Broiler downtown. The dinner conversation was animated, and they went dancing afterwards. Tess liked Connor and agreed to see him again. Soon they were an item. Darcy was not interested in any of Connor's friends and chose not to waste her time on them. She wanted to enjoy the night life of San Francisco with no strings attached, so she often went off on her own.

Time went by, and they settled into a routine. Tess was a good, decent girl and had not let things get out of hand with Connor. Over tea one afternoon, he told her he loved her; she was the only girl for him. Not long after, she let her guard down and spent the night with him. Soon after, she realized she was pregnant. When Tess told him, Connor took her in his arms and again told her he loved her. He said nothing of marriage but expressed great delight in becoming a father. He told her that he had always wanted a son.

It was about that time that Darcy, the free spirit, said she wanted to move on. There were other places to experience, she told them. She had heard a great deal about Lake Tahoe and would like to go there. Would Tess consider leaving San Francisco? Tess did not know what she wanted to do. She was pregnant by a beau who had not committed to marriage. Would she stay with him or go with her friend? The matter was decided when Connor suddenly chose to quit his job and go with them to Lake Tahoe. Darcy was delighted, and Tess was relieved. Darcy had friends at the lake, and the three became their house guests for a few weeks. The weather was warm, the lake was breathtakingly beautiful, and the wine flowed freely. Their hosts were affable and welcoming. The threesome stayed until they all knew it was time to go.

Connor suggested Carson City because he needed to get a job, and he could certainly find one there. So, the three friends moved to the territorial capital and stayed there a few months. Connor worked at the local bank. They left Carson City and moved south to a place called Bodie only because Connor had caught the gold fever and wanted a chance to prove himself. Tess had not heard of Bodie but was expecting his child, and so she agreed to go with him. She believed he would marry her before the baby came.

Darcy was a good sport about moving again and said, "Why not? We're all in this together. Let's go see what Bodie has to offer."

Connor rented a two-bedroom house for them all, and they settled in again. He planned to work in the mines but soon realized what dirty work it was. He found a job at the assay office instead. Darcy took a job as a saloon girl. Tess stayed home, kept the house, and prepared meals.

As her due date neared, Connor became more and more enthused about parenthood, and he often suggested names for their baby. Connor liked the name Aidan, but Tess told him no. The name reminded her of an annoying neighbor back home. Connor did not like the name Raymond. He did not want to name the baby after her father, a man he had never met, he told her. They were at an impasse.

Connor hired a midwife named Prue, and when the time came, she delivered not one baby but two, a boy and a girl. Connor seemed distressed by suddenly being responsible for two children, but Tess was thrilled to be the mother of twins. She checked the babies for fingers and toes and declared them perfect. She fed them, and then because it had been a long, exhausting labor, she slept soundly, while Connor and Darcy toasted to everyone's health in the kitchen. When Tess awoke later, she could hear drunken laughter.

The next morning, when Prue came to check on Tess and the babies, she found the house strangely quiet. Tess was asleep with one of the babies at her breast. The bassinet was empty, and Connor and Darcy were gone. They had taken the baby boy and left before the sun rose.

Tess asked Prue to check the wardrobe, and yes— their clothes were gone. Prue talked to a neighbor who had seen them leave in a carriage before day light. No, the neighbor hadn't noticed a baby with them, but he hadn't been paying close attention. Tess was inconsolable. Connor had gone and had taken Darcy and the baby with him. Or perhaps it had been Darcy's idea to go. Tess had no idea. If her beau and her best friend were romantically involved, she hadn't suspected it. She knew Connor wanted a son, and she thought he wanted to have a family with her. Instead, he had gone off with Darcy. Utterly dejected, she hugged her baby daughter to her and sobbed.

,

CHAPTER 24

What to do? Tess had no idea. She was confronted with the serious issues of providing for a newborn baby and anguishing over the loss of another. She had no friends to help her. While Darcy and Connor had gone off to work each day, Tess had stayed home and cared for their house. She had not gone far and so knew no one in town. Prue proved to be a godsend to Tess. She had a family of her own and other responsibilities as well, but she went to the house every morning to help Tess. She bathed the baby and helped Tess in other ways until Tess was strong enough to do these things herself.

At Tess's urging, Prue sent a telegram to Jeannie. Tess needed help and turned to the one person she knew she could depend on—her sister. The telegram had been futile; however, because Jeannie had been in transit from one town to another, and the message did not get to her. Tess did not reach out to her parents because they were too far away to be of any real help. Also, she was embarrassed that her mother had been right about so many things, especially about Darcy.

Every time Tess thought about Darcy, tears rolled down her face. Darcy had been her best friend. They had traveled together for two years and had grown as close as sisters. At least that's how Tess had felt. They had talked intimately about many things. Tess had opened her heart to Darcy as she had to no one else, not even to her sister. And now, suddenly Darcy was gone. She had taken not only Connor but Tess's baby. Darcy had never wanted to marry or to have children, so how could she want Tess's baby? This made no sense to

Tess. And irrationally, Tess couldn't get over the fact that Darcy had left without even saying goodbye.

The pain Tess felt when she thought about Connor was intense. She had believed he was the love of her life. She had believed him every time he had told her he loved her. Why hadn't she realized that he had no actions to back up his words? A real man would have married her and would not have put her in such an impossible situation. Connor had been excited about the baby and was convinced it was a boy— his boy. He had great plans for the lad. He would teach him to ride a horse, sail a boat, and play rugby. Yes, he had plans for his son, but never had he suggested that these plans would not include the boy's mother.

Tess had desperately wanted to marry Connor and had waited for him to say, "Today's the day. Put on your prettiest dress, and we will walk over to the Justice of the Peace. Today's the day I will show my love for you by giving you my name. Today's the day we will look back on with great happiness for the rest of our days. Today's the day."

But Connor had not mentioned marriage. Tess had been in an unsettled position waiting for him to say, "Today's the Day." When he did not, Tess thought of leaving Bodie. Darcy had dissuaded her.

"Where would you go?" she had asked. "You could never make it home to Butte before the baby comes. Besides, if you leave, you'll never be Mrs. Connor Sullivan. I advise you to stay. I know he loves you and will marry you. And frankly, I like it here in Bodie and don't want to move yet, so you would have to go alone."

So, Tess had stayed, and then it was too late to go. The babies were born, and Connor had indeed wanted his son— so much so that he had disappeared with him in the night. Tess wondered if this had been Darcy's plan all along when she had persuaded Tess to stay in Bodie. Had Darcy also been in love with Connor?

Tess was stunned that she had given birth to two babies. She knew of no other twins in her family, but she had fallen in love with both children instantly. She had never felt such love in her life, not even for Connor. She would be a fierce mother bear in protecting these children, she had determined, but she had failed even at that as she had slept through her baby's abduction. She didn't know where her baby was but knew instinctively that his name was Aidan.

The town sheriff came to see Tess at Prue's insistence. Had Tess had her wits about her, she would not have made the disastrous mistake she did when talking with him. She was exhausted, however, and frightened. She was not thinking clearly.

"What's this I hear about a missing baby?" the burly man had asked her. "Where's your husband?"

Tess had to admit that she and Connor were not married. She felt dirty telling this law man about her unmarried status while she had a newborn lying next to her. A decent woman would have a husband.

"Is this Sullivan fellow the father of these babies?" the sheriff had then asked. This was when Tess made the grave error.

"Yes, Connor is the father," she had replied.

The sheriff became businesslike now. He put his hand up and rubbed the back of his neck as he spoke. "If he is the father, then he can't be accused of stealing his own child, can he? I know this is not what you want to hear, young woman, but these are the facts. A man has the right to take his child and go anywhere he wants."

"What about a mother's rights?" she asked.

The sheriff looked uncomfortable. "I think you should consider yourself fortunate that he didn't take both babies. You each have a child. That's about the best I can do for you. I can't arrest a man for stealing a baby who rightfully belongs to him."

Tess sat up straighter in bed. "What about the baby's welfare? How is Connor expected to feed this baby he so blithely took? I'm certain he didn't think this through. The last time I saw him, he was drunk."

"Drunkenness is not an arresting offense either, Ma'am. And as far as finding milk for the baby… there are plenty of cows around. Goats too. I understand that this Sullivan left with a lady friend of yours. She'll figure it out. Women have a nurturing nature about them."

Tess could hear the condescendence in his voice and couldn't believe that this law man wasn't going to help her. "But my friend never wanted children," she told him. "She won't want this one for long."

"No, I know nothing about that, Ma'am. But I think that if she wants to keep your man, she'll have to care for his child. Maybe that's why Sullivan took her with him. I don't know. I'm just speculating. But it's my guess that they'll go somewhere far from here and pretend to be a married couple with a child. No one will ever know the difference."

"So, you can't do anything?" Tess asked. She already knew the answer.

"I truly am sorry, but I think you've seen the last of them – and your baby. Do you think this was their plan all along? To desert you?"

"I have no idea. I know Connor wanted a son. Maybe the added birth of a daughter was too much responsibility for him. But I never saw this coming. Darcy was my best friend, and I can't imagine that she plotted all along to take my child from me."

The big man looked wary. "Darcy, you say? Did she work at a hurdy gurdy bar?"

Tess nodded.

"Sorry to say this, Ma'am, but this Darcy is a tramp. I'm sorry for you that she's the one with your child. You should have married this Sullivan when you had the chance."

Tess couldn't admit to this rough man that she had never had the chance. Connor had not asked her to marry him.

So, what to do? Tess had no legal means to help her, and she had no money for a lawyer even if the law was on her side. She would get her strength back and then decide what to do. Thank God for Prue. Tess knew no one else in Bodie.

But bad news does not travel alone; it usually arrives with a companion. Tess suddenly found herself in more trouble when the landlord knocked on the door looking for Connor. Tess had to admit that he was no longer in town. The man, a smart dresser by the name of Barrett, got right to the point. The rent was due. Could she pay it? If not, she would have to move. He hated to seem insensitive, but he was running a business, after all. There were plenty of people looking for a house to rent. Perhaps she could move in with a friend, he suggested.

"Three days!" he told her, "You have to be out in three days."

Prue again checked the telegraph office. Nothing from Tess's sister. So, then Prue did the only thing she could think to do; she went to see her cousin Sophie who owned and operated a bordello on Bonanza Street. Sophie was smart, and she had money. If anyone could help Tess, it would be she. Sophie was a wise businesswoman, but she also had a big heart. She listened to Prue's story and understood the plight of this young woman who had been deserted. As long as there were young, naïve women, unscrupulous men would readily take advantage of them. Sophie had heard the story before. It was an old story that usually ended badly. Some of Sophie's "girls" had similar stories. So, Sophie went with Prue to visit Tess.

Tess did not know that Prue had a cousin, but she willingly talked about her situation to the older woman. This was no time for embarrassment because she was in serious trouble and needed help. Sophie asked Tess if she knew what a bordello was. Tess did not, so Sophie explained it to her. She offered Tess a small bedroom in the back of the house for her and her baby.

"What is the baby's name?" Sophie asked while caressing the baby's cheek.

Tess smiled ruefully and shook her head. "I don't know. I haven't thought to name her. We expected a boy so didn't even consider names for girls. I have no idea. Any suggestions?"

"My mother's name was Annabelle," Sophie told her. "She was a great lady of good character and great integrity. She was the strongest person I have ever known and the most respected woman in our town. I miss her every day."

"This baby will need all those attributes, especially inner strength, "Tess said. "Yes, I like the name. Annabelle it is! And her middle name shall be Prudence for you, Prue. You've been so kind to me, and I am so grateful."

Sophie brought the conversation back to business. "Tess, you will have to keep the baby quiet. My girls sleep in the daytime and entertain at night. We can't have a crying baby."

"I understand," Tess said.

Sophie continued, "I can't keep you there forever but am happy to help you until you are recovered. I'll have to charge you for your room and board, but you can pay me when you can. I'll collect later."

Tess was overwhelmed by this woman's goodness. Sophie was taking her in, no questions asked. *The kindness of strangers*, she thought. Certainly, she would go with her. Tess hadn't seen herself ending up in a brothel but knew she had little choice. She wouldn't live there forever, just until she could get back on her feet. Then she would either find Jeannie or find a job.

But the Piper must be paid. Four weeks later, when Tess felt better, Sophie told her the amount she owed for board and room. Tess had not had much money to begin with, and it had been spent on clothes and diapers for the baby. Tess did not have the money to pay Sophie, so Sophie offered her a job in the bordello as a hostess, which was a euphemism for a "Working Girl" or "Upstairs Girl." Sophie might have a good heart, but above all, she was a shrewd businesswoman. She recognized an asset when she saw one and knew that as a prostitute, lovely Tess would attract many customers. She wasn't about to let her go. Prue and her family were no longer in town. Prue's husband had gotten a promotion, and they had moved to Reno. Tess had no one to turn to and nowhere else to go.

"And that, Mary Kay, is how Tess came to live on Bonanza Street," Lex said.

"Thank you for telling me so frankly, Lex. I feel that I can talk with you about anything." Mary Kay stood up from the kitchen table. She smiled sweetly and said, "And now, I am going to show you how Tess becomes a former prostitute."

Lex pointed to Mary Kay's chair. "Please have a seat while I tell you the rest of the story."

CHAPTER 25

"What would you say to having a dozen children?" Nick asked.

"With you?"

"Yes, with me."

"I'd say that we should start sooner rather than later then."

"I'd say so."

"Would that be a dozen children plus Annabelle and Jodie, or a dozen including Annabelle and Jodie?" Tess asked for clarification.

"We'll play it by ear, see how tired you are after ten."

"Would you be putting a ring on my finger?"

Nick grinned. "Yes, definitely a ring. However, in the spirit of full disclosure, I must tell you that I offered the same ring to another lady recently. She turned me down."

"So, I'm second choice?"

"Not second choice. Definitely NOT second choice. You have always been my first choice."

"So, will you be telling me about the other woman, the one who turned you down?"

"Not until you agree to marry me. Then, I'll tell you everything — always."

"I've never been proposed to before, but I expected the fellow to get down on one knee, at least."

"No, the getting down on one-knee technique is highly overrated. I tried it, and it failed, so I've given up on the idea. And because we are presently riding in a coach, there is not much room for the one-knee proposal."

"I see." Tess gave Nick a quick smile but then continued smiling. She had loved Nick for a long time but had never imagined that he might love her in return. They had been good friends and confidants since they had first met, but Tess had never expected it to come to more than that. They had never talked of romance, but she loved this man more fiercely than she had ever loved Connor. With Connor, she had never felt completely secure. She had always wanted and expected more of him than he was willing to give. Now, being older and wiser, she knew that it had been a one-sided romance. He was one of the users her mother had warned her about. But this love she felt for Nick was different. She felt completely safe with him. And happy.

Despite her horrendous week in San Diego, burying her sister and trying to be there for Jodie, she suddenly felt a great burden lift from her shoulders. It had been a long time since she had been happy. She looked into Nick's eyes now. He looked back at her and was just leaning in toward her when Jodie spoke up,

"Oh geez! Just kiss her, will you?" Jodie had been lying on the seat next to Tess, but he sat up now.

"I thought you were asleep, Jodie." Nick was embarrassed.

"I couldn't sleep with all your talk of procreating children," Jodie muttered.

"Procreating children? Where do you get such highfalutin words?"

Jodie laughed out loud. "I read," he said triumphantly.

"Go back to sleep, so I can kiss the lady, will you?"

"Sure thing," Jodie agreed as he curled up again and closed his eyes.

"Come here, you," Nick reached out and pulled Tess toward him. "Listen carefully while I tell you how much I love you, how I have loved you since I first saw you buying liver in the butcher shop years ago. Please tell me that you love me and will marry me." He kissed her and held her tightly despite the closed, cramped condition of the coach.

"Yes Nick, I will marry you. I love you too despite the botched proposal."

"Botched?"

"Yes, and witnessed by a nosy, outspoken boy. Despite all that, I do love you, Nick."

"Yes," Nick agreed, "Jodie is a bit meddlesome. Sadly, that's one of his better qualities."

"Just to be clear," Tess inserted, "it was not liver I was buying. I would never eat liver."

Jodie sat up again and smiled at them both. "Congratulations, you two. Do I get to be the Best Man?"

"Yeah, yeah, you will always be my Best Man." Nick tousled his hair. "Now, will you please go back to sleep? Tess and I have things to discuss before we get back to Bodie in a couple of hours."

"Okay, but first I get to kiss the bride." Jodie leaned over and gave Tess a loud smack on the cheek. "Good job, hooking this big guy, Tess. I didn't think anyone would ever want him. Good night." Jodie lay back down.

Tess and Nick grinned at each other, and Nick reached out and took her hand. It had been a horrible week, but they had weathered it together and had been the comfort and support Jodie had needed. It is difficult to lose your mother at any age but especially difficult when you are so young.

Jeannie had still been alive when they arrived at the sanitarium. The kind doctor had seen to it that she was given a private room, so her family could spend time with her. Jodie had been brave because Nick had told him that he needed to buck up, and he had tried his best. He had almost cried though when he first saw his mother lying on the white sheets on the bed. She looked so small and withered, not the vibrant mother he had known as a young child.

He suddenly wished with all his heart that he had been more loving and attentive to her. Many times, he had bolted out the door to play ball in the streets and had left her to do the chores. She had not complained, but now he wished he had done things differently. When his father had berated and bullied her, Jodie had not come to her defense. Looking back, he was ashamed of himself for allowing his dad to browbeat her the way he had. A good son would have stepped in and stepped up. Jodie had been too enamored with his dad and had always sought his approval, even if it meant keeping quiet and allowing a woman to take the beating. Now, looking at his mother on the last day of her life, Jodie was filled with regret. He did not cry because he knew that tears would have saddened her more.

Tess left the room, so Jodie could have the time he needed with his mother. Jeannie was weak but alert and heard every word Jodie said to her. He told her how much he valued her as a mother and appreciated all the caring things she had always done for him. He talked about specific times they had spent together: the Wednesday afternoons when they walked to the library for story time and then chose books to take home. The many books she had read to him after he had had his bath and was dressed in freshly laundered pajamas. He told her he still used the vocabulary note cards written in her handwriting and that Mary Kay was impressed by his use of big words. And then, Jodie told his mother all about Nick and how kind he had been to him.

"Maybe Nick could come in later and meet you, if you are feeling up to it, that is."

Jeannie had smiled and told him that yes, she certainly wanted to meet this Nick of his.

Jodie reminded her of the beef lasagna she always made for him on his birthdays. He talked of the many themed cakes she had made to celebrate his special day.

"Remember the time you took me to the circus, and when we got home, you surprised me with a clown-shaped cake? And do you remember the day at the lighthouse when we got drenched from the rain? In San Diego where it never rains!" he had exclaimed.

"And the time we went down to the riverbed and caught polliwogs, brought them home, and watched them eventually turn in to tiny frogs?" Jodie had so many good memories of childhood with his mom.

"I remember," she had replied. "Do you remember trying to teach me to play marbles, and I was terrible at it?" she asked.

"I remember the marbles and all the other stuff you made sure I had even though we didn't have much money."

Jodie took her hand. "Thank you, Mom, for everything you did for me. You are the best mom. I have missed you so much."

"Me too, Sweetie, me too," Jeannie said as she wiped tears from her eyes.

"Tell me some more of your life in Bodie," she requested. "I want to know everything."

Jodie told her about school, and about dinners at the Manor, and about Nick's dog, Cindy.

But there were two topics he did not touch. He did not mention getting beaten up by kids he thought were his friends. And he did not tell her that he had run into his dad in Bodie and that dad seemed to have a whole different life now— one that did not include his family back home. Jodie would not tell her how betrayed he felt by his own father, nor would he tell her that she too had been betrayed. She would have been brokenhearted to know that her husband was unfaithful to her. Jodie would never tell her that.

"I know you don't want to hear this, Jodie, but we both know I am not going to make it. The doctor has told you as much. I don't have much time left, and that is why I am so grateful that you got here in time. It has meant everything to me to have you here. You are so loved."

Jodie bowed his head. "I love you too, Mom," he said sadly.

"Why don't you go get your Aunt Tess now, and also bring Nick? I would like to meet him. Gosh, it is so good to see Tess again. I hope you will stay close to her. Always remember how important your family is, Jodie."

Nick came in and sat down next to Jeannie's bed and talked with her as though they were old friends. He had that knack about him and had never met a stranger. After a few minutes, it was not Tess to whom Jeannie turned but to Nick.

"Nick, I know that we have just met, but I am going to ask a huge favor of you, nevertheless."

"Yes, Jeannie. Anything," Nick responded, taking her hands in his.

"I want you to take Jodie, please. Raise him up as your own son. He will need a family, and I want him to be with you. Tess and I talked it over, and we think this is best. Please, Nick, will you do that?"

"Of course, Jeannie. Nothing would make me happier than to take care of Jodie. He's a spectacular young man, and I think you have done a tremendous job with him. I applaud you."

Nick squeezed her hands and looked at her intently. "I will educate him, protect him, and love him. If at all possible, I will someday take him to Butte, so that he can spend time with your parents. I know you would want that. Thank you for placing your trust in me, Jeannie. I am so honored." Tears trickled down Nick's cheeks.

So much for "Bucking up," Jodie thought.

It was an hour later that Jeannie slipped into a coma, and not long after that when she died. Jodie and Tess held her as she breathed her last breath. Then Nick hugged them both to him and let them cry until they could cry no more. As he ushered them out of the room, he thought of Mary Kay and was glad she had urged him to come. She had been right, of course, because both Jodie and Tess had needed him.

It wasn't feasible to send Jeannie's body back to Butte. Nick had talked to the mortician and had concluded that it was far too complicated and costly. He also thought it would be an unneeded burden on Jeannie's parents to have to arrange for the burial of their beloved daughter. No one should have to bury a daughter. Nick talked it over with Tess and Jodie, and they all agreed to bury Jeannie in the Catholic cemetery there in San Diego. Nick made the arrangements and talked to the priest who agreed to say a morning Mass. Jeannie's doctor was the only other person to attend the burial. Because Tess wasn't up to it, and Jodie couldn't do it, Nick gave a short eulogy about this wonderful woman and mother named Jeannie. From the passionate way he spoke, one would have thought he had always known her. Tess, Jodie, and Nick all placed yellow roses on the casket. They thanked the doctor for his many kindnesses, and Nick paid the priest for his services. And then, hand-in-hand, the three walked away, knowing they had done their best for Jodie's mom. There were no more tears. They were all cried out.

CHAPTER 26

"Now what?" Nick asked as they walked into the hotel lobby a few minutes later.

Jodie surprised him. "Would you take me to the beach?"

"The beach?"

"Yes, it was my mother's favorite place. We went often and took long walks or played in the sand," Jodie said quietly. " I thought we could each look for a seashell to remind us of this day."

"The beach it is! If that's okay with you, Tess?" Nick responded.

"Yes," Tess said. "I want to see my sister's favorite place."

"If you like, I could make you each a shadow box to display your shells," Nick offered.

Tess and Jodie both thought this was a good idea.

And then Nick spoke again. "We will go to the beach this afternoon, but Jodie, we probably won't be back in San Diego for a while. What other places would you like to see while we're here? You can show Tess and me the town you grew up in. We have time. We don't have to leave for Bodie until we're ready."

Jodie thought about this. Nick was a good guy to offer. "Yes," Jodie told him, "I would like to visit my pal Ian who lives in the old neighborhood. Maybe we could see my old house too. It's right next door to Ian's."

"Anywhere else?" Nick prodded.

"I would like to show you the lighthouse out at Point Loma. Mom and I used to go there and take picnics. If we go, we would have to leave fairly early in the morning though because it's a dirt road going up, and it takes a while. But it's worth seeing.

"The lighthouse keeper, Captain Israel, is a nice man, and he doesn't mind if we are on the grounds up there. His wife, Mrs. Maria, was his assistant for a couple of years. They have three sons who used to row across the bay to go to school in the old town.

"Maybe we would run into Captain Israel if we went, and you would be able to talk with him about carpentry because at one time he was a chair maker." Jodie ran out of breath, so Nick was able to ask Tess her thoughts on a day trip to the lighthouse.

"Yes, I want to see everything that is important to Jodie," she answered.

Jodie spoke again, "You will like seeing the lighthouse, and you won't believe the view of the bay from up there!"

Nick did not tell him that he knew San Diego well because he had good friends who lived there, and he often visited them. Yes, the view from Point Loma was spectacular, but he said nothing because he wanted Jodie to be able to show it to him.

Nick had a thought. Jodie had mentioned his mother's and his favorite places. He had not mentioned his dad going to any of these places with them. That spoke volumes. Nick knew better than to ask Jodie about his dad's favorite places which he figured were the saloons. Nick did not know Jodie's dad, but he disliked him. Nick was feeling a bit jealous, and he was still irritated about Jodie's remark to him a couple of months back: "You are nothing like my dad." Nick wished Jodie would think as highly of him as he thought of the scoundrel who had deserted him. Nick hoped the dad was gone for good.

They changed from their Sunday clothes to casual clothes and drove down to the beach in their rented buggy where they scoured the sand for hours searching for just the right shells. They were pleased with their individual finds and looked forward to displaying them. The hot sun rejuvenated them after such a depressing morning.

Tess sat on one of the boulders and put her face up to the sun and thought about the last time she had been on a California beach. She had been with Darcy and Connor in San Francisco. That seemed like a lifetime ago. A lifetime of heartache. A lifetime of longing for her little boy, whom she knew she would never see again. Life did not seem fair, she thought. But she realized that she had brought on most of the heartbreak herself. She should have listened to her mother who had only wanted the best for her.

Oh no, she suddenly thought to herself. *My mother! How am I going to tell her and Dad about Jeannie's death? I can't share such devastating news in a telegram. A telegram is too impersonal and inappropriate for announcing a daughter's death. No, I will have to write them a letter, something I have not done in a long time.* Tess sighed. She hadn't known how to explain her circumstances and so had put it off. Because she was too ashamed to tell her parents that she had a child born out of wedlock, she had not written to them since before Annabelle was born. Now she regretted the pain she must have put her family through and wished she would have done things differently.

While Tess was lost in her own thoughts, Jodie waded in the water, grabbing handfuls of water and splashing it everywhere but mainly on himself. Then he and Nick chased each other up and down the shore, tackling each other whenever they could. Nick was careful not to injure Jodie's arm where the cast had recently been removed.

"Too bad Cindy isn't with us," Jodie said as he threw himself down on the hot sand. "Cindy likes a good run."

"Yeah, yeah, maybe we can bring her next time," Nick said. He smiled to himself. He had purposely chased after Jodie knowing that a brisk run was a good stress reliever. The hot sun and the exercise might help Jodie sleep tonight. He and Nick were sharing a room, and Nick knew that Jodie hadn't slept much the night before with the upcoming funeral on his mind.

They were staying at the Horton House in New Town, San Diego's grand hotel. After they returned from the beach in the late afternoon, they had dinner in the dining room there and then retired to their rooms early. It had been a long day. After Jodie was asleep, Nick told Tess he was going out for a while to visit old friends. Did she mind?

"Of course not," she said. "I'll come sit in your room and watch Jodie sleep. I have a book to finish, so I won't be in a hurry for you to return. Take all the time you need."

So, Nick spent the evening with his friends whom he visited every time he came to town. They were old pals from his Grass Valley days and were the same men who had been keeping an eye out for Jodie's father.

"Sorry, Nick, nothing to report here," Ryan said. "We go to the old neighborhood every week or so and talk with the neighbors and the fellow who owns the corner store. They haven't seen him."

"I left my calling card with them all, so they could contact us if he showed up," Rob said. "Not a word. No one has seen nor heard from him since he left here over a year ago."

Dave spoke up. "Maybe something's happened to him. Maybe he actually is gone for good. I know you just went to his wife's funeral. Where does that leave the boy? He could be an orphan and not even know it."

"No, he has me. I promised his mother that I would take care of him, and I intend to do just that, but I still want to know where his dad is. I have no legal right to Jodie, and if his dad shows up, he could take him. Frankly, that would break my heart. I love the kid."

"Would Jodie want to go with his dad?" Rob asked.

"Probably. He adores his dad, as misguided as that is."

Nick would have been surprised to know he was wrong. Jodie had been relieved when his mother had asked Nick to take him, and he knew he wanted to stay with Nick forever. Jodie had been relieved because he had been living in a state of limbo for months, not knowing where he was going to end up or with whom. He had lost all trust in his dad, whom he now considered a liar and a cheat. If he never saw his dad again, that would be fine with him. His future was settled, and it was with Nick.

"Well, maybe we're looking at this all wrong," Rob said now. "If we find the dad, he'll take Jodie. So, let's quit looking for him."

Nick smiled ruefully. "Be careful what you ask for, huh?"

"Right. You take the boy and go back to Bodie. He's better off with you than with that rogue who deserted him."

"Yeah, I bet the scoundrel doesn't even know his wife is dead," Dave added.

Nick sat up straighter. "Okay, new plan— I'll take Jodie home, and you stop looking for his dad." The four men clinked glasses. The matter was settled.

* * * * * * * * * *

The next day, Nick drove Jodie and Tess in the buggy to Jodie's old neighborhood. Ian answered the door when Jodie knocked, and he joined Jodie outside.

"Oh no, not your mom." Ian was dismayed. "I loved your mom. She was always so nice to me." Ian didn't know what to do with his hands, and so he kept patting Jodie on the shoulder. Eleven-year- old boys did not hug each other, but Ian felt close to tears. "I knew your mom was sick, but I thought she would get better."

"Me too, "Jodie said.

One of the best times of my life was the day we caught the polliwogs with your mom down at the river. I'll always remember that day."

"Me too," Jodie said.

"When my dad would come home roaring drunk, I would run next door to your house, and your mom always took me in. Remember the time she hid me under her bed, so he couldn't find me and beat me?"

"I remember," Jodie said. "She always liked you too. Said we were two peas in a pod."

"She had lots of those funny sayings. She made me laugh sometimes." Ian sat down on the front step of his house. "Wow! And now she's gone! What are you going to do?"

"See that man and woman in the buggy over there?" Jodie pointed across the road.

"The lady is my aunt, and the man is my very good friend. I'm going back to Bodie and live with him."

The two young boys talked for a long time, promising to always stay in touch. They made plans to go away to college together and be roommates. The boys didn't realize that Ian was never going anywhere except to a menial job someday. His family, with their many children and deadbeat dad, had no money for education or anything else.

Jodie walked Ian across the road and introduced him to Tess and Nick, and then the boys said their goodbyes. Ian did reach out and hug Jodie then, and Jodie hugged him back. They had been best friends for a long time. Jodie knew he would return to San Diego sometimes to leave flowers on his mother's grave. If it were springtime, he would leave daffodils, his mother's favorite. He would look Ian up then.

"Ian, you are always invited to visit me in Bodie, of course. My friend, Mary Kay, owns a boarding house there. She would welcome you to stay with us."

Jodie looked across the street then at the yellow house that had been his home for most of his life. The yellow organdy curtains were no longer in the windows, and the house itself looked neglected and rundown. The grass needed cutting, and miscellaneous items lay in piles on the side of the house. He did see a dog's water bowl on the front porch, and this made him sad. New people had moved into his house; there would be no going back. There was nothing to go back to. His mother was dead.

CHAPTER 27

"Insufficient loyalty! What are you talking about?" Jodie asked. "I'm loyal."

"No, you aren't. Most times you side with Tess," Nick told him.

"I side with her because she's usually right, and you're not."

"You're just a sucker for a pretty girl, that's all." Nick laughed.

"Yes, she's certainly better looking than you. And I guess she's not bad for an older woman and an aunt."

"She's not that old, Jodie. She's twenty-five."

"Yeah, not as old as you, but she's a lot nicer than you."

"Yeah, yeah. You say that because I make you toe the line. I'm just keeping you out of trouble, my friend."

"Well, I do like her better than I thought I was going to," Jodie added. "I was scared of her at first."

"What are you talking about? Tess isn't scary."

"Well, you know! I thought she would be loud and vulgar because she's a prost. . . Whoops!"

"A what?" Nick looked at Jodie carefully.

"Never mind."

"What word were you going to say?" Nick insisted.

Jodie knew he had blundered and wished he had kept his mouth shut. "I don't want to tell you."

"Well, you started to tell me. What word, Jodie?"

"Prostitute," Jodie whispered.

"You know about prostitutes? How do you know?"

"My friends told me about them."

"So, all those times I sent you outside to play baseball, you and your so-called friends were talking dirty instead? What the hell!"

"They explained things to me because I didn't know anything."

"So, why do you think your Aunt Tess is a prostitute? Did they tell you that?"

"No, but they took me down to Bonanza Street, so we could look at the prostitutes, and I saw Tess there. Annabelle too. They didn't see us because we were hiding behind some old junk in the alley."

Nick sat down on the hotel bed. He rubbed his hand through his hair and looked at Jodie. "When was this?"

"Never mind, Nick. I don't want to talk about it."

"Not an option. Tell me when you saw them."

Jodie was scared now because Nick wasn't kidding around any longer. He wanted answers to his questions. "I saw them a couple of months ago."

"So, you have known that Tess was in town all this time. Why didn't you say anything to me?"

"Why didn't you say anything to me?" Jodie countered. "You must have known she and Annabelle were in Bodie. Why didn't you tell me?"

Now Nick found that the shoe was on the other foot; Jodie was questioning him. "She couldn't take you in, Jodie. Not down on Bonanza Street. That's no place for a child."

"Annabelle lives there. She's a child."

So, you saw them and then just went back to the Manor and didn't say anything?"

"I did say something. To Coosie."

Nick was flummoxed. This conversation had taken quite a turn. "Coosie knows you saw Tess in Bodie, and he didn't say anything to me?"

Jodie looked Nick in the eye. "I asked him not to tell you. You're always saying how important it is to keep your word. Coosie promised not to tell, and he kept his word. But he told me I had to tell you."

"But you didn't tell me. Were you ever going to?"

"I don't know. I don't think so. I like living with you and thought I would have to leave and go live with my aunt if you knew I knew. Prostitute or not."

Nick sat on the bed and stared at the palm fronds blowing in the wind outside the window. He had no idea what to say next. Jodie's logic was sound. He had obviously thought things through. But two months of lies! Nick was just as guilty of lying as Jodie because after all, he had lied first. But this was not the relationship he wanted to have with this boy. Before he could respond to Jodie, a knock came on the door. Tess stood there with picnic supplies. Nick didn't know who was more relieved at the interruption, he or Jodie.

* * * * * * * * * *

The view of San Diego Bay was as beautiful as Jodie had told them it would be. Nick and Jodie had joined Tess, and they had driven up to Point Loma in their rented buggy, each pretending there was nothing wrong between them. They avoided looking at each other and didn't have much to say. Tess sensed there was a problem but said nothing. She knew they would figure it out when they were ready.

Tess loved the quaint lighthouse. "It looks like a sentinel sitting up on the hill," she had exclaimed.

She told Nick and Jodie that it was built in the Cape Cod style of architecture. Jodie added that the roof was actually made out of tin but was red because it had been painted with red lead. Tess was surprised to see chickens and goats wandering around the grounds. Jodie told her that sometimes one could see pigs and horses too. No one seemed to be home at the lighthouse; the Keeper and his wife weren't needed until nightfall, and the quiet suggested they were gone for the day. Because school was in session, the children were also away. Nick, Tess, and Jodie had the place to themselves.

Tess had thought to bring a hotel blanket, and they spread it on the grass far from the lighthouse and pinned it down with the heavier picnic items. Even though it was September, the weather continued to be warm here, but San Diego was also visited by Santa Ana winds this time of year. A warm, gentle breeze blew steadily now.

While Nick and Jodie had argued in their hotel room, Tess had gone off in search of food for their outing. She had found a market and had purchased foods she knew both Nick and Jodie would enjoy. They both liked to eat, and both usually ate a lot. Today, neither seemed to be too hungry, however.

"Do you want an apple, Jodie?" she asked.

"No thanks, Tess. I'm not hungry."

"Is something the matter, Honey? Do you feel unwell?" She asked.

"No, I'm okay."

"I'll tell you what's the matter," Nick spoke up. "Jodie thinks you are a prostitute."

Jodie was horrified. He started to get to his feet, but Nick grabbed him and sat him back down. "You told her," Jodie sobbed, "You weren't supposed to tell her."

"I did tell her. I think it's time we stopped all the lies and told each other the truth. We all deserve to know the truth, don't you think?" Nick looked at Tess. "Are you up to the truth too?"

"I guess I am. I don't know what's going on between you two, but yes, let's talk it out."

"I'm sorry, Tess. I didn't want you to know. I wouldn't hurt your feelings for anything. Oh, please don't be angry with me," Jodie pleaded between sobs. He had just been reunited with this thoughtful, loving aunt; and now Nick had ruined everything. She would hate him now.

Nick looked at both Tess and Jodie. "We are going to have a family meeting, right here, right now. I've called the meeting, so I get to make the rules. The first rule is that no one is allowed to get up and leave." He looked pointedly at Jodie. "We all have to stay here, even if we don't like what we hear." Nick looked at them both now. "Okay?" he asked. They nodded.

"The second rule is that no one is allowed to interrupt when someone is speaking. Do not think about what you plan to say next, but instead, listen to the one who is speaking. Really listen. We will each get a turn to talk. Any questions?" Tess and Jodie both shook their heads. "No? Okay, I'll go first," Nick said.

"This is a mess, and I take full responsibility. It's my fault because I told the first lie. When I met you on the stage, Jodie, I realized you were Tess's nephew. Yes, I knew Tess and knew she lived on Bonanza Street. Because she lived in a brothel, I realized you couldn't live there with her, so I took you in. I should not have told you she was out of town. That was a lie. But to explain myself, I thought you were too young to know the truth— about prostitutes and such. In my own way, I was trying to protect you from harsh realities you were too young for. Do you understand?"

Jodie nodded.

"Okay, who wants to go next?" Nick asked.

"I do," Tess said. "I have to think I also lied to you, Jodie, because Nick told me you were in town looking for me. I allowed you to think I was gone all these many months. I do live in a brothel and did not want you to know me as your promiscuous aunt. I was embarrassed. Humiliated, actually! In my own defense, I have been trying to pay off my debt, so I could move out of there and away from Bonanza Street. Then, you could live with me. I was hoping that you, Annabelle, and I would come here to San Diego together. I thought your mother would get better, and we would come then. I am sorry, Honey. I was embarrassed by my circumstances and did not know what to do. Please forgive me." Tess looked down at her lap.

"May I speak?" Jodie asked.

Nick nodded.

"Tess, did you know I was with Nick at the Manor?"

"Yes, I knew from the first day, and that's why I didn't worry about you. I knew you were in good hands with Nick. He reported to me regularly about you."

"Thanks. Now it's my turn to tell you about my lie. Tess, I did know you were in town because I spied on you one day. We fellows were messing around, and we hid behind some furniture in the alley. We saw two little girls sit on the back steps, and then you came out and called them in for dinner. You called one of them 'Annabelle.' I knew right then that it had to be you. But I didn't tell Nick. I was too upset – discovering you were one of those ladies and all." Jodie looked embarrassed.

"Tell Tess who it was that you did tell," Nick directed.

"I told Coosie. He's one of our boarders. He talked me through it, and then I felt better."

"I know Coosie," Tess said.

"You do? Really? OH! I never thought about Coosie going to Bonanza Street." Jodie was embarrassed again.

"No, Sweetheart, I don't know Coosie like that. Coosie and I are friends, that's all. He's teaching Annabelle how to ride his horse."

Jodie looked at her. There were so many things he did not know.

"Nick, I think it's time I told Jodie my story. If we are going to have a relationship, I think he should know how I ended up where I did."

So, Jodie listened, and Tess told him about growing up in Butte, Montana with his mother. She told him about leaving her parents to go see the world. It wasn't the world she found but false friends who told her lies and led her on. Tess did not try to make herself look better in Jodie's eyes but told him the truth about how gullible she had been. She told him she had been selfish and thoughtless in leaving her parents who were still grieving for him and his mother. When she got to the part about her babies, she began to cry. Jodie scooted over and sat next to her while he listened to her describe the worst day of her life, the day Aidan was taken from her.

When she finished speaking, Jodie sat still. He had never heard anything so horrible, and he couldn't talk or offer her words of encouragement because he was too stunned. Having a baby stolen from you! He couldn't even imagine and was profoundly sad.

Nick got up and pulled Tess to her feet. "Let's take a break. I know how hard this is for you." He wrapped his arms around her as if protecting her from the cold. Jodie got up and stood close to them because he too needed a safety net. Nick reached behind him and folded Jodie into the embrace. Jodie was shaken. Grown-up matters were too much sometimes. Scary even. Nick was right about him being too young to know everything.

"I need to finish," Tess said, breaking away from Nick. She did not sit down again but told the rest of her story standing, looking at the lighthouse framed against the blue skies of San Diego. When she got to the part about recuperating at Sophie's, she said,

"I'm sorry that you had to learn about prostitution so early, Jodie. And I am sorry you learned about me in such a disagreeable way. I can see why you were distressed." Tess turned then and looked straight at Jodie. "But you have to know that I am not a prostitute. I have never slept with a man for money."

Jodie gazed at her. He wanted to believe her, but the facts did not add up. "But you live in that house on Bonanza Street. Don't prostitutes live there?"

"Yes, Jodie. You're right. Prostitutes do live there. And in the beginning, that was what was planned for me. Sophie expected me to work for her as soon as I recovered from childbirth, but I didn't know that and thought she had taken me in as a favor to Prue. I had been there several weeks when Sophie told me I owed her money for room and board. I had no money, of course. So, that's when she told me I could work for her as one of her 'upstairs girls,' to pay off my debt. She acted like she was doing me a favor. I was absolutely appalled. It was one of the low points of my life."

"What did you do?" Jodie whispered.

"For the first time in my life, I stood up for myself. I told her, 'No.' I simply looked her in the eye and said, 'No.' I told her I was a good Catholic girl who had temporarily lost my way. But no more! I had been used and misused, and I would never put myself in that position again. I told her I would not be one of her 'upstairs girls.' I told her I could be of help to her, however. You see, I had lived in that house long enough to realize that it was all about the money. Sophie was a smart businesswoman who just wanted to make money. She could have made a fortune from me if I had been willing to go upstairs and be one of her 'girls,' but I refused."

Tess stopped long enough to catch her breath, and then she continued. "I explained to Sophie just how I could be of value to her. I sat her down in the front parlor and told her I had observed her business for the last few weeks, and what she needed was a vivacious, gracious hostess. I have good people skills, and so I told her I could chat with her customers while they waited to go upstairs. I could charm them into buying me drinks and make sure they bought drinks for the other girls. The bar itself could be a lucrative operation. Sophie had a fancy piano that collected dust in the corner, unused. I sat down at it then and pounded out loud, lively tunes that would attract customers. Sophie liked that.

"I told her I would expect her to give me a clothing allowance, but I would be the one choosing what I wore— nothing skimpy, risqué, or gawdy. I told her I would help her anyway I could and that I could even do her bookkeeping for her, but under no circumstances would I ever go upstairs. If she did not agree to my offer, I would leave, and she wouldn't be able to stop me because she couldn't keep tabs on me all the time.

"If she consented to my offer, I would be available to her in the evenings after Annabelle fell asleep and not before. If Annabelle were ill or needed me, I wouldn't be in to work at all. I spoke with confidence, and Sophie agreed to all my terms. I have made a great deal of money for her, but I have never been upstairs. I have kept my virtue and my dignity."

"Good job, Tess." Jodie smiled at her. He loved this new aunt of his. Then he looked at Nick.

"Did you know that Tess wasn't a prostitute, Nick?"

"Yes, I knew. But she still wasn't in any position to take you home with her. You couldn't live in a bordello."

"Why are you still in debt, Tess?" Jodie asked.

"Excellent question, Jodie. I paid off my debt to Sophie, but then Annabelle got sick. She's healthy now, but I had many doctor bills to pay. Sophie lent me the money. You will find this hard to believe, but Sophie has been very good to me. She loves Annabelle like a grandmother would. Over the years, Sophie and I have become good friends. She may run a brothel, but she's a good person."

Jodie knew there was a lesson here, and usually Nick would be the first to point it out, but for some reason, Nick wasn't talking just then.

When he did finally speak, he gruffly said, "Meeting is adjourned."

CHAPTER 28

Neither Tess nor Jodie was surprised when Nick excused himself, said he needed to take a walk, and loped off down the road. They both knew he walked when he needed to think. Tess and Jodie cleaned up the picnic supplies and chatted about inconsequential things. Jodie again turned down the offer of an apple. Trying to lighten the mood, Tess said,

"I think we should both mind our P's and Q's, so Nick won't call any more family meetings. What do you think?"

"It was pretty dreadful."

"Agreed. But necessary, don't you think?"

"Yes. Nick is always right about everything." Jodie sighed. "I hurt his feeling bad, I think. I shouldn't have lied to him."

"You can fix it, you know," Tess suggested.

"How?"

"Just talk to him, Jodie." Tess pulled him toward her. "That's the best thing."

"He won't listen."

"Oh yes, Sweetheart. He'll always listen to you."

"I don't think I'll ever feel the same about this place because this is where Nick got mad at me." Jodie sighed again.

"Technically, Nick got mad at you hours ago back at the hotel. This is where we talked it out. So, this is still a good place."

Jodie looked at her. "Thanks Tess. That makes me feel better because I've always loved this place with my mom. Now, I'll also love it because I was here with you and Nick."

"Family Meeting included?" Tess smiled.

"Family meeting included," Jodie said and smiled back at her. Then he grew serious again and said, "Thank you for telling me about your life, Tess. I'm glad you are my aunt, but just so you know, I would have loved you even if you had been a prostitute."

"Good to know." Tess hugged him again. "I see Nick standing over there near the lighthouse. Now is as good a time as any to go talk with him."

When Jodie reached Nick's side, Nick did not acknowledge his presence. Instead, he continued to stand with his hands in his pockets, looking out over the bay.

"Are you okay?" Jodie asked him.

"Yes."

Jodie looked up at Nick. "Are we okay?"

Nick still did not look at Jodie. "I don't know, Jodie. Are we okay? You tell me."

Jodie remained quiet for a minute before saying, "No. I know we're not. But I don't know how to fix it."

Nick finally turned and looked at him. "Don't you really?"

Jodie shook his head. "No, I'm confused. I want to be loyal to you, but you tell me to be a man of my word and not break confidences. I don't know how to do both."

"I just don't want any more secrets and lies between us. I know there are things you still aren't telling me."

"Like what?"

"Like who beat you up and left you for dead."

"Okay."

"Okay? Why would you keep your assailant's name a secret from me?"

"I can't tell you." Jodie was on the verge of tears again. "You want me to tell you things I can't tell you. I'm afraid you're going to send me away, but I just can't tell you."

"Damn it, Jodie. Damn it all to hell!" Nick was more than frustrated. "Why won't you listen to me? I'm not going to send you away. I don't know how to make you believe me."

Jodie was crying in earnest now. Nick took him by the hand and walked him over to where Tess stood by the picnic basket. "Let's go. I think we're all tired. Let's get back to the hotel and rest a bit."

As they walked back to the buggy, Jodie turned around for one last look at his beloved lighthouse. No matter what Tess said, Jodie knew he was never going to feel the same about this place.

* * * * * * * * * *

Jodie slept all the way back to town, his head on Tess's shoulder. Tess took Jodie up to his room and left him on his bed to rest while Nick walked to the stagecoach office to purchase tickets for the next day's trip back to Bodie. It was time to get home, Nick reasoned. He had work responsibilities. School had started, and Jodie needed to get back to his lessons.

And then there was Tess! Nick had made a decision. He was going to persuade her not to return to Sophie's when they arrived back in Bodie. Annabelle was already at the Manor, so Tess would not have to go back to the bordello to retrieve her. Tess needed a clean break, and Nick intended to pay off her debt in order to make that happen. He had offered to give her the money twice before, but she had been too proud to accept his offer. This time, he would reason with her and insist. If Tess agreed with his plan not to return to Bonanza Street, she would need lodging for one night. Then he would find more permanent accommodations for her and Annabelle elsewhere. He considered putting her up in a hotel for the one night, but then he changed his mind. He would take her home. Mary Kay had one unoccupied guest room, and he would take her there. He was playing with fire; he knew. He had already brought home a young boy and a young girl. Now, he would be asking Mary Kay to accept a full-grown adult. She would surely kill him! One more thing to worry about.

Nick had made another decision, as well. Although he wasn't a gambler, he had decided to risk his all and ask Tess to marry him. He had loved her since the first day he met her. They were good friends, and he did not want to chance ruining that friendship by proposing to her; but his instincts told him she would be receptive to his offer. She had never indicated that she wanted anything other than friendship from him until this trip. Even now, she hadn't said anything nor led him on in any way, but Nick sensed that things were different between them now. This trip had thrown them together in a whole new way. Tough decisions had had to be made, and they were like-minded in making them. They definitely shared the same philosophy on most matters. He loved her and wanted to spend the rest of his life with her. He was twenty-seven years old, and she was the only woman he had ever loved.

Yes, he had proposed to Susanne, and he now knew he would have destroyed that friendship had they married. She had been wise to turn him down and encourage him to find his real love. He hadn't had to search— he had always known it was Tess. So, he was going to gamble and propose to her. She could reject him with a firm, "No." But what if she said, "Yes"? Could she possibly say, "Yes"?

He would find out. He wasn't sure when he would ask her, or what words he would use. He wasn't a ladies' man and did not feel confident in matters of the heart. He did know that somethings in life were worth the risk though. If Tess accepted his proposal, he would give her his grandmothers' ring, the one Susanne had declined. His grandmother would have loved Tess, and Nick was sorry she wouldn't ever get to meet her. Gran had died four years ago, soon after giving him the ring.

* * * * * * * * * *

It was after they had rested, after they had eaten a quiet dinner at a nearby restaurant, and after they had returned to the hotel that Jodie asked Nick and Tess if they would come up with him to the room he and Nick shared. Nick and Tess had no idea what Jodie had in mind, but they went with him. After they were seated in the comfortable, upholstered chairs on either side of the table, Jodie sat down on the bed Indian style with his legs crossed in front of him.

"I am calling a family meeting," he said. Nick groaned, but Jodie continued, "and because I called the meeting, I get to make the rules."

"And what rules would those be?" Tess asked.

"Same rules that Nick made."

Both Nick and Tess smiled. Jodie continued, "I have been thinking about what you said up at the lighthouse, Nick. I want to tell you about the day I got beat up. I didn't tell you before because I knew you would go after the guys who did it, and I couldn't let that happen. Will you promise not to go after them?"

"No, no promises. But let's hear what you have to say," Nick said.

Jodie sighed but plunged into the story of his friends hurting the dog and how they had turned on him when he had tried to stop them.

"I don't understand," Nick told him. "Why couldn't you tell me that?"

Jodie looked shaken, but he continued. "Walter said that if you came after them, they would find you when you weren't expecting them, and they would throw acid in your eyes. They laughed about you being a blind carpenter, but I know they meant it. Don't you see, Nick? I couldn't tell you, or they would have hurt you."

"I see," Nick said quietly.

"So, please, I'm asking you. Don't do anything. Stay away from them. Please!"

"Okay, Jodie, if that's what you want. I don't want you to spend your time worrying about me." Nick could sit no longer. He got up and began to pace around the room. He stopped in front of Jodie and said, "Sometimes we do the wrong thing for the right reason, like when I told you the lie about Tess being gone. It was wrong to tell you, but I did it for the right reason. Can you understand that?"

Jodie nodded.

Nick continued, "When you didn't tell me who hurt you, you also did the wrong thing for the right reason. You were trying to protect me."

Jodie nodded again. "Can you ever do the right thing for the wrong reason?" Jodie asked.

"Sure, of course. But let's not get into that right now," Nick said.

Jodie sighed. He had stalled long enough. "Okay, I guess we need to talk about me being disloyal to you. Not like this morning when we were just kidding around. You feel that I was disloyal to you when I didn't tell you I saw Tess and Annabelle."

"Yes, but it goes deeper than that. I wonder why you trusted Coosie with your story, and yet you couldn't trust me. There, I've used the word: trust. I don't feel that you trust me."

"No, Nick. It wasn't like that. I was upset and crying and ran into Coosie on my way home. Literally ran into him. I was really mad at you because I knew you had lied to me all along. Coosie talked me down. I don't think that I would have told him if he hadn't been there. I trust you."

"No, Jodie, you don't. You told me again this afternoon that you thought I would send you away. It's like you wait for me to say, 'Enough, Jodie! You've finally done it this time, Jodie. This is what it has taken to drive me away. I'm sending you away now.'" Nick continued to stand in front of Jodie. "I don't know what to say to you, so you will trust that I won't send you away. Why can't you believe that I want you in my life?"

Jodie was trying his best not to cry. He wanted to tell Nick everything but wasn't sure how to do it. Finally, he said, "It's because my dad doesn't want me. If my own dad doesn't want me, how could anyone else want me? Especially you, Nick."

"I don't know about the 'Especially you, Nick' part, but I think it took a lot of courage for you to say that about your dad just now. Do you really believe your dad doesn't want you?"

"Yes," Jodie whispered. Nick went over and sat next to him on the bed and put his arm around him. He took Jodie's chin in his other hand and tilted his head up, so he was looking at Nick.

"I want you. I will always want you. I will never throw you away. There is nothing you can do to drive me away. You have a family now with Tess and me. Isn't that right, Tess?"

"Yes," Tess said.

But now Nick was not quite so sure of himself. He knew he had to tell Jodie the truth. "Jodie, there is one thing that could ruin all this. I might as well tell you what I'm thinking, so here goes. We don't know where your dad is, but if he should show up and want you, you would have to go with him."

"But Mom said I was to go with you."

"Yes. You're right. That's what she wanted for you, but I have no legal claim on you. If your dad came for you, I couldn't stop him."

"But the judge would let me go with you."

"No, we would lose in court because your dad has the law on his side. But we'll be fine as long as your dad doesn't show up. He doesn't know where you are, so we're probably safe."

Jodie trembled. He had to tell Nick. He thought he would vomit; he was so scared. But hadn't Nick just told him to trust him?

"My dad knows where I am," he whispered.

"Your dad knows you live in Bodie?"

"Yes." Jodie started to tremble more.

Nick tightened his arm around the boy. "I won't be mad. I promise. Just tell me."

"One day last June, right after school got out, I saw him ride into town on his horse. I was having lunch with Susanne, but I ran out and talked to him. He said he was just there for the day on business, and then he was leaving again. He was surprised to see me."

"I bet."

"I told him I was staying with friends at a boarding house but would go with him instead."

Jodie did not see Nick frown, and he continued, "But Dad said I couldn't go. He said he would come back for me when he finished his business, and then we would go home to San Diego together. He told me to stay with you until he returned. He didn't know Mom was sick or that Tess was supposed to be in Bodie but had left."

"Did your dad act like he knew me? You said he told you to stay with me."

"No, he just said to stay at the boarding house with you. He didn't act like he liked Tess much though."

"No, he wouldn't," Tess said. "The last time I saw him was the day he took you and your mom away. No one liked him very much that day."

"Are you angry?" Jodie looked at Nick.

"No, Jodie, I'm not angry, but I am wondering why you wouldn't tell me. Finding your dad was a big deal for you, so I know you must have been happy. Why wouldn't you tell me about it?"

"I wanted to tell you, more than anything, but Dad told me I couldn't tell anyone he was there. That if you knew, you wouldn't let me stay with you anymore. You would expect him to take me, but he couldn't. He had business."

"What kind of business?"

"He didn't say."

"So, you saw him in June. Did you ever see him again?" Nick asked.

Jodie looked uncomfortable and did not say anything but sat looking down at the floor. Nick picked his chin up and made him look at him again. "You can trust me, Jodie. Just tell me."

Jodie couldn't help himself, and he began to cry. Nick was going to be so mad at him. Nick held him for a few minutes and then told him to buck up and tell them the rest.

"I saw him on the Fourth of July. He was going into the dance at the Miner's Union Hall. He didn't see me, and I was surprised to see him, surprised that he was back in town."

"Any other times?"

"Just once more. The morning after the dance, I got up early and went and stood outside the hotel and waited to see if he would come out. He was pretty mad when he saw me and yelled at me. He told me he was in town only because he had taken the wife of a friend to the dance as a favor, and he was leaving again immediately. Told me to stay put until he came back for me. He said he would whip me bad if I told anyone he was in town. I know he would have too. I was afraid of him that day."

"Had he been in contact with your mother?" Nick asked.

"No, and I was disappointed in him because I had told him in June that she was sick. He didn't even write to her."

"I imagine that made you sad."

"Yes, very sad. There is one other thing I should tell you. When he talked about the boarding house, he called it the Manor. I wondered how he knew to call it that."

"That is odd. Anything else you want to tell Tess and me?" Nick asked.

Jodie shook his head. "No, that's all. I think I've told you everything."

"No more secrets, okay?" Nick asked.

"Okay."

"And no more lies."

"I promise." Jodie looked up at Nick. "Are we okay?"

"We are okay, Buddy. Better than okay. Tess and I are proud of you, aren't we Tess?"

"Absolutely! Very proud. You showed a lot of courage in talking with us tonight."

"Thank you. I trust you, Nick. Always, from now on."

"Bedtime?" Tess suggested.

"Yes," Jodie said.

"No," Nick said.

They both looked at him. Nick looked at Jodie. "Aren't you forgetting something?"

"What?"

"Come closer, and I'll remind you." Nick leaned in and whispered in Jodie's ear.

Jodie sat up straighter on the bed and announced, "Meeting is adjourned."

"Thank God! "Tess said, and they all laughed.

What a long day it had been, but everything had turned out well. One question had been answered for Nick. Now he knew why Jodie had stopped talking of going home to San Diego to find his dad. Jodie had known where he was all along. Nick would not remind Jodie that he could be in danger of his dad taking him away because he didn't want Jodie to worry about it. Frankly, it didn't sound like the dad wanted to be burdened with the young boy, so perhaps he would never come for him. They would just hope for the best.

But in the meantime, and without saying anything to the others, Nick decided to see what he could find out about the dad. He would start in Bodie with the hotel register of July Fourth. Billy Burke's name must be written there. Nick should have thought to ask Jodie if Susanne had seen his dad that day at lunch. Had Nick talked with Susanne, she might have told him the truth about Liam's real identity. That would have changed everything.

CHAPTER 29

Had Nick asked the right questions, he would have discovered that Jodie's dad was not only a deserter, but also a liar, a fraud, and a manipulator. Most people are not born liars. Most people tell the truth when it matters and do their best to live every day without inflicting pain on others. But not everyone, and certainly not Billy Burke. Billy was undeniably a narcissist. Psychiatrists could argue over whether he was a psychopath or a sociopath, but either way, he suffered from a personality disorder. He was born with it, and he used his manipulative skills daily to his advantage.

Billy had learned to lie when he was just three years old. He accidentally told a mistruth to his mother and was surprised when she did not question him. He tried it again, and again he was not found out. He tried it on other family members with the same result. He was so successful that he became almost proficient by the age of five. No one considered that this sweet child could have an evil thought in his head. Billy was too young to recognize evil but found lying a fascinating game. He lied when he could easily have told the truth. Mostly, he made up stories about people who shopped in his father's store. One time he told his dad that Mrs. Wright had put a packet of buttons in her skirt pocket and had walked out with them. Dad kept a watchful eye on her after that. Billy would tell his dad tidbits of gossip he heard as farmers' wives shopped, all of it fabricated. He talked about old Mrs. Blake whose son mistreated her. He told the secret of a respected church elder who drank too much and battered his wife. Billy's dad, a Christian man, felt saddened by these revelations.

Billy, a beautiful child with black curly hair, green eyes, and rosy cheeks, had a winsome smile. He smiled as often as possible because he learned early on that adults prefer pleasant, happy children. He purposely charmed everyone he met. No one suspected that beneath this sunny exterior beat the heart of a young degenerate.

Billy did not care about other children his age. The only boy he had prized was his childhood friend, Drue Bailey, and look how that had turned out! No, Billy preferred adults who could give him things or provide opportunities for him. But again, he figured out that in order to make it in this world, he needed the help of others— no matter their age or station in life. So, he cultivated the friendship of classmates he considered tedious because someday he might need their help, their money, or their vote.

Billy looked upon women with contempt. The females he knew, including his own mother, acted subserviently toward the men around them. In his mind, men were in charge; they chaired the meetings and made the decisions. Their women were the stewards of their homes, the mothers of their children, the caregivers of their elderly. It was the woman's job to run a man's household and to have a hot meal on the table when he returned home. She was to keep his social calendar in the morning and be available to him for romance at night, when he desired her. A woman's lot was to be of assistance to men, so men could be about the business of running the world. The women in Billy's life would have been surprised to know the distain he felt for them. He never let on.

Several local girls in their teens had marriage on their minds, and each hoped Billy would cast his eye on her. He flirted and danced with many of them and took more than a couple up into the barn loft. Both of his parents would have been horrified to know he was having sexual relations outside of marriage. "Holy Mother of God! What are you thinking?" they would have cried as they reached for their Bibles. Billy would have dismissed their distress with the old joke: "It isn't premarital sex if you don't intend to get married." He had no plans to get married. Eventually, he left to fight in the war and did not return home afterward. He left behind several shattered dreams.

Billy's Irish family was deeply religious. As tired as they were after a long day's work, father and mother always knelt in prayer with their children after the evening meal. They recited the rosary, and each child learned to lead in saying the prayers. Billy and his siblings knew how to say "The Lord's Prayer" before they were out of diapers. Billy noted his parents' devotion and as a young boy tried to share their enthusiasm for the Good Lord. He wanted to feel toward God as his parents did, but he felt nothing. He knelt in prayer with his family and went through the motions, but it was a sham. It was what his dad expected. His mother would have been sickened to know that a child of hers did not love God and loathed attending the many religious services. Mass filled their Sunday mornings. They worshipped at St. Bruno's Church, two blocks from their home. His mother walked to church early on Sunday mornings to take the altar linens that she had washed and pressed the day before. Anything for Father Daly!

Billy's mother, Bridget, was a practical woman who brooked no nonsense from her children. Life was too busy and difficult; she had no time for waste or silliness. Her one shortcoming, as far as Billy could see, was her stubborn adherence to the local priest. Father Daly had been pastor of St. Bruno's for many years. Bridget and several other devout Catholic women tended to him. If he even hinted that he needed something, these women took care of it. Sometimes, there was a bit of good-natured competition for the priest's attention, but overall, these reverent women worked together to help him and their parish.

The annual bazaar on the church grounds kept them busy. Planning meetings began almost immediately after the last raffle prize was won. Who was going to run the cakewalk? Who was going to chair the apron booth? All of this was unnecessary, of course. Edith Drury always ran the cakewalk, and Kiera McKay would never allow anyone but herself to take charge of the aprons. So, meetings were scheduled, events were planned, and everyone stepped up to do her part.

Every Thursday, Father Daly came to the Burke home, for that was the night when Billy's dad, Sean, hosted the weekly poker game. Six men played cards: the priest, Sean, and four other parishioners. The game was always in Sean's kitchen. Liquor flowed, problems were discussed, and deals were made. The men raged about politics and often cussed out the imbeciles who ran the government. The running of St. Bruno's was of prime importance. Father Daly was certainly in charge, no doubt about that, but he was wise enough to listen to his parishioners. They often heard rumors or knew of problems within the community that could have caused unrest. This crusty, old pastor could not allow unrest. His parish was a well-oiled machine, and he needed to keep it that way.

Billy was just a lad when he spied on this poker group. Sitting on the back steps, he listened attentively to the men's conversation and occasional bragging. He learned the ways of men and of life and how best to maneuver through them. He learned about people and how to outwit them. Billy realized that he needed to listen to people, both to what they said and did not say. One learned much by listening. Instinctively, he studied body language too and learned that a person with crossed arms gave off negative vibes and would be resistant to whatever you were suggesting. He learned to read men, and then he used all he learned to his advantage. Always careful when he spoke, no one ever knew what he was thinking.

For a brief time, Billy considered the priesthood for himself— not for the spirituality nor because it would bring joy to his mother but because he could see the power that a priest held. Billy coveted power and the prestige that accompanied it. Father Daly had both. Billy came to his senses soon enough and realized he did not want a hierarchal system giving him orders. These men of the cloth could be both inflexible and downright authoritative. No one was going to tell Billy Burke what to do.

No one had ever told him, "No," until he ran across Mike Julian. Mike's rejection of him, and thus Drue's rejection, still festered. Someday, he would get even with Julian. But not yet. Now, he had bigger fish to fry.

Billy had changed his name to Liam when he moved to Bodie. But neither in Butte nor in Bodie had he ever wanted to get married. Lust had driven him to it the first time. Money drove him to it now. He was determined to get Susanne to marry him as soon as possible because his plans had changed, and he needed her financial assets and connections. A buddy of his, a gambler from New Orleans, had given him the inside scoop on a South American oil company that had offices in New York. Those who invested in it now, on the ground level, could expect immediate wealth. Liam had decided to give up the gambling circuit in order to see this investment through. However, he would have to move to New York in order to accomplish it.

It was time for a change. Living out of a suitcase in a hotel room had lost its luster, and gambling had lost its shine. Loose women had lost their charm. Unknown to Susanne, Liam had been living with a buxom little gal with a lusty laugh whenever he was in Reno. Although she had fulfilled all his sexual needs, he was bored with her and needed a change. He had given this a lot of thought and was ready to settle down with one woman. Liam wasn't so naïve as to think that Susanne would go along with all he suggested, but once she married him, she would answer to him. He would control her money, and that, if nothing else, would keep her in line. One of the things he liked least about her was her strong sense of independence. She was too damned self-reliant for his taste. But he knew he could charm her and eventually convince her to do things his way. He had seduced her to his bed, hadn't he?

He had been patient and had even encouraged her to work on that silly photography project she was enthused about because it had occupied her time while he was away. Now, he would urge her to either complete it or discard it because time was of the essence. He feared that she would resist and tell him she needed more time. But they had no time to waste. He needed her to understand the urgency of getting to New York. He would invest her money and watch it grow, and he and his new bride would be wealthy beyond all expectations. He was ready for riches. He had had enough of these small-time cities and small- time yokels. Even Denver seemed pedestrian to him now.

Liam craved life in a cultured city, and he eagerly looked forward to moving to New York with its art museums, numerous theaters, and fine restaurants. He wanted to meet sophisticated people with whom he could share a bottle of merlot and stimulating conversation. He was certain that Susanne would enjoy this too. She was, after all, a big-city girl from St. Louis. Certainly, she would like a more civilized lifestyle! However, first he had to marry her. Only then could he get her out of Bodie.

Once in a while, he gave Jodie a brief thought. He hadn't wanted children, and having such a weak son was a great disappointment. Jodie was always sniveling about something. Even back in San Diego, Jodie had been a pain in his side, always wanting him to play with him or wanting to go places with him. Christ Almighty! Liam had felt smothered.

Jeannie hadn't been any better, always wanting him to come home for dinner. He was a busy man; he didn't have time for nightly dinners. But she couldn't understand that. No wonder he had left her! But by God, he hoped she recovered and got out of that hospital soon! She had responsibilities. The sooner she recuperated, the sooner he could send Jodie home to her. He would put Jodie on the fastest stage out of town. Those snooty folks at the Manor wouldn't even know the boy was gone – until he was. Now, Liam chuckled as he realized he didn't need to stick around until Jodie left. He was certain Nick Pratt would put Jodie on a stage bound for San Diego whenever Jeannie sent for him. Nick would most likely be as relieved to be rid of the boy as he was. He and Susanne could leave any time.

But then everything changed! Liam was in Sacramento when he received a telegram from his old pal Del. He and Del had been on the circuit together until Del banged up his leg while drunk one night in Bodie. He was still there recovering. Liam always looked him up when he came to town. They would sit and drink all afternoon while Susanne worked. Del kept Liam apprised of Bodie's goings on. The telegram from Del was concise. "Your girlfriend is pregnant."

"Christ Almighty," Liam had roared after reading the message. "Damn it, go to Hell!" What was she thinking? Liam had no doubt that the baby was his, but he did not want a damned baby. If he wanted a child, he would go home with Jodie. Didn't Susanne know better than to get herself pregnant? Liam had rarely been this angry. He stuffed the telegram into his pocket and stomped away from the telegram office. "Damn it," he kept muttering. This would change all his plans. What would New York be with a small child in tow? It would be hell, that's what! It was inconceivable to even consider taking a baby. He headed for Murphy's Pub to think things through.

The next morning, Liam shopped at an exclusive jewelry store in downtown Sacramento and then left for Bodie. He wanted to find out all he could from Del before he saw Susanne. When he arrived, he went straight to Del's house and demanded answers.

"Got it straight from Doc himself," Del told him. "Doc said he examined Susanne in his office and that she is definitely in the family way. Baby's due in February. Is it yours?"

"Hell yes, it's mine! How could she do this to me? The last thing I need is a baby. I have big plans, and they do not include a baby."

"Well, Doc said to tell you, said you would want to know. Said we men have to stick together. Can't let any conniving broads play hell with our lives." Del shook his head in disgust before he continued, "But when you see your little lady, don't let on that you heard it from Doc. Medical ethics and all!"

"Sure, sure," Liam had responded, lost in thought. He still needed Susanne, baby or no baby. Because he needed her money, he would revise his plans. He couldn't wait until after the baby's birth to move to New York. He would have to get Susanne to go now while she could still travel. Maybe Susanne would have a miscarriage enroute; journeys by train were quite strenuous. He could hope for that. Perhaps the baby could have an unfortunate accident after he was born. Liam smiled at the thought— an easy solution to his problem.

He needed to marry Susanne quickly. He would propose to her, get down on one knee and tell her he loved her; women always wanted to hear those words. He would give her the expensive ring he had just purchased. He would not mention her pregnancy but would act surprised and pleased when she told him. She would certainly jump at the chance to get married, now that a baby was involved. Perhaps, with the prospect of a new baby, and with a sparkly diamond engagement ring on her finger, Susanne would give up her project, marry him, and go with him immediately. He hoped so. He did love her.

"Luck be with me," he murmured.

No, Nick Pratt had not asked the right questions, or he could have prevented Liam's proposal and the hurt and heartache that followed it.

CHAPTER 30

Nick and Tess talked amiably as their stagecoach neared Bodie. It was late in the evening, and they were eager to get home. It had been a long trip. Jodie slept on the bench seat next to Tess. Curled into the fetal position, he looked young and vulnerable.

Nick smiled at Tess. He had smiled all evening. "I've decided to call you my 'Downstairs Girl,'" he told her now.

"Are you making fun of me?"

"Not at all. Someday I will call you my 'Upstairs Girl.'"

"Oh, and when will that be?"

"When I call you my wife. Only then will I take you upstairs."

"I like 'Wife,'" Tess said.

But Nick wasn't finished. "I think I'll shorten it from 'Downstairs Girl' to 'D.G,'" Nick continued, "and I'll shorten that to 'Deeg.' It will be a term of endearment known only to us, and every time you hear it, you will know I love you."

Tess smiled at him. "'Deeg' it is! I love you too."

Nick had more to say, "And when I am old and incontinent, and I'm gasping for breath, I'll still utter, 'Deeg, Deeg;' and you will know I love you still, even in my advanced age and infirmity."

Tess laughed. "Fancy words, Mister. You certainly know how to win a girl over."

It was dark in the coach, but Nick could see her face, and he told her, "You roll your eyes almost as well as Jodie does. It must be a family trait."

"Old family trait," she murmured as he reached for her. They were quiet for a few minutes.

Nick stroked her cheek. He was glad Jodie slept soundly, and they had this time to themselves. They had much to talk about and had spoken openly and candidly about this new life they would share. They wanted no secrets or lies between them. There had also been a bit of kissing— now that Jodie was asleep.

Again, and again, Nick expressed his love for her. Tess had never felt such exhilaration. She thought to herself how much she had changed. Earlier in the evening, she had spontaneously asked Nick if he were giving her a ring, thereby making an honest woman of her. She had never had the courage to ask Connor that question. When he had not committed, a strong woman would have spoken up, demanding to know his intentions. Would there be a marriage to go along with the baby he was giving her? But Tess had not considered it her place to question him. She had been brought up to always be the proper lady. Proper ladies did not initiate conversations about marriage. That was a man's prerogative. It was the same as at a school dance: girls had to wait for the boys to ask them to dance. In the meantime, the girls were expected to sit along the wall and pretend to be cheerful and carefree. Wallflowers indeed! It truly was a man's world. Today she would have asked Connor his intentions and forced an answer. Then she could have made her own plans. After all she had been through, Tess was a different woman now— stronger and more self-confident. She would never let a man push her around again.

Had Tess known that Connor had no intention of marrying her, she would most likely be in Montana now, mothering twin children. She might be married to a miner or a barkeep, and she might even be content. Providence, however, had not led her back to Butte, and for a long time she had been depressed and unaccepting of God's plan for her. She had been abandoned and had felt totally alone. Only Annabelle's dependence on her had kept her going when she wanted to give up. Only when she had stopped trying to orchestrate her life and had allowed God back in, had she found the inner peace for which she had been searching. And then she had found two good friends: a miner and a carpenter. It was the carpenter who had declared his love for her, and she knew she wanted to be nowhere else but with him. God had placed her right where He intended her to be.

Tess would enjoy being married to Nick. What happiness it would bring her to be married to her best friend. Life would certainly not be boring with Nick who was slightly crazy but also the most caring man she had ever met. She would never try to change him. She understood him and his need for sociability. Because he enjoyed people so much, she would never expect him to give up his friends or the after-shifters at Wagner's that he looked forward to each night. Tess wanted him just the way he was.

Tess pinched her cheek to make sure she wasn't dreaming. No, Nick wanted her and had asked her to marry him. Unbelievable! Tess blushed slightly as she realized she looked forward to going upstairs with him. It had been a long time since she had slept with a man, not since Connor. But she couldn't wait to be intimate with Nick. If he actually wanted a dozen children, (One never really knew with Nick) then, that's what she wanted too. Wouldn't it be wonderful having a big, noisy family? Nick would be a terrific dad. Wasn't he already a terrific uncle? Would Annabelle call him "Daddy," or would he always be "Uncle Nick" to her? Tess would let Annabelle decide. The child already loved Nick, so the title wouldn't matter.

Tess had another thought now. Nick already had a family—extended as it was. Would these people accept her? Could they like her, even? She already knew Coosie, of course, but it was Mary Kay she was worried about. She knew from Nick that Mary Kay was very religious. Would such a devout Christian accept a sister-in-law who had lived on Bonanza Street? Could they even be friends, much less sisters? She hoped so. Tess shook her head again. She would let go and trust that God would help her. God had led her to Nick, so she had to believe He would help her with Nick's family.

But what of her own family? She owed it to her mother and father to tell them of her sister's death. They deserved to know what had happened to their eldest daughter. They also deserved to know that Tess was alive and well. Certainly, they should know they had a granddaughter. How much unnecessary worry she had brought on them because of her selfishness and neglect! She longed suddenly to see them again. Tomorrow, she decided, she would write to them and tell them everything. She would let them know that Jodie was fine and was living with her. Butte was a long way away, but she would talk with Nick about taking the children and going home to visit her parents. Only after she apologized to them would she feel truly cleansed of her bad character.

* * * * * * * * * *

And then the stagecoach had arrived in Bodie, noisy bustling Bodie— a town that never slept. From the coach window, Nick could see Mary Kay standing on the wooden sidewalk waiting for them. Lex was with her, and they looked chummy. This surprised him. Nick had been gone less than two weeks, and now Lex looked like part of the family. Good for him! Lex had his hand on Mary

Kay's elbow and was leaning down, listening to something she was saying. *Mary Kay always has something to say*, Nick thought.

What would she say, he wondered, when he told her about him and Tess? Would she be happy for him? For them? Perhaps he should tell her about their engagement before he asked for the use of her guest room. Nick's heart softened, and he knew he was being unfair to Mary Kay because she definitely was a brick. She had been patient with him when he had brought home other people's children. He had been like a little boy bringing home stray pets.

"Here's another one, Mary Kay," he would say. "Got room for one more?" He hoped Mary Kay would make room for Tess.

The boarding house belonged to Mary Kay — no strings attached. The only thing Nick had asked in return was the use of one bedroom for himself. Mary Kay had gladly given him his choice of rooms and had been delighted that he wanted to live with her and her children. That had been three years ago, and in the meantime, they had acquired boarders who were now an integral part of their family. At that time, Nick had not given any thought to marriage. Now he knew he and Tess could not possibly share his small room in the Manor after they married. They would need larger accommodations, but they would figure all that out later. Now he had to secure a room for Tess for this one night. Tomorrow, he and Tess would go to Sophie's and get her belongings and move her and Annabelle elsewhere.

Nick was surprised to see Jodie climb down from the coach and immediately run and hug both Mary Kay and Lex. *What is going on?* Nick wondered. *When had Jodie and Mary Kay gotten so friendly that they hugged?* He helped Tess down, quickly greeted the others, and went to fetch their bags and thank the driver. He could hear the conversation behind him. Jodie was speaking,

"Ham? We get ham? Now? Good! I'm famished!"

"Well, actually ham sandwiches because it's so late," Mary Kay told him.

"Potato salad too?"

"Of course. I know you like potato salad."

Mary Kay could not know that only a couple of days before, Jodie had not been able to eat a thing. He certainly hadn't been hungry up at the lighthouse. That had been a tough day for them all, but Jodie had recovered his good humor and was looking forward to starting a new life in Bodie— a permanent one this time.

When he had arrived here five months earlier, he had thought it would be for only a brief time. Then he would return to his mother and hopefully his dad. Now, he knew he would miss his mother every day of his life, but he was grateful to be going home with Nick and Tess. Annabelle would be part of this new family too, and Jodie was excited about that. He would play with her, take her places, and look out for her as an older brother should do. Would there be a dozen more children to come? He had no idea but knew he would happily be the big brother to them all.

Mary Kay had the food ready when they reached the Manor. Tristan, Nessie, and Annabelle were all asleep in their beds, and the boarders had gone to their rooms earlier in the evening. The others gathered around the dining room table. Tess noticed Cindy as the dog stood as close to Nick as possible and never took her eyes off him. Cindy was relieved to see Nick. Twelve days was a long time for a dog to wonder if her master was coming home. Jodie thought back to his first trip with Nick and decided that Nick had described his dog perfectly that day on the coach, even if he had tricked Jodie into thinking Cindy was his wife. And now, Nick was actually going to have a wife!

While they ate, Nick told Mary Kay and Lex about their trip. He hit only the main points because he did not want Tess and Jodie to have to relive the sad parts. He would give Mary Kay and Lex details later.

Lex poured more coffee for Nick. "You look tired, Buddy. I imagine it was a long trip."

"Yeah, yeah, I am tired tonight, and I feel old." Nick acknowledged.

"You are old," Jodie reminded him.

Nick swatted him. He was glad to see Jodie back in good form. "But not too old to make an announcement," Nick said. He got up and stood behind Tess and put his hands on her shoulders. "I have asked Tess to marry me, and she has agreed." He held up both hands now and looked at his friends. "Please, do not try to talk her out of it." He smiled. "I want the world and all of you to know how much I love her. I hope you will be pleased for us."

They certainly were pleased. After a stunned silence, Mary Kay and Lex both jumped up. Lex shook hands with Nick, and Mary Kay hugged Tess. Then they switched places, and everyone hugged again. Jodie sat at the table and grinned.

Lex thought to himself, *If* you can get a girl *to marry you by taking her on a trip, then I'll purchase travel tickets tomorrow.* He thought he might want to marry Mary Kay someday, but for now he was happy for his good friend. He had known for a long time that Nick loved Tess.

Jodie said good night and went up to bed. He knew the grownups wanted to talk about weddings and mush like that, and he was too tired. It would be good to be back in his own bed.

Nick did come up for a minute. "Just to tuck you in," he said.

"You tuck me in every night," Jodie murmured, and then he was asleep.

Jodie had been right to go to bed. The talk continued of weddings and such, and he would have been bored. Tess and Mary Kay got along well. They talked easily together and even laughed a bit. Mary Kay did all she could to make Tess comfortable and to feel welcomed.

"So, Mary Kay," Nick spoke up, "now that Tess has agreed to marry me, I don' t want her going back to Bonanza Street. It wouldn't be right. Have you ever heard of Bonanza Street?"

Mary Kay nodded. "Yes, Lex told me." She wasn't going to admit to Nick that she had known about Bonanza Street for years.

Nick continued, "Would you consider putting Tess up? It would be for just this one night."

Lex and Mary Kay looked at each other and smiled. Then Mary Kay looked at Tess and said, "Yes, of course I am expecting you to stay with us, Tess, but I am hoping it will be for more than just one night."

"Why is that?" Nick was surprised by her answer.

"Tess, I am hoping that you will stay with us permanently, especially now that I hear you and Nick are getting married."

"Thank you, Mary Kay. I would like to stay."

Nick looked at his sister-in-law. "Thank you, Mary Kay. We will collect Tess's things from Bonanza Street tomorrow."

"Oh, no need for that." Mary Kay smiled sweetly at him. She was enjoying herself because she didn't often get the best of Nick. "Lex brought all her belongings here last week." She looked now at Tess. "Sophie packed your things herself. They are upstairs in the guest bedroom. I hope you will be comfortable there."

Nick was confused. Mary Kay did not often surprise him. "How did you happen to meet Sophie?" he asked.

"Oh, Sophie and I are old friends now. When I told her about Jodie needing his aunt, Sophie graciously agreed to let Tess go."

"You know Sophie?" Nick asked again.

"Yes. Lovely lady. She speaks highly of you, Tess."

Nick was still having a problem understanding how Mary Kay could possibly know a madam.

"Again, how did you meet Sophie?" he asked.

"I invited her to tea last week. We sat right here at this table, drank tea, nibbled on delicious little cucumber sandwiches and cute little iced tea cakes, and had a lengthy talk on a variety of subjects."

Nick looked at her, but Tess spoke up, "Sophie agreed to let me go, is that right?"

'Yes." Mary Kay smiled at her. "She has forgiven you your debt. She told me she would like to see you soon, so she can tell you herself. She said you are like a daughter to her and that she will dearly miss little Annabelle. Yes, Sophie really is a lovely lady. Shall we invite her to tea again soon?"

Nick sat down heavily in his chair. He had underestimated Mary Kay. He wondered just what she had offered a madam that she was willing to forgive a sizable debt?

Lex spoke up now, "Yes, Sophie is a special lady, bless her heart!" He and Mary Kay looked at each other and dissolved into laughter. They wished Jodie had been in the room.

CHAPTER 31

Nick and Mary Kay were drinking coffee in the kitchen when Tess walked in early the next morning. She was dressed and groomed, ready to put her best foot forward in her new home.

"Good morning, Mary Kay," she acknowledged her hostess.

Then she bent and kissed the top of Nick's head. "Good morning, my love."

"Good morning, Deeg," Nick replied.

"Deeg?" Mary Kay inquired.

"It's a word Nick uses when he's feeling incontinent," Tess replied. Nick smiled happily up at her.

Mary Kay stared at her. Was Tess going to be as quirky as Nick? Good Lord, she hoped not!

Mary Kay turned her attention to Nick. "Please make sure Susanne is available for dinner, so you two can tell her of your engagement," she ordered.

"Ah, the "Other Woman," Tess said.

"You know about Susanne?" Mary Kay asked, looking at Tess again.

"Of course," Nick chimed in. "Tess knows everything. Between us, we have no secrets and very few lies."

Mary Kay put her hands to her face. She was suddenly getting a headache.

"I can see what you've been dealing with all these years, Mary Kay," Tess said. "Nick won't behave for me either. My sympathies are with you."

"You talk about me as if I weren't in the room," Nick complained.

"Why don't you go to work?" Mary Kay suggested.

"Can't. I'm waiting for Tristan and Jodie. I'll walk them to school."

The boys came down soon enough and they all left, but not before it was settled that Susanne, Lex, and Casey would all be invited to dinner. Nick and Tess would wait to tell the boarders of their engagement until then too. It would be a real celebration. Tess was going to talk to Annabelle about her plan to marry Uncle Nick this morning. Since Annabelle would be a principal player in their marriage, she should be told before the others. And yes, Annabelle could keep a secret.

The fall semester of school had begun before their San Diego trip, and it hadn't been as bad as Jodie had feared. Walter had left town with his dad, and without him, Marty seemed far less menacing. Marty hadn't mentioned the beating, nor had he issued another warning of any kind. He was, in fact, cautiously friendly— as if he hoped Jodie would forget the whole thing, and they could be friends as before. Jodie would never trust him again but was wise to let the incident slide. To openly hold a grudge would serve no purpose. He still had to go to school with all these fellows, and he didn't want them having to choose sides in a confrontation. He hoped to play ball with them again when he was able, so he kept his own counsel. This had been Nick's advice, and Jodie was glad he had taken it.

Because Jodie was smart and well spoken, he had emerged this school year as one of the scholars and was respected by his classmates. Even the class clowns and bullies didn't bother him. It didn't hurt that Jodie excelled in sports and had a keen sense of humor. He was in class with kids of different ages, and because they all liked him, he had become a school leader. Jodie had enjoyed this new role and took it seriously. He had often helped younger students with their reading or arithmetic. He always looked forward to recess and lunch, although his arm had not healed enough to play ball. That would have to wait, but it was marble season now, and Jodie could play that. So, today he looked forward to returning to school, even though it had been a late night, and he was tired.

Unknown to Nick, Jodie read everything he could get his hands on and had acquired quite a bit of knowledge on many topics. He particularly enjoyed reading about history. He perused the newspaper and kept up on political issues, so he could contribute to dinnertime discussions. He would never let Nick know he read so avidly because he had his image to protect and relished Nick's calling him an "illiterate." Nick badgered Jodie, and Jodie gave it right back to him. It was a game the two played, a game they both enjoyed. Mary Kay didn't understand their constant barbs, but she couldn't have. It was a "guy thing."

Jodie diligently studied the maps in the back of one of his schoolbooks because he wanted to know geography, but also in an attempt to outshine Nick. He and Nick often challenged each other at the dinner table, each hoping to claim bragging rights. Nick would never let on how much he looked forward to these contests with Jodie.

Jodie might begin with, "I have a geography question for you, Nick."

Nick would pretend to be vexed. He would sigh dramatically and put down his fork.

"Don't you be wasting my time with dumb, asinine questions. Ask me something difficult." He would shake his head as if baffled and say to the others, "Can you believe that Jodie asked me the location of the Appomattox Court House last week?" Nick would shake his head again. "Every damned Civil War veteran knows the answer to that."

"You aren't a veteran," Jodie would remind him.

"You talking back to me, Lad? You better not be talking back to me! Now, if you have a worthwhile question, go ahead and ask it. Otherwise, let me eat my dinner in peace."

Other times, Nick would pretend not to know an answer, so Jodie would think he had him stumped.

"The Great Smoky Mountains run through two states. I bet you don't know which two," Jodie challenged one night.

"Bet I do," Nick retorted. "Tennessee and . . . hum, better let me think about this for a minute." Nick knew the answer, of course, because he also studied maps when Jodie wasn't around. In fact, he had an atlas hidden down at his shop where Jodie would never see it. Nick would pretend to be thwarted, and Jodie would get excited, thinking he had him. Nick would scratch his head and stare into space. Finally, he would hesitantly ask, "Is it North Carolina?"

Jodie's shoulders would slump; he had hoped that Nick would incorrectly answer, "Kentucky." Foiled again! Until the next time.

Nick had tried to include Tristan in these challenges, but the boy was unwilling. He wasn't competitive and disliked confrontation, so he preferred to watch. Besides, he knew he could never outsmart his Uncle Nick. He shared a bedroom with Jodie, and they had become buddies, but he secretly rooted for Nick.

Before they left for school today, Mary Kay had warned both Nick and Jodie that there would be no geography challenges this night. She would not permit it.

"You are to be on your best behavior. Both of you! This is to be a celebratory dinner honoring Tess and Nick, so save your shenanigans for another time."

"Yeah, yeah, okay." Nick shook his head sadly at Jodie. "That woman runs a tight ship." Jodie giggled.

The little girls awoke and came downstairs to find Mary Kay and Tess busy in the kitchen. Annabelle was thrilled to see her mother and hugged her tightly. She had never been separated from Tess before and had missed her. Mary Kay had coddled her and had been sweet to her, and so Annabelle had settled in comfortably at the Manor. She and Nessie were friends and playmates now.

Nessie had not met Tess before and did not realize she was to be her aunt. In later years, Nessie would always refer to Tess as her favorite aunt. Now, Tess smiled at her encouragingly and spoke softly to her.

"Good morning, Darling. I am so pleased to meet you, Nessie. Thank you for being so nice to Annabelle and sharing your bedroom with her. You are such a good girl. Could you possibly come over here and sit next to me for a minute, so we can get to know each other?"

Nessie got up and sat next to Tess on the kitchen bench. Tess asked her questions about her favorite things and the names of her dolls, and soon they too were friends. Nessie decided she liked this pretty lady very much.

"Did you stay here at the Manor last night?" she asked Tess.

"Yes, Darling, I stayed in the guest room."

Nessie looked at her, eyes wide. "Gosh, I never met a real guest before!"

Both Tess and Mary Kay laughed heartily. This was Tess's first encounter with Nessie's literal thinking, and she found it endearing.

Nessie wasn't offended by their laughter because she liked to see her mother happy. Sometimes, her mother could be so sad.

Mary Kay said to Tess, "Nick has that odd nickname for you— 'Deeg.' You call Susanne, 'The Other Woman.' I shall nickname you, 'The Guest.'" They laughed again. Tess enjoyed Mary Kay's pleasant company and was encouraged that they could become friends.

Annabelle had news for her mother.

"Sophie was here. She came to tea, and she brought dolls for both Nessie and me. See." She held up a beautiful porcelain doll wearing a lavender dress. "Show her yours, Nessie."

Nessie held up an equally beautiful doll, this one dressed in green.

"So, Sophie really was here," Tess mused. "I wasn't sure I believed you when you were teasing Nick. Did you like her?"

"Yes, very much. She does think the world of you, Tess."

"I care for her too. She has been good to both Annabelle and me. I know it is hard to believe because of her occupation and all, but she is a good person. I'm not sure where I would have ended up if she hadn't taken me in. My time there was rocky at first, but it all worked out. Someday, I will tell you my story. Not today when we are so busy, but soon."

Mary Kay looked her in the eye. "You can tell me anything, Tess, and I won't judge. I want us to be real sisters." Mary Kay put her hands up to her mouth. "Oh gosh, I shouldn't have said that! I'm sorry if I overstepped. I know your sister just died. Tess, I am so sorry for being insensitive."

Tess began to cry. "No, Mary Kay, you have it all wrong. I want nothing more than to be your sister. Excuse my tears, please. This romance has happened so quickly that my head is still spinning. Nick and I have been friends for a long time, but I never expected more. And now to find out he loves me and wants to marry me— it's almost too much. I am feeling a bit overwhelmed. I never thought I would be happy again."

"Sisters it is!" Mary Kay said. "I am so glad because I can see how much Nick loves you. I have waited a long time for him to be happy, and here you are! Selfishly, it will be good for me to have another woman in the house, what with all these men! I could use an ally." She smiled at her newest sister. "Now, why don't you take Annabelle upstairs? I know you want to talk with her. Come down when you're ready, and we'll talk about dinner preparations. No hurry."

"I want to write a letter to my parents after I talk with Annabelle. I will be down as soon as I have it written. Thank you, Mary Kay."

Dinner that evening was a raucous affair. Everyone at the Manor toasted the engaged couple, and there was champagne for the adults although Mary Kay did not have any. Good-humored speeches followed. The children were excited to have everyone home again. Nick had brought gifts for them from San Diego and gave them out after dinner: a set of knucklebones for Tristan and colorful scarfs for the girls. He had also bought them all a piñata but would save it for Christmas. He wasn't sure they would know what to do with it.

The three boarders were wise enough to see that change was coming to their small community, but so what? Sometimes change was good. Thornton and Wiley had introduced themselves to Tess. It seemed as though they had not met her before. Jodie wondered if they had been customers at Sophie's and were not letting on now? He dared not ask.

"You will have to give up your cussin' now with all these young'uns here," Coosie told Nick.

"What the hell are you talking about?" Nick asked. "I don't cuss."

Everyone looked at him. Nick smiled, but he was glad when Annabelle changed the subject.

"Mama is going to marry Uncle Nick," Annabelle reported happily.

"So, you are pleased about that, are you?" Thornton asked.

Annabelle nodded. "Now I get to stay with Uncle Nick always, not like before when he went to San Diego."

"And I get to stay with Aunt Tess," Nessie said. "She's the only one who calls me 'Darling.'"

"I call you 'Sweetheart.' Doesn't that count?" Nick asked her.

"No, it's 'Darling.' She calls me 'Darling.'"

Susanne had spent the afternoon in the kitchen with Tess and Mary Kay. She was happy to meet Tess and liked her quiet, unassuming manner. Tess was easy to talk with, and they had talked a lot. Last week, Mary Kay had confided in Susanne about Tess's background, and Susanne was aware of the deal Mary Kay had made with Sophie. This afternoon, Tess and Mary Kay told Susanne about the engagement. Susanne had been genuinely happy for both Nick and Tess. She had hoped that Nick would find the right woman for himself, and it seemed that he had. Tess would now be part of all their lives, and Susanne instinctively knew that she and Tess would be good friends. The three of them— Mary Kay, Susanne, and Tess would be lifelong friends and allies. They would weather sad times together and celebrate the good ones.

After the engagement party ended, and everyone was grabbing jackets and wraps, Wiley took Susanne aside.

"Why isn't Liam with you tonight?" he asked.

"Liam's not in town."

"Yes, he is. I saw him yesterday over on Green Street. Are you two getting along?"

"I have no idea." Susanne looked at her good friend. "I was not expecting him to return to Bodie for a while. Why would he come to town and not let me know? I wonder if I have done something wrong?"

"Put that thought out of your head, Susanne. If that were the case, you would know it."

"I am going to have his baby, Wiley. I haven't told him, but maybe he found out and is avoiding me."

Wiley was fatherly toward her now. "Susanne, don't worry about what he is going to do or not do. If this is his baby, he needs to step up. You will want to marry him, won't you?"

"No, I have no intention of marrying him. I was already pregnant when I found out he had a wife. I feel so stupid." Susanne shook her head. "I asked him the first day we met if he was married, and he assured me he was not. I'm beginning to hate men. At least I think I hate him."

"Wiley patted her arm. "How can I help?"

"No, there's nothing you can do. Just know that I don't plan to marry him."

"Well, you have plenty of friends in this house who will be looking out for you. That's for sure!"

Susanne smiled weakly up at him. "Thanks, Wiley."

"Come on, Thornton and I will walk you home tonight."

Jodie did not mean to eavesdrop, but he had been standing nearby and had heard every word. So, Susanne had not been trying to steal his dad away! She hadn't known he was married. That changed everything. He suddenly felt sad because he had dismissed Susanne three months ago and had had nothing to do with her since. She hadn't deserved that. She had once been a good friend to him.

Jodie rubbed the back of his neck, which he unconsciously did when trying to comfort himself. He was disgusted with his dad. How could Dad deny being married? His wonderful mother hadn't deserved that. In a way, it meant that Dad was also denying Jodie's existence. He certainly was a liar! Jodie sighed. Another night of going to bed with heavy things on his mind!

CHAPTER 32

"Hi Dad," Jodie said when he saw his dad emerge from the staircase. It was still early morning, but Jodie had been sitting in the hotel lobby for over two hours. The elderly clerk had not noticed him back in the corner in the overstuffed chair because Jodie had been quiet, lost in thought, but also determined to have this talk with his father. Jodie wasn't certain that his dad was staying at the hotel, but he knew he wasn't staying at Susanne's. So, he had waited because he had no other plan.

"What are you doing here?" his dad asked him.

"I was hoping we could talk."

"How did you know I was in town?" Dad asked.

"It doesn't matter how I know, but I know you have been here a couple of days."

"Don't talk back to me. What do you want?"

"I thought we could talk," Jodie said again.

"Okay, let's talk. Now's as good a time as any. Let's go up to my room."

Jodie followed him up to room 212. The bed was made. A white chenille bedspread was pulled up, barely revealing the corner of a white cotton pillow case underneath. Billy's clothes were folded neatly, lying atop his satchel. A bottle of whiskey sat on the bureau with an empty crystal glass standing at attention next to it. An orderly room for an orderly man.

Jodie's dad did not invite him to sit down, so they faced each other standing in front of the open window where white organdy curtains blew in the breeze. Jodie would think back on those curtains when he recalled this day.

Billy Burke faced his only son, knowing that the confrontation that had always loomed in the background was finally at hand.

"So, what's on your mind, Son?" Billy then held up his hand to stop Jodie before he could speak. "Never mind, let me go first, if you will. There have been some changes in my life lately, some good changes. I have an opportunity to go to New York and be part of an oil investment there. Get in on the ground floor, so to speak. It's an unbelievable opportunity— one that I can't turn down."

"Are you planning to take me?" Jodie asked.

"That's the thing, Jodie," his dad hesitated, "I can't take you. New York is no place for a boy, and I will be busy; I would not be around for you much. You will be better off going back to San Diego. You mother should be recovered soon, and you can go home."

Jodie was silent as he stared up at his dad.

Billy continued, "This is an incredible opportunity, as I said. I will come out of this a very wealthy man. But Jodie, you and I want different things now. I'm not the same man I was before. I can't go back to a life with your mother. Frankly, she suffocated me, Son. Nothing I did was ever good enough for her. I'm not cut out to be a husband or a family man. You're old enough to understand this, don't you think?"

Again, Jodie said nothing. He stared up at his dad.

"I expect your mother will be sending for you any day. If I have already gone to New York, I know your friend Nick Pratt will see that you get home. There's a stage leaving almost every day from here, and I know he'll make sure you get on it."

Jodie was stunned that his dad was so unaware. How could his dad did not know that his mother had died more than a week ago?

That she was buried in a grave in a cemetery, miles from here? How could he be so selfish as not to know this? Jodie did not cry. The former Jodie would have cried and begged his dad to take him with him. His dad would have sworn, and shaken him, and told him to grow up. Jodie almost smiled now. If his dad only knew how much he had grown up! How much he had matured without his dad's help. It was Nick who was teaching him to be a man, not this self-centered egotist standing in front of him. His dad was not finished; however, and Jodie looked him in the eye and took in every hateful word.

"The thing is, Jodie, your mother and I have not been together in a long time. In the meantime, I have met someone else— someone who understands me. Your mother and I never saw eye to eye on anything. You remember how we used to fight, don't you?"

Jodie nodded. "I remember."

Billy looked uncomfortable as he told Jodie the next part of his plan. I am going to marry this woman. I know you don't want to hear this, that you were hoping we could be a family again. But that is just not going to happen."

"How can you marry another lady when you are already married?" Jodie wanted to hear his dad say the words. He wanted his dad to admit that he would divorce a very sick woman. But Jodie knew what his dad did not know. He knew that a death also ends a marriage, and his parents' marriage had ended last week. No divorce needed!

"I am going to divorce your mother, Jodie. As soon as she's better, of course. I will wait to file the papers until your mother is better. After all, I am not heartless."

Jodie knew his dad would not tell him, but he asked anyway. "Who is the other lady? The one you are going to marry?"

"Someone I doubt you know, so there is no reason to give you her name."

Jodie wanted to catch him out in his lie. He wanted to tell his dad that not only did he know Susanne, but that he knew her well. Had Dad forgotten that he lived at the boarding house, the place where Susanne spent most of her evenings? But Jodie kept his thoughts to himself.

"Any more questions?" Dad was getting impatient.

"Will the lady be going to New York with you?"

"That's the thing, Jodie. I do plan to take her. You see, Son, she is going to have a baby, and I need to be there for her."

"You are having a baby?"

"We didn't plan for this to happen. But yes, there will be a baby, and the baby will need me."

"What if I need you?" Jodie wanted to see where this would go. He had never before seen his dad squirm. It was a new experience because his dad was always in charge, always in control.

"That's the thing, Jodie. You don't need me now. You are twelve years old, practically a man. This new baby is just starting out and will need a father to watch out for him."

Jodie shook his head in disbelief. "So, if I hear you correctly, you are choosing this new baby over me."

"Don't think of it like that."

"Did you ever love me?"

"Sure, I did. I love you now."

"It sounds like you are divorcing me too." Jodie looked at his dad. "Have you asked the lady to marry you yet?"

"'Tonight. I plan to ask her tonight. Then we will be leaving for New York soon."

"Will I ever see you again?" There was no emotion in Jodie's voice.

"Certainly, you will. When I get settled, I will send for you. You can spend vacations with us."

Jodie knew this was never going to happen. His dad was trying to exit his life with as little drama as possible.

Billy was surprised at Jodie's calm reaction; he had expected hysterics and a tantrum from the boy. That's why he had delayed this conversation as long as possible. They were having it now only because Jodie had forced it. If Billy had had his way, he would have left town without seeing Jodie. He felt no love, regret, or guilt when he thought about either Jodie or Jeannie. They had been a pain in his side for a long time, like a dog he couldn't shake loose.

"Okay, Dad. I will be at the boarding house if you ever want me."

"Frankly, you are taking this better than I expected," his dad said.

Jodie looked him straight in the eye. "A friend told me I needed to 'Buck up.' I'm just following his advice. Have a good life, Dad, and good luck with your investment. I hope you make a mint." Jodie turned and walked out.

Jodie was shaking when he reached the lobby. He again crawled into the overstuffed chair and tried to catch his breath. He was suddenly cold, and he wrapped his arms around himself. Even though Jodie continued to shake, he was calmer than he had ever been in his life. He felt as though he were experiencing all this from a distance. His dad had finally put into words what Jodie had dreaded this entire last year; he did not want Jodie. Oddly, Jodie felt at peace with this. It was out in the open now, and Jodie could deal with it there. It had been the uncertainty that had stymied him.

A few minutes later, Billy walked down the staircase and out the front door. He did not see Jodie. The overworked desk clerk puttered around behind the desk and did not notice the young boy either.

Jodie sat in the chair for a long time and thought back on the conversation. It was probably the last talk he would ever have with his dad. How could his dad not know about his mother's death? Well, Dad wouldn't be asking her for a divorce after all, and Jodie was relieved that his mother would be spared that humiliation.

Jodie looked up and stared into space. He thought of his dad's words. Dad had not only chosen another child over him but had planned to desert him, the one child he did have. How could a father go off and leave his only child far from home? What father wouldn't ensure that his boy got home safely? Who would leave the responsibility of getting his son home to another man, one he barely knew? Jodie shook his head. He understood many things now, but he could not understand such a dad.

It also bothered Jodie that his dad had gotten his age wrong. He was only eleven. Jodie realized that this was petty but felt that a dad should know his child's age. Dad had forgotten Jodie's birthday last year, along with everything else he had forgotten about his family, so Jodie shouldn't have been surprised. He hoped Dad would treat his next child more lovingly than he had treated him. And then Jodie thought of Susanne and knew what he must do next. He hadn't been able to save his mother or even himself, but he could save Susanne. He owed her that.

* * * * * * * * * *

"Got a minute?" Jodie asked as Susanne opened the door of her studio.

"I always have a minute for you, Jodie. Let's go in the back room, so we can talk." Susanne thought about the last guy she had brought to the back room of her studio. He had unsuccessfully proposed, and look at him now— happier than she had ever seen him. Susanne locked the front door, so they wouldn't be disturbed and invited Jodie to sit down. She put a quilt around his shoulders because she could see that he was shaking. She thought he was cold.

Jodie looked so serious. She smiled at him and said, "I am glad to see you, Sweetheart. Don't get me wrong, but aren't you supposed to be in school?"

"Yes, but this is more important. I want to apologize to you, Susanne. I have treated you bad for months, and you never deserved that." Jodie looked miserable. "You have always been decent to me. I want to tell you the whole story, and then I am hoping you will want to be friends with me again."

"I'm listening." Susanne smiled at him encouragingly.

"I always knew that Liam was your boyfriend, but I never met him because he was always away. What I didn't figure out right away was that Liam was also my dad - my dad with a different name. His real name is Billy. Did you know Liam was my dad?"

Susan looked at Jodie and had a decision to make. She wasn't a liar because she had never been put in a position where she had to lie. If she admitted to Jodie that she had known Liam was his dad, it would be unforgivable. It would look as though she had indeed been stealing his dad away. If Nick found out she had known the dad's whereabouts— after he had spent months searching for the guy, he would never speak to her again. She would lose both Nick and Jodie. Fortunately, she did not have to lie now because Jodie took her silence as a "No," and he went on talking.

"I am sorry. I did not mean to listen in on your conversation last night with Wiley, but I heard you tell him you are going to have Liam's baby. My dad just now told me his lady friend is going to have a baby. So, it has to be you. Right?"

"Right. But how did you know I was seeing your dad?"

"I saw you together on the Fourth of July. As you were going into the dance, I saw him kiss you. I didn't realize then that you thought you were with Liam. You didn't know that Liam was really my dad. But I saw you kissing my dad, and I thought you were stealing him away from my mom. That's why I have hated you all these months."

Susanne chose her words carefully. "Jodie, I did not know it was your dad at first. Yes, the man I knew called himself Liam. And if you listened last night, you heard me say that I asked him if he was married, and he told me no. He lied to me. I would never try to steal another woman's husband."

"I hate that he lied about being married to my mother. She was a good wife to him, and he didn't deserve her. He lied to me too. He's good at lying. He let me down."

"He let us both down," Susanne agreed.

"I want to apologize and tell you that I am really sorry I treated you so shabbily. Will you forgive me?"

"Of course. I was deeply hurt when you rejected me, but I understand now that you were trying to protect your mother. I respect that. You are a good boy, Jodie."

"There's more, I'm afraid. Dad wouldn't tell me your name, but he is coming here to propose to you tonight. He said he plans to divorce Mom, so he can marry you. My mother died, and he doesn't even know! I didn't tell him either. I just let him go on with his plans to take you to New York, so he can invest in an oil company."

"I didn't know."

"I didn't think you did. But before you agree to marry him, I want you to know the truth. He's a mean guy, Susanne. I never told this to anyone before, but he treated my mom terrible. He bullied her all the time, and I saw him slap her more than once. Mom told me he wasn't like that before they got married. So, I have come to warn you that he is not a good man. I don't want you to think I am just saying this, so you won't marry him. I am afraid for you."

"Thank you, Jodie, for trying to protect me."

"I couldn't help Mom. I realize that now; I was too young. But I can help you. That's why I'm here. Both to apologize and to tell you the truth about my dad before you make your decision."

"You have come a long way since you first moved to Bodie," Susanne told him now. "The little boy I first met months ago didn't care much for women. I can see that you have changed your views on that. You have matured."

"Nick helped."

"Yes, I know that. You have grown very close to him, haven't you?"

"Nick's been more of a father to me than my real dad ever was."

"Have you told him this?"

"No, as I told you before, we don't have that kind of relationship where we say nice things to each other."

"I suggest you give it a try. You might be surprised."

Jodie nodded.

Susanne smiled at him. "Okay, just so you know, I have no plans to marry Liam— baby or no baby. Be assured that when he proposes tonight, I will tell him, 'No.'"

"So, can we be friends again? Like we used to be? Please say, "'Yes.'"

"Absolutely! There's nothing I would like more." Susanne hugged Jodie to her. "But Jodie, we are going to be much more than friends."

"What do you mean?"

"You and I are going to be related because I will be the mother of your half-brother or sister."

"Wow! I didn't think of that. I always wanted a brother or sister. Wow!" Jodie smiled happily. "Susanne, I will like being related to you."

"And I will like being related to you! Now listen, and I will tell you a secret how we are going to make this all work out." And Susanne told him that Nick had agreed to claim the baby as his own. That way, Liam would have no say over her or the baby.

CHAPTER 33

It was midmorning when Nick looked up to see Jodie standing in the doorway of his shop.

"Playing hooky?" he asked.

"Yes," Jodie replied. He paused and then added, "Are you angry?"

"Do you have a good reason?"

"Yes."

"Then, I'm not angry."

Jodie flung himself at Nick, hugging him tightly. "It's been a bad morning."

"A long one too, I suspect. I got in from my morning walk and saw your note saying you were leaving early and would see me after school. It was not even six then. Do you want to tell me about your bad morning?"

Jodie nodded. They walked over to the table by the back door and sat down.

"I talked with my dad this morning," Jodie began. He told Nick about confronting his dad at the hotel. He told Nick everything he could remember of the conversation, and then he added,

"I have something else to tell you. It's important." Jodie took a deep breath. "You know that I saw my dad in town last summer. I told you that I had seen him again on the Fourth of July, right?"

"Right."

"Well, I knew Susanne was seeing a man named Liam, but I had never met him because he was always away. On the Fourth of

July, I saw Susanne with my dad outside the Miner's Union Hall, and I wondered why she was with my dad instead of with her beau, Liam. Then, I saw Dad kiss her on the lips, and I thought Susanne was trying to steal him away from my mother. I was so angry that I stopped speaking to her."

Nick asked, "Why were Susanne and your dad outside the Miner's Union Hall?"

"Dad escorted her to the dance."

"No. It was Liam who took Susanne to that dance, "Nick pointed out. "I was there and saw them there together."

"No, she went to the dance with my dad. I saw them go in."

Nick did not speak for a minute as he digested this information.

"Mother of God!" He then exclaimed, "You're telling me that Liam is the same man as your father?"

"Yes."

"Holy Hell!" Nick breathed. "Your dad is Liam?"

"Yes, Dad changed his name from Billy to Liam."

"It's no wonder we couldn't find Billy in San Diego. He was here, right under our noses."

Nick looked at Jodie. "When did you figure out that your dad and Liam were the same person?"

"Not until last night when I heard Susanne talking with Wiley. She said she was going to have Liam's baby. Only then did I realize that she thought my dad was Liam. She told me that when she first met him, Dad introduced himself to her as Liam. So, she didn't know he was actually Billy, my dad. He tricked her. And to think I have been angry with her all these months!"

"And all the time I was searching for Billy, he was here," Nick said again.

"Today, Dad told me his lady is having a baby, and he is planning to propose to her tonight and then take her to New York where he is investing in an oil company. He's talking about Susanne! He loves Susanne now. But the worst part for me is that Dad doesn't even know my mother died. He plans to divorce her. What a jerk!"

"Agreed. I'm glad he didn't file for divorce while she was so sick."

"At least he can't ask her for a divorce now. That helps."

"Will you ever tell him she died?"

Jodie shook his head. "I don't expect to ever see him again, but if I did, I would never tell him. He doesn't deserve to know."

"He doesn't deserve you, Jodie." Nick reached over and covered Jodie's hands with his own.

"Dad is going to propose to Susanne tonight, like I said; but Susanne told me that she's not going to marry him. Then he will leave for New York."

"You talked to Susanne too? You have had a busy morning! I want to hear about that, but let's concentrate on your dad for another minute. The Liam I know gambles for a living. He must do well because he always has money for poker or faro. He buys stylish clothes for himself, and he brings Susanne flowers and expensive presents. However, I don't think he has the kind of money it takes for a serious investment. At least, that's the way Susanne described him to Mary Kay— pocket money but no serious money. Certainly not old family money like Susanne has. Did he have much money when you lived in San Diego?"

"No, we were poor."

"That's what I thought."

Jodie sighed. "It's hard to tell you this, but when he left that July, we never heard from him again, and that includes not sending us any money to live on. I think I told you that my mom had to get a job."

"That's despicable! What kind of a man does that? He deserted you and your mom, started a whole new life, and even took a new name."

"He is a jerk!" Jodie said again.

"Okay, here's what I am thinking," Nick said. "I suspect that he needs Susanne's money for his investment. If she turns down his marriage proposal, he won't have her money to invest." Nick looked Jodie squarely in the eye. "That means he won't be going to New York. He can't go without the money, see? There's no telling what he will do then. He could change his mind and decide he wants you, and he could come here to take you away. You need to buck up, Jodie, and get ready for whatever comes next. But know he will have a fight on his hands. Even if he wants you, I won't let him take you."

"He doesn't want me," Jodie said, "but more importantly, I don't want him. It feels good to be able to say that."

"Jodie, a man like your dad can be dangerous when he's crossed. You must be careful, and I must warn Susanne to be careful tonight too."

"I am not going anywhere with him. Not ever! He would have to kidnap me."

Nick stared into space for a minute trying to decide what to do. Then he reached into his left-hand pocket and extracted a ten-dollar coin. "When I left home to seek my fortune, my dad gave me this coin. He told me it wasn't my money. It was his money, and I was to keep it in my pocket always in case of an emergency. Only in an emergency would I be allowed to spend it. Fortunately, I have never needed it." Nick then withdrew another coin from his right-hand pocket. "So, with my dad in mind, I want you to take this Gold Eagle. Keep it in your pocket. It's mine, not yours. For emergencies only. If something ever happens, such as a kidnapping, you can use it to send me a telegram telling me where you are. Then I'll come for you. Okay?"

"Okay." Jodie nodded. It gave him some comfort, and he put it in his pocket. "Thanks, Nick. I hope I never have to use it."

What Nick didn't tell Jodie then was that he had another coin just like it in his bureau drawer. Until yesterday, it had sat next to his grandmother's ring. The coin had been his brother Ed's emergency money. Ed had not needed it, and so Nick was saving it for Tristan. He looked at Jodie now.

"I also hope you never have to use it, but we'll call it 'insurance,'" Nick said. And then more forcefully, he added, "By God, I wish I were unethical!"

"Unethical how?" Jodie asked.

"If I were unethical, I would check the hotel register. I would find your dad's signature and study it long enough to be able to copy it. Then, I would forge a letter from him to me asking me to raise you, so he could go to New York. I'd have him practically giving you to me. We would have a better chance in a court of law with a letter like that. If the judge thought your dad had deserted you, he would hand you over to me in a heartbeat."

"Would this be one of those times when you do the wrong thing for the right reason?"

"Hell yes! It would be."

"Too bad you are ethical." Jodie sighed. "You are ethical, right?"

"Sorry, yes. I am ethical. But it was a good plan, even if inoperable."

"What now?"

"Now, tell me about your visit with Susanne."

"Two really important things happened today. First, I apologized to Susanne, and we are friends again. That means everything to me. And second, her baby is going to be my half brother or sister because my dad is the father. I will be a big brother, and that will make me a relative of Susanne's. Isn't that great?"

Nick grinned. "Looks like our family is expanding daily. What are we going to do with all these young'uns underfoot?"

"Love them," Jodie said simply.

"My darling, Jodie! You are a wonder!"

"Did you just call me, 'Darling?'"

"What? Do you think Nessie has a monopoly on that word?"

Jodie laughed at Nick's joke, but he remembered a time not long before when both Nick and Mary Kay had called him, "Darling." He had been lying on Nick's bed, badly hurt. They had called him, "Darling," and had held him, and he had felt so loved and protected. He sat for a moment lost in thought. Nick brought him out of his revelry.

"I bet Susanne was glad to see you. I know she missed you."

"I missed her too even though I was angry at her. I was mean to her, Nick, and she didn't deserve that. I have a lot to make up to her."

"You are growing up, Jodie. I'm proud of you."

"I've learned a lot, mostly from you, but also from the other men at the Manor. You all think and act differently from my dad. I've learned that Dad is a selfish man who believes he's better than everyone else. People should be treated with respect, not the way he treats them. Why would he think he is better than Coosie who is such a great man? And why should my dad consider the Indians, or the Chinese, or women inferior?"

"Agreed."

"You know you also have a problem, right?" Jodie asked. He glanced quickly at Nick.

"What are you talking about?"

"You don't have such a high opinion of women, yourself. It shows whenever Mary Kay talks about women having the right to vote. I know you told me once that you thought Mary Kay was smart, but I wonder if you think all women are smart? Or smart enough?"

"Jodie, I am just kidding Mary Kay. You know how I like to tease her."

"Are you really teasing, or does a part of you think women are inferior?"

Nick sat back in the chair, cupped his chin in his hand, and looked at Jodie. He had never given women or women's issues serious consideration. True, he enjoyed tormenting Mary Kay about her suffragist views, but did he really believe women weren't smart enough to vote? Or to hold public office, for that matter? Should women have the same opportunities as men? He had never actually thought about these things, even when Mark Kay was adamantly trying to make her views heard.

Nick continued to sit at the table, looking at Jodie all the while. Men ruled the world. That was the way it was and had always been. True, he had underestimated Mary Kay in her ability to deal with Sophie. He also had never given Tess enough credit for taking care of herself and her baby daughter during the worst time in her life. She had landed on her feet, even in a brothel. Susanne was the other woman in his life. She was strong and independent and quite capable of taking care of herself.

"You know, Jodie, you might be right. I've never seriously thought about women's rights, and I have been content to go along with the status quo. Why not? As a man, the advantages have always been in my favor. You asked me a reasonable question, but I can't answer you right now; I need to think about it. Let me do that, and then we'll talk. Okay?" Nick smiled at Jodie. "It took courage on your part to point this out to me."

Jodie nodded. He couldn't imagine having this talk with his own dad. His dad would have stormed out of the house after having slapped him and left him in a heap on the floor. Jodie couldn't remember one meaningful conversation he had ever had with his dad. His dad had kept him off keel— sometimes he had treated him well, sometimes not.

Jodie had no idea what had kept him so loyal to his dad. Maybe he had thought his dad's way was the way of all dads. Ian's dad was drunk most of the time, and he too had used the belt on his children for the least infraction. Jodie hadn't known the dads of his school friends, and he had no nearby relatives as role models. He simply hadn't known that good dads existed.

Now he said to Nick, "I've changed my views on women since I've been here. I used to think they were supposed to just clean and cook and so on, while men did the important work. You men at the Manor never treat Mary Kay like that. You compliment her on her cooking and thank her for the many things she does for you. No one ever yells at her or treats her like a servant. In fact, you all pitch in and help her. Wiley dries the dishes for her most nights, and Thornton sweeps the floor. And they pay to live there! My dad never helped my mom in any way. He usually just sat in his chair and hollered at her to bring him things. It's been good for me to see how decent men act."

"What? I don't get any credit for helping Mary Kay?" Nick joked.

"You pay the bills. That's enough," Jodie said.

"Actually, Mary Kay pays her own bills. The boarding house is self-sustaining." Nick smiled. "You've come a long way, Jodie. You have earned the respect of everyone at the Manor."

"Thanks, Nick," Jodie paused before saying, "so, since it has already been a long day, I am wondering if I have to go to school today? It's noon. I would rather spend the afternoon with you. Can I?"

"Don't say, 'Can' when you mean to say, 'May.' May I spend the afternoon with you?"

Jodie rolled his eyes. "May I?" he asked.

"Hell, why not? No school for you today. If you are going to play hooky, then you have to do it right; no one plays hooky for only half a day. Damn, I wish we had a good fishing hole near here. There's nothing like fishing to improve a mood. Let's go rustle up some lunch instead."

"Good. I'm famished."

"After we eat, you can help me over at Peterson's. They have a few things that need fixing."

"The first job I ever went on with you was to Peterson's to fix their porch. Remember?"

"I do," Nick said. "We were just getting to know each other. It seems like a long time ago."

"It was. A lot has happened— that's for sure!" Jodie paused. "Nick, I do have something else on my mind. I have been meaning to bring this up, but life has been crazy."

"Yes?"

"I lied to you, and I stole from you too." Jodie went on to tell Nick that he hadn't lost the money for the wood at the ball field last April but had pocketed it in order to go back home. "Did you ever suspect?"

"I knew you took it all along."

"How could you know?"

"Occam's Razor," Nick said, smiling.

"What does that mean?"

"It means that the simplest explanation is usually the right one. So, I figured you had just kept the money."

"Really? You've got to be kidding! You knew all along?"

"Yes. Besides that, you are a terrible liar."

"And you let me stay with you? Even when you thought I was a liar and a thief?"

Nick smiled at him. "People do things to survive, Jodie. I knew you would come around. Besides, Cindy liked you, and she is a good judge of character."

Jodie was touched by Nick's revelation but decided to joke, "Occam's Razor! You sure know about a lot of odd things." Jodie immediately regretted his words. He knew what was coming.

"I read. Not like some illiterates I know."

"Yeah?" Jodie responded as he walked over to Nick's desk where earlier he had noticed a book. "Are you reading this?" He held up Nick's atlas.

CHAPTER 34

Nick and Jodie spent more time at lunch than they'd planned because Nick talked at length about an old friend. Jodie had teased Nick about having to clean up his language because of the young, impressionable children at home. That reminded Nick of Philip Deidesheimer, a mining engineer he knew in Virginia City.

"I brought him home for dinner one night. Mary Kay can cook anything, and she made a traditional German meal of sauerbraten."

"What's that?"

"It's a beef stew. Most times when she cooked for him, she made pork and sauerkraut because that was his favorite. He also liked cruller, a dessert of some sort. I think he appreciated everything she cooked for him. Philip is an interesting fellow. He's much older than I by about twenty years or so. He came around 'The Horn' from Germany to California when he was just nineteen."

"I don't know what you mean when you say, 'To Come around the Horn,'" Jodie told him. "I remember that Uncle Billy also talked about that."

"At the very tip of South America, there is land that extends out into the ocean. It is known as Cape Horn. So, to 'Come around the Horn,' means to travel by ship around the southern tip of South America. This is the only way to get from the Atlantic Ocean to the Pacific Ocean by water. Prospectors, on their way to the gold fields, are specifically interested in getting to the west coast of California by water. Another way to get to California is to cross through Panama, and many of the forty-niners who were in a hurry to get to the mine fields chose that land route instead," Nick told him. "'Going around The Horn' takes longer than going through Panama, but the land trip is more difficult because of the swamps, mosquitos, snakes, and so on. Also, you have to travel on mules, and that's tough going. There is talk of building a canal through the isthmus there for ships to get through to the Pacific Ocean, and from what I read, construction should begin in a couple of years. We will have to watch in the newspaper for word on that."

"Is Mr. Deidesheimer still living?"

Nick nodded. "He sure is. He has been superintendent of the Ophir Mine in Virginia City for the last three years. Do you know about the Comstock Lode?"

"No, not much."

"It was a huge silver discovery in Virginia City, Nevada, a few years back. You know that I lived there before I came to Bodie, right?"

Jodie nodded.

"Virginia City was a jumping place when we lived there. It still is, but I think it's dying down some now. Thousands of people live and work there. Like here, it's busy twenty-four hours a day. Millions of dollars of gold and silver have been taken out of those mines, making some men enormously wealthy."

Nick stopped speaking as he thought back on his former life. He considered his time spent with Ed and Mary Kay in Virginia City a treasured time. So many great memories of carefree days, good friends, and many social activities. Nick smiled when he remembered his brother in his square dancing "duds." He would give anything to have his brother back again.

Jodie waited patiently for Nick to resume the conversation. Nick sighed and continued.

"But what I want you to know about Philip is that he is famous for his invention that braced up the mines that were constantly caving in there. These cave-ins not only killed miners, but they were bad for business. Philip was hired to solve the problem. This was back in the early sixties. He knew a lot about engineering because he had attended a prestigious school back home in Germany. Smart guy!"

"What was his solution?"

"His bracing system was built of wooden cubes and designed like a honeycomb, which made it quite sturdy. It was all in the design! It's known as 'The Square Set.'"

Jodie was impressed. "I bet he got rich."

"No. He chose not to get a patent for his invention, so he received no money at all. He didn't care. He often went to other mines in the area and showed their miners how to build it, so they could prevent cave-ins too," Nick said. "I'm telling you, Jodie, he's a nice guy. Philip's invention enabled the mines to produce tons of rich ore, but it saved plenty of lives too."

"Nick, you said that Philip had something to do with swearing."

Nick chuckled as he thought back. "When Philip got impatient or frustrated, he would mutter, 'Hucklesacrement!' We knew for certain that he was swearing under his breath, but we didn't know which vulgar word he was saying exactly. Finally, an old timer explained it to us. He told us, 'Hucklesacrement,' merely means 'Holy Sacrament!' To this day, we don't know for sure which language Philip was speaking, probably not even German. But all that time we thought he was uttering obscenities. So, the joke was on us, and we all got a good laugh from it.

"Philip moved to the Montana Territory in '64. He designed and supervised the construction of the Hope Mill and Smelter there in Granite County. I think that's about fifty some miles from your hometown of Butte. A town evolved there and was named Philipsburg after Philip Deidesheimer in 1867. They called it Philipsburg because the word 'Deidesheimer' was too long. Eventually, he came back to Virginia City. Because I was a carpenter, I often got to work with him, and I sure enjoyed that. I'll take you to meet him next summer when school is out."

"That would be great. Thanks for lunch."

"Yeah, yeah. You're welcome. Okay, we'd better get back to work. Are you ready?"

Jodie jumped up. "I'm always ready."

"We have to stop by Susanne's studio on our way. I want to warn her about Liam."

They spent some time with Susanne discussing Liam's expected proposal. Liam had sent her a message inviting her to dinner, but now that she knew of his marriage plan, she had decided not to dine with him that evening. She was afraid he might propose to her in public, in a restaurant perhaps, and this would embarrass them both when she declined his proposal. She had a different plan.

When Liam arrived at her studio, she would sit him down and explain to him that she did not want to see him anymore. She would simply tell him that her feelings for him had changed, and she wanted to end their relationship. She would tell him quickly before he could speak of marriage. She had not told him of her pregnancy, so that would not be an issue.

"What will you do if he doesn't accept your plan to end the affair?" Nick asked her.

"I don't expect there to be a problem, Nick. I really don't because he has always been a gentleman around me. He won't be happy about the break-up, but he can't fight it. I am a grown woman, and I make my own decisions. I will be resolute in my decision and he will leave. I'm certain he won't give me a problem."

"I wish I were as assured as you are, but I am concerned. He is going to propose. We know that. He will probably do it here in the studio. I know he wants you to marry him because you are both beautiful and bewitching, but I suspect he is also after your money for his investment. That worries me because a man desperate for money is unpredictable. He could become violent and hurt you when you reject his proposal. Would you like me to be here with you when he comes? I could be your safety net in case he reacts badly. What do you say? I would like to do this for you."

"No, Nick. Liam won't be a problem. If he mentions the baby, I will tell him it is not his. He won't argue with me about it. How can he? So, he won't have any hold on me. When I ask him to leave, I am certain he will go. Please, go spend a pleasant evening with Tess. I liked her very much, by the way."

Jodie had a request. He reminded Susanne that his dad did not know about his mom's death, and he hoped his dad would never find out because it was no longer any of his business. Jodie asked Susanne not to tell him. Susanne promised not to mention it.

Nick and Jodie left then, assuring her they would both come should she send for them.

Nick had to bow to her wishes, but he was unhappy about it. The more they had talked, the more danger he felt she was in.

Nick and Jodie repaired several things for Hal Peterson that afternoon and then returned to the shop and worked on projects there. Nick always took the time to teach Jodie the tricks of the trade, and Jodie was an apt student. Because he helped Nick so often, he would be able to find a job as a carpenter, should he ever need to. The plan was to have Tristan join Nick the following summer and learn the carpentry trade as well. Neither Jodie nor Tristan expected this to be their life work, but knowledge of carpentry would benefit them when they owned their own homes.

The plan was for the boys to go to college. Both were intelligent boys who would thrive in college and have successful careers afterwards. Nick thought Tristan would do well as an engineer. He didn't know what Jodie would choose to study yet. Jodie was interested in both history and politics, so perhaps a degree in law. They had time to figure it out.

When the workday ended, Jodie walked home alone. That morning, Tess had insisted that Nick meet Casey and Lex for an after shifter at Wagner's, their usual ritual. She had no intention of coming between him and his friends. Besides, she told him, she would be busy at that time helping Mary Kay in the kitchen. There were many people to feed, and Nick would just be in the way. Tess had assured Nick that she would miss him but wanted him to go to Wagner's. Who was Nick to argue with a woman?

After dinner, he and Tess planned to take a walk, so they could have some private time to themselves. The prior evening, before the engagement dinner, they had walked over to a rock wall a short distance from the Manor. There in the semidarkness, while Tess sat on the wall, Nick had indeed gotten down on one knee and had slipped his grandmother's ring on her finger. Tess had tears in her eyes when he told her how much he loved her and how much his grandmother would have loved her. So, tonight they would again walk to the rock wall where they could be alone. One could find no privacy at the Manor—what with Mary Kay, Lex, three boarders, four children, and a dog.

So, Jodie walked home alone and had time to think about his day. He wished Nick would let him play hooky more often, but he knew that was not going to happen. When he rounded the corner, he spotted Nessie and Annabelle out front playing with their dolls. Jodie talked with them for a few minutes. Annabelle was still shy around him. She had been told that he was her cousin, but she wasn't quite sure what a cousin was. Jodie decided it was time to get to know her better. And Nessie too. Jodie had lived at the Manor for months and had given the young girl little thought. She was just another person at the dinner table who sometimes made him laugh by the things she said. Now these children were to be his family, so it was time he got to know them.

Jodie went up to his bedroom where he found Tristan.

"Let's play jump rope with the girls," Jodie suggested. "I know there's some rope out in the shed. You can swing one end, and I'll swing the other."

"I make it a habit of never playing with girls," Tristan said and picked up his book.

"Come on, Tristan. It will be fun. I need you to help me." Tristan reluctantly followed Jodie down the stairs and out to the shed. "Why are we doing this?" he asked.

"I think we need to step up as big brothers and cousins and do the right thing, that's all."

Jodie showed the girls how to jump the rope. He and Tristan swept the rope on the ground, and the girls caught on, slowly at first. Annabelle had more natural skill than Nessie, so Jodie found himself helping Nessie more. Both girls practiced while Jodie chanted some popular jump rope songs that helped them keep cadence with the rope. The young girls giggled at the witty songs, which often included the word, "Kissing." Another day, after the girls became more competent, Jodie would teach them to jump with the rope up in the air. Much later, he would introduce Dutch Doubles, a game he and Ian had excelled in together. After a while, even Tristan began to enjoy the game. Jodie and Annabelle swung the rope for him, and he did better than he thought he could. He too had never jumped rope before.

"Look, I've really got the swing of it now," he exclaimed before adding, "Pun!"

Jodie laughed. He had never spent much time with Tristan because Tristan usually had his nose in a book, or he was engineering something out of wood. Tristan didn't care about sports, and so they hadn't had much in common. But now, Jodie decided he would teach Tristan to play marbles next. He even had a boulder he would give him. Today, as the four children played together, Annabelle overcame her shyness around Jodie.

"Jodie, can we play this game tomorrow again? Please, Jodie, can we?" Annabelle tugged on his sleeve to get his attention.

Jodie smiled to himself as he listened to Annabelle's word choice. He decided to skip the grammar lesson on "Can and May." Even Nick would consider that too advanced for these young children. Instead, he said,

"Yes, let's play again tomorrow. I want to spend time with you too."

Jodie was learning how to be a big brother, and he decided he liked it. He certainly liked his new family, although he mourned his mother and thought of her often. He had landed on his feet, and he realized what a fortunate boy he was – all because he had gotten on the same stage as Nick months before.

Random? Nick would think not!

"I'll come and swing the rope again," Tristan offered. He had also liked being the big brother and had liked spending time with Jodie.

These four children would grow up together and forever be close friends. More children would come into the family, as Nick hoped they would. "The Core Four," as Jodie, Tristan, Annabelle, and Nessie would later dub themselves, would be there to teach the new "young'uns" to skip a rope and to play many other games as well. True, the games would not always be played in Bodie because the ore in Bodie, like in Virginia City, would one day run out, leaving this bustling city nothing more than a ghost town. But that was a time in the future. For now, these were the good times.

CHAPTER 35

That afternoon, Susanne was agitated and could get nothing done. She had sufficient work to keep her busy for months but had fidgeted for an hour after Nick and Jodie left. Jodie had rattled her this morning by all he had said against his dad. The one thing she kept going back to was that not only had Liam hit his wife, but he had done so only after she married him. Only after he had taken her away from her family, her support system, had he felt he could hurt her. What kind of a man did that?

Nick's comments this afternoon had also made her uneasy. Was Liam committing to her now because he needed her money for an investment? He had never mentioned marriage. Sure, he was foot loose, but she had thought he would eventually settle down with her. Then in June, when she had discovered he was Jodie's father, she had realized he was no family man. He had deserted his family. What kind of a man did that?

Susanne put on her hat and cloak and went for a walk. It was autumn now, and the wind swept through the open landscape. She walked to the small cemetery on the hill where she sometimes did her best thinking. If she was going to be honest with herself, she would have to admit that there was a time when she had wanted Liam to propose to her. She had loved him since the first evening they met.

Susanne had a close college friend whom she had met at Vassar. She and Lydia had kept in touch after graduation, and Susanne had stood up for her when she had married Arthur in Newport, Rhode

Island. Arthur was an engineer, and the young couple had soon found themselves living in the mining town of Aurora, only twelve miles away. Lydia knew Susanne was living in Bodie and had invited her to come for a visit. Lydia and Arthur enjoyed entertaining, and because they both came from money, they knew how to throw lavish dinner parties. It was at one of these parties that Susanne and Liam met. The guest list that evening had consisted of Susanne, Liam, and three married couples. Susanne had immediately suspected that her old friend was playing matchmaker. Liam had been seated next to Susanne at the table, and Susanne had wondered if he too realized this was a set up. If he noticed, he made no comment.

Liam had been traveling around the West for only a month, but he knew entertaining stories that made the region seem so real. He told her of Black Bart, the stagecoach robber, who sometimes left short poems at the site of his robberies. Liam made her laugh when he talked about the sixty-three camels the army had brought to Texas before the War. He described Buffalo Bill and other interesting characters. He enchanted her, and she fell for him.

After graduation, Susanne had first worked in Brady's studio and had then come west to pursue her photojournalism project. She had been too busy to think about marriage, and although she had many admirers, she had not been attracted to any of them until she met Liam. To her credit, she had asked him if he was married that very first evening, and he had told her no. He described himself as a Southern Gentleman, who having survived the war, had come West. He was self-deprecating when he told everyone at dinner that the Confederacy had lost the war, and this certainly was the reason why he drank, gambled, and dipped his toe in the waters of debauchery. All at the dinner table had laughed and were charmed by him and his stories.

Susanne did not realize that Arthur had not known Liam long. She incorrectly assumed that he was an old friend. But no, the two men had met right there in Aurora a few weeks before and had become friends because they shared similar interests. They both belonged to the same fraternal organization, and they played chess together on Saturday afternoons. Because Liam was a guest at their dinner table, Susanne incorrectly assumed that Arthur and Lydia vouched for him.

Susanne's family was wealthy, and she herself had come into a fortune when she turned twenty-one. In the year that she had known Liam, she had not told him of her financial assets. A well-bred woman would never discuss such matters. But Liam knew. Liam had asked what seemed to be innocuous questions, and Arthur had unwisely told him all he knew.

So, even though Liam never wanted to marry again, he knew that someday he must marry Susanne to get his hands on her money. He and Susanne had known each other for over a year, and neither had spoken of marriage. In the meantime, Liam had courted her. He had taken her to dinners, to concerts, and to the theater. He had danced with her long past midnight and had escorted her afterward to late-night suppers. He had wanted her in his bed and had patiently waited for that. She was a good girl, and he knew he could not rush her. When he finally succeeded, it had been magical for them both. Susanne loved him. He was her first love, and she had fallen hard. She loved when he held her hand in public and kissed her lips in private. She relished waking up next to him and seeing him staring into her blue eyes in a manner that told her he loved her too. She enjoyed having coffee and reading the morning newspaper with him across the kitchen table. Susanne and Liam shared different views on a variety of subjects, and they debated the pros and cons of these. She loved both his mind and his body. She loved the marvelous way he made her feel. In bed, he constantly whispered that he loved her and would love her forever. He told her he wanted to be with her always. Susanne loved him completely and expected to someday marry him.

And then came the day in June when she found out who he really was. He was a young boy's father and another woman's husband. He was not the decent, trustworthy man she thought she knew. On that fateful June day, when she had seen Jodie run to Liam, she knew her dream had ended. She immediately resolved to end things with him because she certainly couldn't be involved with a married man. However, when she tried to break away, she found she was weak willed. When Liam would suddenly appear in her doorway, her heart would melt, and she would once again find herself in his arms and in his bed. She was weak, and her mother would be disappointed in her. Elizabeth had raised Susanne to be a strong woman. She would not recognize her now.

Susanne knelt down now at one of the graves and cried, not for the deceased who occupied that lonely spot, but for herself and for the irresolute, immoral woman she had become. That evening, Liam would be standing in her doorway, and she knew it would be for the last time. She would be strong that night and send him away. She did not understand a man who would propose to a woman knowing he had a wife back home. Again, she thought, *What kind of a man does that?*

Susanne cried more tears for herself because she loved Liam! She had never loved another man. How does one say goodbye to a dream? Susanne knew she was about to find out.

It was true that she could have gone to New York and started a new life with him there. She had thought about this all afternoon. They could leave tonight and be married enroute or even when they reached New York. No one would know them there and realize she had been Liam's mistress. They would be Mr. and Mrs. Liam Burke. She would have his baby, and they would be a happy family. A nagging thought tugged at her, however, and would not leave. Away from her friends and family, would Liam turn on her and hurt her when he was provoked or angry? Would he harm her baby? Jodie had told her that his dad had often hit him. Jodie's mother must have been tortured to see her little boy hurt. Susanne drew in her breath. What was she thinking? She could not marry this man even though she loved him beyond measure. She must muster up the courage to send him away. She could never trust him. Hadn't he deceived her from the beginning? But God, it was so difficult to think she would never be held by him again. Putting her forehead down on the ground, she cried herself out.

Fortunately, no one came up to the cemetery that cold, blustery afternoon to witness her tears and self-doubt. She had the time to come to grips with this impossible decision. She had to do it correctly, she determined, or Liam would see right through her. She would simply say that she had changed her mind. She would never tell him about the baby. He would not leave if he knew, and it would be his hold on her. Tonight, she needed to be strong. Finally, she picked herself up from the grave. She would always remember her time up there and even bring flowers to that lonely grave many times afterward. Now, however, she wished she too were dead.

* * * * * * * * * *

And then it was evening, and Liam was there, standing in the doorway with lush red roses in his arms and a warm smile on his face.

"Good evening, my angel. I have looked forward to seeing you all day." He leaned across the flowers and gave her a peck on her cheek. "Why don't you put these petals in a vase, so I can kiss you properly?"

Susanne took the flowers and walked to the back room. Liam followed her. She did not reach for a vase but laid the flowers on the counter instead. As she turned around, he asked,

"Did you forget our rendezvous? You aren't dressed for dinner."

"Thank you for the lovely roses, Liam. Let's sit for a minute and talk."

"Do you mind if I fix myself a whiskey?" he asked as he strode over to the cabinet. She didn't reply, and he poured himself a stiff drink. He did not offer Susanne a glass because he knew she drank only wine and that only sometimes with dinner. She kept no wine at the studio.

"I made dinner reservations. Is there a reason you aren't ready?"

"Yes, Liam. I have decided not to have dinner with you, and I wanted to tell you why in person. Hear me out, please."

Liam sat forward in the chair and looked at her intently. He had a sudden premonition but shook it off.

Susanne smiled at him, but her words were less than friendly. "I have been thinking about us, and I have decided that I would be happier if there were no 'US.' Because you are rarely here, I find that my feelings for you have changed. I have fallen out of love with you, and I want us to go our separate ways."

Liam stood up abruptly from his seat and reached out to pull her up also. He wanted to hold her and kiss her to prevent her from saying another word. What could possibly have come over her?

Susanne avoided his embrace and remained seated. Liam sat down again before he spoke.

"I'm sorry, my angel. I wanted to wait for dinner to talk with you. I had hoped for candles and atmosphere, but now seems like the right time." He stood up again. "I have given up gambling and life on the circuit because I want us to be together. I can't live another day away from you."

"No, Liam, you don't understand. . . ," Susanne started, but before she could finish her sentence, Liam was down on one knee. He held a jewelry box in his hand. Her thoughts went quickly to Nick who had been in this same room in this same position not long before. She wished he were here with her now because she suddenly felt frightened.

"Susanne, please, not another word! Listen instead. I have come to tell you that I love you above all else, and I am asking you to marry me. I promise to make you happy."

"Liam, please get up! My feelings for you have changed. I do not love you, and I do not want to marry you."

Liam was appalled. He had expected her to readily say yes to his proposal. "You can't mean that! We love each other."

"No, Liam. Not anymore. Frankly, I can't see you as a married man living here in Bodie."

"Oh, my angel! We don't have to stay here. I was thinking I would take you to New York where we could live splendidly with museums and the theater right at our fingertips." Liam opened the box and took out a gold ring with several large diamonds and rubies.

Susanne was extremely disturbed now. She had intended to say her piece and send him away, but he was not going, and he certainly was not listening to her. He had a ring in his hand and was presenting it to her, probably expecting her to swoon at her good fortune. She stood up now and shook her head, rejecting the ring. "No, Liam. I insist that you listen to me. I do not want to marry you.

I do not want to move to New York. Please leave and do not come here again."

Liam was not prepared for her reaction. "Are you rejecting me or are you rejecting the idea of moving to New York? Bodie is a small town without much to offer. Surely, you don't intend to stay here forever?"

"Yes, I love it here in Bodie, and I intend to stay. I have my work here, so I couldn't possibly leave even if I wanted to."

"Surely, you can give up that photo project. You can find a new project in New York, or you can do no work at all. I thought we would find a place near Central Park. On Fifth Avenue, perhaps. You would like the park."

"Stop it! You haven't heard a word I said. I want out of our relationship."

"What if I don't want out?"

"It's my decision. You must accept it."

"No, by God, I will never accept it! You know I love you. Why won't you marry me and come away with me?"

"I want more out of life than a husband who is gone all the time. As a gambler, you were seldom here. I don't know what you plan to do in New York, but I believe you would be buried in your work there, as well. I do not want that kind of life."

"But we would have wealth beyond compare. You could have any kind of life there you chose."

Susanne shook her head. She was becoming weary. "The answer is no. I want you to leave now."

Liam came over and stood in front of her, "What about the baby?" he asked.

"Baby?"

Liam smiled at her, but there was no warmth in his eyes. "Don't play coy with me, Susanne. I know you are carrying my baby."

"How could you possibly know?"

Liam would not betray his buddy, Doc. "Trust me. I know."

"I still refuse your proposal." Susanne looked up at him. "I insist that you leave."

"No, I won't go. I love you and plan to marry you."

"No, we will not be getting married."

Liam grabbed her by her shoulders and shook her. "Stop it, Susanne. You can't have a baby without a husband. People will think you are a hussy."

"I am a hussy," she replied, looking him squarely in the eye.

The irony was not lost on Susanne. Tess had a bad reputation as a hussy, but she had never gone upstairs with a man. Susanne, who had gone upstairs many times with Liam, was still considered pure. She almost smiled.

Liam knew he shouldn't have handled Susanne so roughly, and he tried a softer tactic now. "Sweetheart, I can't leave you here alone to have this baby. You need me. You must marry me, so I can take care of you."

"No."

"You can't keep me from my child," he said coldly.

Susanne was exasperated and wanted this ordeal to end. So, because she had no choice, she played her trump card. "The baby is not yours, Liam. I didn't want to have to tell you, but it is not yours."

"Of course, it is mine," Liam roared. "Whose baby is it if not mine?"

"That is none of your business, frankly. You didn't expect me to remain faithful to you when you were away most of the time, did you?"

"I was faithful to you."

"Nonsense," Susanne replied, and she suddenly knew this to be true. "I want you to go now."

"I am not leaving until I know who the other man is. Tell me, damn it." Liam grabbed her arm.

Susanne shook herself free from his grasp. "All right, if you insist on the truth, I will tell you. The baby is Nick's." There, she had said it. She had been hoping not to have to lie.

"Nick Pratt? You have got to be kidding! You got yourself pregnant by that twit? Impossible! Even you have more sense than that." Liam shook his head in disbelief.

Susanne looked at him, thoroughly frightened, and before he could grab her again, she slipped out of the back room and out the front door to safety. This proposal was over.

CHAPTER 36

Susanne ran to the Manor, looking over her shoulder to ensure that Liam was not coming after her. She burst in the front door, winded and crying. She was badly shaken. Nick grabbed her before she could collapse and held her. He knew things had ended badly and was impatient with himself for not insisting he be with her when she met with Liam.

Mary Kay shooed the children out of the room, telling them to go play in their rooms. Susanne sat down on Mary Kay's rocking chair and tried to catch her breath. Jodie came back into the room, and no one told him to leave. He went over and sat on the floor next to Susanne's chair.

"Did Dad hurt you?" he whispered.

"No, but he grabbed me, preventing my leaving. He was hostile, and I was afraid."

"Did he propose?" Nick asked.

"Yes. He had a ring and got down on one knee. He told me we should marry and leave Bodie. He thought New York would be just the change we needed. I told him no, that I did not want to marry him. I wanted to complete my photo-journal project." Susanne stood up and began to walk around the room. "Liam became impatient and refused to listen. It was as though he had an agenda and would stick to it. Things got bad, and I slipped out before he could grab me again. I ran here to safety."

"You left him there?"

"Yes, in the back room. I am scared to return there because he might corner me. He was not going to take 'No,' for an answer and was angry when I wouldn't agree to his proposal."

Nick spoke up, "He needs your money, Susanne. If you don't marry him, he can't get his hands on it."

Jodie agreed, "Dad was excited about the investment. That's mostly all he talked about this morning."

Susanne began to cry again. "I certainly am a poor judge of character."

'No, it was not your fault. He certainly is charming, and I can see how you misjudged."

Mary Kay spoke up now. "Well, you can't go back there tonight, and it is certainly not safe to sleep there ever. You must stay here with us, but let me think for a minute. I have to rearrange bedrooms."

"Why don't I move to the studio?" Nick offered. "Susanne can have my room."

"No, Nick," Thornton spoke up. "Better that you are here in case of trouble. Allow me to go. Susanne can have my room. I don't think Liam would mess with me if I ran into him there."

And so, it was settled. Susanne moved into the Manor. She continued to work on her photo project and even met clients in the studio, but she was never in the studio alone and never at night. She took many photos out on the streets and in peoples' homes and businesses, but she was never alone.

No one knew where Liam was. He had disappeared. Coosie went to the livery stable and found that he had taken his horse. Nick talked with the hotel clerk and then told the others that Liam had checked out of there as well. Nick was worried, however. He did not expect Liam to give up so easily. Thornton reported that when he had gone to the studio that night, he found roses strewn on the floor and saw that a whiskey glass had shattered on the wall— A show of temper from an unhappy man.

All of the Manor men were determined to keep Susanne safe. They had no idea what Liam might do next. Force would get him nowhere; he couldn't make Susanne marry him. He did seem intent on her money though. He needed that, and time was a factor. Wiley thought perhaps Liam had found the investment money elsewhere and had moved on, but then he dismissed the idea as too convenient. In his experience, he didn't believe in either coincidence or convenience. Happy endings were saved for fairy tales.

Everyone was concerned about Jodie's safety as well. Would Liam use him to get to Susanne? Or as revenge? As far as they knew, Liam still thought his wife was alive. Just to get Jodie away from his new family, Liam might come for Jodie, telling him he was taking him home to see his mother. He would expect Jodie to jump at the chance. So, Nick told Jodie to be on high alert and not to go off anywhere by himself. If he saw his dad, he was to quietly run in the opposite direction and hide. Jodie often fingered the ten-dollar gold piece he kept in his pocket. Nick had not meant to frighten him by giving it to him, but Jodie now worried he might need it someday, and he was always touching it for reassurance.

Two weeks went by with no word of Liam. It was worrisome not knowing where he was, and his absence hung about in a threatening manner. The autumn days were brisk and considerably shorter. Night came early, and it was cold out there on the high plain. Bodie residents, who had only recently sweated in the hot sun, now donned fleece-lined jackets and knew they had to get their winter gear out soon. Old timers were predicting a bad winter "full of weather." Yes, life was unsettled this October.

But life went on, and there was much to look forward to. One had a wedding to plan. Tess insisted that it be a low-key event. She wanted to marry Nick without a lot of the spotlight on her. No drama, she insisted. Bodie had no church, so the ceremony was to be at the Manor with Father Cassin presiding. Since Tess was marrying a non-Catholic, she would not have been permitted a church wedding even if Bodie had possessed a church. The Church frowned on its members marrying outsiders.

Queen Victoria had popularized the white wedding dress when she married her beloved Albert. Tess, however, refused to marry in white even though it was now the fashion. White symbolized purity, a quality Tess knew she did not deserve. Instead, she was making her own wedding dress from a forest green taffeta material that Mary Kay and Susanne had bought for her. The dress would be lovely but also practical, and Tess would be able to wear it on other dressy occasions.

Mary Kay saw that Nick's suit was cleaned and pressed, and she ordered flowers for Tess and the bridal party. Mary Kay, of course, was going to make the wedding cake— chocolate with butter cream frosting, which was Nick's favorite. He groused that this was the only decision he was allowed to make, as the women virtually asked him nothing. He pretended to be frustrated that no one sought his advice.

"I could be of great help to you ladies. I know quite a lot about weddings," he told them.

"Nonsense, you know nothing," Mary Kay said. " You have been a groomsman in four weddings, but that doesn't count because you did nothing but stand around awkwardly with your hands in your pockets. I was there. I remember. In fact, one of those weddings was my own. No, we don't need you."

"Tess needs me. Don't you, sweetheart?"

"No, Nick. Mary Kay is right. This is a job for women. Your only job is to show up at the appointed hour. I certainly hope you are not going to be gawky and awkward though. You will remember to keep your hands out of your pockets, won't you?" Tess teased him. "I will see you on October 19," she added sweetly.

Mary Kay looked on approvingly. She had found an ally.

So, Nick took the ladies at their word and spent his time working and drinking beer with his buddies. Half the town heard about his upcoming wedding when he went into Wagner's and loudly proclaimed, "I'm getting married; drinks are on me!" This announced to all that Nick was buying! His friends and acquaintances wished him well. They all drank to his good health, and he drank with them.

The wedding was to be five weeks before Thanksgiving and seven weeks before Jodie's twelfth birthday. Christmas would then be right around the corner, a big day in a house with four children. So, no one knew where Liam was, but life went on, and everyone was busy.

Nick owned the house next door to the Manor. He had bought adjoining lots and had built large homes on both. Recently, he had given his renters notice and was preparing to clean the house and move his new family in. Tess was thrilled to be getting her own home at last. Jodie and Annabelle would move next door with them when Nick and Tess returned from their honeymoon.

After Nick told Mary Kay that he would be moving out with Tess and the children, Mary Kay consulted Tess about an idea she had. She then called a family meeting, boarders included.

"I called this meeting to say that I can't imagine having nightly dinners without Nick and his family here with us," Mary Kay began. "Nick, it would be strange not having you here interrupting me whenever I speak and always asking for more gravy and just one more biscuit."

"And more dessert," Nessie piped up. "Uncle Nick likes dessert."

Everyone laughed. "You're right, Nessie. Uncle Nick does like his dessert," Mary Kay agreed. "So, I propose that nightly dinners should continue as usual here at the Manor with all of us present. Instead of cooking in her own kitchen next door, Tess would cook here with me."

Tess nodded. "Yes, I would like that."

Mary Kay continued, "Thank you, Tess. And Nick, as a concession, I am even willing to put up with the geography challenge nonsense you and Jodie like to play. What do you say? Will you come to dinner?"

Nick looked at Tess who nodded again. "Yeah, Yeah, you bet! You couldn't keep us away."

The three boarders spoke up then, saying what a fine idea it was. The children cheered. All present agreed that dinners were necessary because as extended family, it was important they spend time together. Dinner time at the Manor was special, and they all relished the camaraderie. Yes, the children would continue with their Thursday facts, and the card games would also go on. Nothing would change except for the presence of new, cherished, and very loved family members. And Lex! Nick told Mary Kay that he hoped Lex would also be included. Mary Kay nodded and blushed.

When Nick and family moved next door, Thornton would move back to the Manor to his old room. Susanne would move into Nick's room, and her baby would be born there. Susanne was expecting the baby early in February. So, even though no one knew where Liam had gone, they carried on despite him, but always on the lookout.

* * * * * * * * * *

Nick was in his shop building a new, oak dining-room table, and Jodie was helping him. The old, rectangular table was now being replaced by a large, round table that would comfortably seat twelve. Jodie joked now.

"King Arthur wanted everyone to be equal. That's why his table was round. However, I can't see you wanting to be equal with others."

"Well, you are correct about that. I am certainly not equal with you because you are an illiterate." Nick smiled. "It is a damn good thing I am keeping this old table though, so I can sit at it and remind myself that I am the head of this family. You often forget my importance here."

Jodie rolled his eyes. The old table would go into the dining room of the Nick's new residence, "The Annex," as the family was already calling it.

"The old table will suit us for a while. It seats ten, and we already have a family of four." Nick shook his head in disbelief. Just last month, he was a family of one. Things changed so quickly.

"After Tess and I have our first four children, I will have to build yet another table. You won't always be home because of college, but we will always have a place set at the table for you."

Home! What a sweet sound it made! It didn't matter whether home was at the Manor or next door at the Annex. Home would be wherever Nick and Tess were. Now Jodie had a family, a large extended family. It was comprised mostly of men and women who were of no blood relation to him, but a family by choice. Even

Coosie, a Negro, was part of this family, and Jodie couldn't be prouder than to consider Coosie both his family and his friend. Jodie had come a long way in his thinking.

Jodie had also given some thought to Nick's philosophy on church attendance. Even though Jodie would always attend Mass, he knew Nick was right. Being a good person meant more than sitting in a pew on Sundays. It meant helping the less fortunate on the other days of the week, and treating others kindly every day. It also meant respecting women and not thinking of them as second-class citizens. Jodie now believed that Mary Kay and all women deserved the right to vote. Because men denied this to them, it showed men's insecurity. Men were afraid of losing power. They were afraid to share and be found wanting.

It wasn't only women who were treated unfairly. Since knowing Coosie, Jodie realized that minorities everywhere were mistreated. Negroes, Chinese, and Indians had few rights. White men were not about to share power with them either. Even the Mexicans had been tromped on and their land taken away. It seemed that treaties were made only to be broken.

Nick talked often of the children going to college. Jodie had no idea what he would study when he got there. It was still a long time away. However, Jodie knew he wanted to help the less fortunate. He read the newspapers daily and kept up with the Indian problem, as it was called. Jodie knew the Indians needed help now before all their bison were slaughtered and their lands confiscated. He was frustrated because he knew he wouldn't grow up in time to help them.

In the meantime, he would take Annabelle and Nessie under his wing and teach them things. They also would be expected to attend college, so each could live up to her potential. Then they could go on and help other women. Mary Kay was an advocate of strong women enabling other strong women.

Jodie followed Mary Kay's lead in hoping that one day women would not only vote but would serve in Congress, helping to make the laws. The House of Representatives had nearly 300 members. The Senate had seventy-six. Surely, some of these Congress members should be women. If Mary Kay were an example of an enlightened woman, then women should have a say in their own lives and that of their country.

Jodie's new way of thinking had begun with Nick who had told him that very first evening:

"Don't be the man whom women fear. Instead, help women."

Jodie did not know how Nick had gotten so smart. He had never been to college, but he was worldly wise. Jodie suspected that Nick had gotten some of his wisdom from his brother Ed. Jodie wished he had known Ed. He was sorry that next week when Nick married Tess, Ed would not be there to stand up for him as his Best Man. Jodie would not be the Best Man either because he was too young. Instead, Nick had asked Coosie to stand up for him. Jodie wasn't surprised because he knew Nick and Coosie had a strong bond. It looked as though Lex would someday be part of the family; he and Mary Kay were courting properly now, but Lex understood Nick's choice and had no expectations.

So, Nick was busy building a table and twelve chairs to match. He had other jobs he had committed to as well, so he spent long days in his shop. Tristan and Jodie attended school but helped him when they could. Nick knew that his only other job was to show up at the wedding on time. He was not to stand around awkwardly with his hands in his pockets. He could do that! He would marry Tess in style.

CHAPTER 37

"Miracle of Miracles!" was Earl Pratt's response when he received the telegram from his youngest son telling his parents of his engagement. Upon reading the telegram for herself, Nick's mother, Rose, sat down at the piano and with gusto played Beethoven's "Ode to Joy." Neither Earl nor Rose had thought that Nick would ever get married, so his announcement was met with great enthusiasm. *Who could this woman be?* They wondered. Who could capture their son who until now had had no sense of urgency concerning matrimony? Nick's telegram gave no details. He just wrote that he was engaged. So, Rose did what women always do when they want facts— she asked another woman. It took a couple of weeks for Rose's letter of inquiry and Mary Kay's letter of response to reach appropriate postal boxes.

Although Mary Kay found her mother-in-law exasperating at times, she and Rose had remained close after Ed's death. So, Mary Kay was happy to provide the information. She spoke in glowing terms of Tess and omitted any reference to Bonanza Street or a job in a brothel. Instead, she told Rose how well-suited Nick and Tess were. She described Tess as a beautiful person, both inside and out. She talked also of Jodie, Tess's nephew, and explained that Nick and Tess would raise him as their own along with Annabelle, Tess's daughter. Mary Kay told Rose she looked forward to seeing her at the wedding and gave her the date. Tristan and Nessie would also look forward to a visit from their grandparents, she told her. Rose wrote back to Mary Kay, thanking her for her informative letter and saying that yes, they would be coming, and as a bonus, Mary Kay's parents would be accompanying them. Mary Kay was delighted, and the children would be thrilled to see both sets of grandparents.

Rose then wrote to Nick and told him how happy she and his dad were for him. Tess sounded like the perfect match, but Rose certainly hoped Tess was not divorced. She asked Nick to please assure her that he was not marrying a divorcee. Where was Annabelle's father? Rose went on to say that while bringing two children into the marriage was a bonus, she did hope that one day Nick would consider having children of his own— to help carry on the Pratt name, she said. Nick shook his head. He had three older brothers and seven nephews, so the Pratt name was not in jeopardy. It was his mother giving him her two cents, butting into his business. As usual! Rose obviously did not know Nick's plan for an even dozen. She and Earl already had several grandchildren, but she said they always had room in their hearts for more. She asked Nick to reserve rooms at the hotel for them and for Mary Kay's parents. Good friends all, they could hardly wait to kiss the bride.

Nick reserved the rooms and three more for the Doten Family and other Virginia City friends. It was proving to be a larger wedding than they'd first planned.

Tess expected no out-of-town guests. Her parents were in Montana and too elderly to travel such a distance. She told Nick she had all the family she needed right there at the Manor. However, she did plan to invite two guests. One was Sophie, and Nick readily agreed. He knew the two women were close friends. He also was not surprised by Tess's other guest. She wanted to invite Rex, a miner from North Dakota whom she had known for three years. He was such a staple at Sophie's that he went for ice when they ran out, and he often emptied the trash when needed. He did odd jobs around the place to keep it running smoothly. The ladies who worked there relied on him to put up a shelf or to fix an appliance. Nick knew Rex from Wagner's but not well. Nick never went to Sophie's.

Tess and Rex were friends. He knew her story. Three years before, Tess had confided in him that she had lost contact with her sister, Jeannie, and was at her wit's end trying to locate her. She told Rex that her letters were always returned, marked "Not at this address." Shortly after, Rex did not show up at the brothel for several days, and Sophie told the girls he was away on business. Without a word to anyone except Sophie and his boss, he had hired a horse and set out for Southern California. He went first to the small mining town of Julian and asked for Drue Bailey. Drue explained that Billy Burke and his family had been there but had moved on to San Diego. He believed Billy was tending bar somewhere there. Yes, he had had a wife and young son with him.

Perhaps Rex was lucky. Perhaps his timing was right, but within a week he had located Jeannie's husband. Now to find her! He found Billy tending bar in a shabby saloon. Rex nursed a couple of beers and watched Billy as he interacted with the customers. One petite blonde must have been a very good customer because Billy had his hands all over her. Rex did not like Billy, but he had not expected to from Tess's stories of him in Butte. After observing Billy, Rex decided he couldn't trust him to give his wife Tess's address. So, after Billy locked the bar, Rex followed him the six blocks to his house. Billy was drunk and did not notice Rex.

The next evening, Rex poked his head in the saloon door just long enough to ensure that Billy was working. Then he retraced his steps to the house he had seen Billy enter the night before. He knocked, and when Jeannie opened the door, he introduced himself.

"My name is Rex Lancaster. I am hoping you are Jeannie Burke?"

Jeannie nodded. "Yes. I am she. How may I help you?"

"I have a message from your sister Tess."

Jeannie felt weak in the knees. She had given up hope of ever hearing from her sister again. Her parents had not heard from Tess either.

"Please come in," she said and opened the door wider. A young boy sat on the sofa with a book. He looked at the visitor curiously; they rarely had guests. Jeannie introduced him to Mr. Lancaster.

Rex told Jeannie that Tess was living in Bodie and had sent many letters to her in various places but with no luck. He handed Jeannie a paper with Tess's address on it. "Now you know where she is."

Jeannie remembered her manners. "Thank you, Mr. Lancaster. Let me pour you some lemonade. Sit down please, and make yourself at home. If you don't mind waiting a few minutes, I would like to write a quick note to Tess. Is that convenient for you?"

"I may be overstepping here, Mrs. Burke, but I thought perhaps I could take you and your son to Bodie. I have arranged for a carriage, and we could leave tonight. It would mean the world to Tess if you two came." Rex didn't say that getting her away from her two-timing husband was his first priority. He didn't say he had watched enough of Billy's antics in the saloon to realize what an immoral man he was. Nor did he did tell her that Tess worked in a brothel. Rex was reserved, a man of few words. However, he was a man of action. First, he would get Jeannie out of San Diego, and then he would figure out living arrangements for her and her boy in Bodie. Getting her away from her husband and into the arms of her sister seemed like the right thing to do.

Jeannie put down the lemonade pitcher and looked at this man who was offering her a way out of her lonely marriage. How could he possibly know how unhappy she was? But he knew! Otherwise, why would he offer her this way out?

"No," she whispered, "I can't. Jodie needs his father. We can't leave, but I thank you kindly for your offer of help. Please, give me a minute to write the note to Tess."

Rex acknowledged her request with a nod, and he and Jodie played a game of checkers while Jeannie wrote the note. Jeannie often looked back on that night and regretted her decision to stay. Things might have turned out differently for her had she gone.

In her excitement at finding her sister, Jeannie made the mistake of telling her husband about Rex's visit. Billy did not understand how a stranger just happened to knock on the door of his home to give his wife an address. It had been years since the sisters had been in contact, and Billy wanted to keep it that way. "Who is this man?" he demanded.

Jeannie did not know, just a man with a message. No, of course she had not known him before. He was a stranger. Billy slapped her anyway. And then he slapped her again and warned her to never again invite a stranger into his home. Her sister was a busybody, and they didn't need her in their lives. Forget about her! Jeannie memorized the address and tore up the paper. Billy had been drinking and forgot about the incident. Jeannie picked up Tess's letters at the post office, and Billy was none the wiser.

Rex returned to Bodie with Jeannie's letter in hand. Tess was speechless when he handed the letter to her but so grateful to this kind man who had gone out of his way for her. So now, of course, she wanted him at her wedding. Nick had a suggestion for Tess:

"It's traditional for a fatherly figure to give away the bride. Perhaps Rex is the ideal one to walk you down the aisle. What do you think?"

Tess nodded. "Oh yes. I would like that," she said as she wiped a tear from her eye. Nick was so accepting of her and her friends. He never stopped surprising her.

* * * * * * * * *

Although Nick was busy, he spent some time researching a certain college in Iowa, and then without a word to anyone, he sent the college a sizable cashier's check. He smiled to himself as he thought, *"The check is in the mail. Won't Mary Kay be surprised?"* In June, Standard Mine stock had gone from fifty cents a share to fifty dollars a share almost overnight, and Nick had made quite a large sum of money. He was superstitious about bragging about his windfall, so he banked the money and said nothing. Now he was giving it away, and he felt good about his decision. Jodie would be pleased.

When he wasn't acting the philanthropist, Nick worked in his shop. Besides a new dining room table and chairs for Mary Kay, he wanted to make a wedding gift for Tess, something special from his heart. After much thought, he decided upon a rocking chair with a footstool to match. He studied the available wood and chose a rich walnut. He visited the tin shop and ordered an engraved plaque that he would screw onto the back of the chair. Tess had orders to stay away from the shop.

"Big things going on down there," he told her. "No engaged women allowed." Then he would kiss the tip of her nose and smile at her. He hoped that someday soon Tess would rock a baby in the chair— the first baby of many. Nick Pratt was a happy man with much to look forward to.

Tess had tried to get a job soon after she moved into the Manor. She wanted to pull her weight and be dependent on neither Nick nor Mary Kay. She had changed her mind about being a seamstress. After mulling it over, she wondered why she would sew when she knew bookkeeping. After all, she did have a degree in accounting. So, she went to several businesses downtown and applied for book-keeping jobs. Each time, she was told no, she need not apply. One hotel owner brusquely told her to go home.

"I would never hire a woman to do a man's job. What are you thinking? — trying to steal a job from a man? Men are the breadwinners of the family. Decent women should stay at home. Go along now."

Other business owners asked her if she had experience. She couldn't tell them she had kept the books for a successful brothel for years. When she told Mary Kay she couldn't get a job in a man's world, Mary Kay suggested that perhaps Sophie would hire her. Sophie still needed to have her bookkeeping done and maybe she had not hired anyone to replace Tess.

Tess was amused. "Are you suggesting I go back to Bonanza Street? I just escaped from there, and as you know, proper ladies do not frequent such a place. I am trying to be proper."

"You're right. You can't go back there," Mary Kay said. "So, let's invite Sophie to meet us for lunch at the hotel. You can ask her then."

The three ladies had a pleasant lunch together talking and laughing. Sophie was delightful company and told witty stories. When asked, Sophie said she would be happy to hire Tess as her bookkeeper. Sophie had been keeping the books herself, and she found the process extremely tedious.

"BORING," she exclaimed, throwing her hands up in the air. "My skills are best suited elsewhere, if you get my meaning!" She smiled mischievously. "I have hated every minute of bookkeeping since you deserted me." She put her hand on Tess's arm and smiled at her.

"Yes, I said that out loud," she said. "Deserted me! But I can't blame you. That fiancé of yours is very good looking. And sexy! So, I can't blame you for deserting me." She winked at Tess who was very much like a daughter to her. "Just so you know, I had never seen your beau before you introduced him to me last week. Too bad too! He's a looker!"

Then she sat up straight and got into business mode. "What if I ask Rex to pick up and deliver all the paperwork involved? He could go to the boarding house once a week, and you would not have to come down to Bonanza Street." And so, Tess got herself a job.

Mary Kay found a small desk and had it put in a corner of the library, and she bought a ledger for Tess. Soon, more ledgers were needed as Sophie's friends offered her bookkeeping jobs from other "establishments." It seems that the Ladies stuck together and helped each other out. Tess had become self-sufficient.

* * * * * * * * * *

But no sign of Liam! Wiley had been correct in thinking Liam had gone in search of other funding. Liam had walked out of Susanne's studio that night outraged that Susanne had been with another man. How dare she? Women were supposed to stay home and wait for their men to return— put a light in the window and wait! The irony was lost on him that he had been unfaithful to Susanne every time he left town, and yet he was incensed that she would welcome another man into her bed. And that man was Nick Pratt! That do-gooder!

What happened to platonic friendship, for God's sake? Susanne had made a fool of him. Liam's mood changed between anger and self-pity. Anger that she had played him for a fool. Self-pity because he loved her, and he still needed her money. And to think, of all the eligible men in town, she had turned to Nick Pratt! Unbelievable!

As he traveled toward San Francisco, the financial capital of the west coast, Liam had a nagging thought. What if Susanne were lying to him about the baby? What if it were indeed his baby? The timing was right for it to be his. If the baby were due in February, as Del had told him, then he knew he had been with Susanne nine months earlier, in May. He had spent a week with her then. If she had been interested in Nick back then, surely she would have broken it off with Liam. Intuitively, he was convinced the baby was his. So, why would Susanne lie? Liam could claim the baby, but with no proof, a judge would not listen to him. Liam did not want the baby anyway. To hell with the baby! But he wanted Susanne, and he needed her. Damn Susanne! Damn Women! He hated it that women had all the power.

But still he mused. Why would Susanne break off with him now? Could she have known he was marrying her for her money? Had he said too much to Jodie that morning about his investment opportunity? Had Jodie told Susanne, and she'd figured it out? Had Susanne realized that Liam was leading a double life? Liam was filled with "What ifs." He had no answers but instinctively knew Jodie was involved in this somehow.

Unable to secure financial backing from Crockett in San Francisco, Liam had no recourse but to return to Bodie and try Susanne again. Time was running out. Liam had pledged the money and needed to secure it. Maybe Susanne had had a change of heart. She had told him more than once that she loved him, so maybe she had changed her mind. He did regret grabbing her the evening of the proposal because he had frightened her. He would have to be more careful. Never before had he let his emotions interfere with business. He needed to pull himself together.

He arrived in Bodie to find the hotel almost completely booked. Many guests were there to attend a wedding. When Liam discovered that the groom was to be Nick Pratt, he almost lost his self- control. What the hell! Nick was stealing both his girl and his baby. He would not allow Susanne to marry this loser. He walked over to Del's house to think things through and find out what Del knew. Liam realized he had to get his anger under control.

CHAPTER 38

The stars were out of alignment the day Nick planned to marry Tess. They had been unaligned for several days, but no one knew, at least no one at the Manor. There, they worked tirelessly, so Tess and Nick could have the wedding of their dreams. To be accurate, this was not the wedding of Nick's dreams. He had never been a dreamer; he was much too practical to spend his time dreaming. He knew that social events ran smoothly because of organization and hard work. He had only recently learned another great truth: Men might rule the world, but women took charge of matrimonial affairs.

So, Nick cut, sanded, nailed, and polished wood instead. An elegant table with matching chairs emerged for Mary Kay. A rocking chair was completed for Tess. Nick was pleased with both projects; both were works of love. Nick carefully screwed the tin plaque on the chair back. It simply read, "Deeg."

Tess also had not expected a dream wedding. After Connor deserted her, Tess had given up on any dream of marriage. Weddings were for women who remained chaste and deserved to walk down the aisle in a white dress. Tess had no dreams of a "Happily Ever After." Instead, she had worked every day to ensure that her child had a home and nourishing meals, even if these were provided under the roof of a brothel. She had given up the idea of marriage with a decent man like Nick, so she pinched herself because she knew she did not deserve such happiness.

Tess smiled as she looked at Rex, her good friend. She did not deserve his friendship either but knew that God must have one day said to Himself,

"I can't take everything from Tess. I do not intend to break her completely— just tax her enough to make her strong and to build up her character. So, I will add people into her life, but slowly this time."

Tess now felt she understood God and His decisions for her. She had come a long way since she had gone down the wrong path with Darcy. What hubris she had had— throwing her morals away and turning her back on decency and the values her parents had tried to instill in her! She had fallen far from grace, but with God's help, she had picked herself up.

She sighed as she looked at Rex again. He had graciously accepted her request to walk her down the aisle. He would be honored he had told her. He had then gone to the tailor and had a suit made just for this occasion. He sat in his new clothes now at the table in the Manor and waited for the ladies to get ready. He could hear them upstairs. He never understood why women talked so much. They always reminded him of nervous chickens in the coop, but he had a soft spot for them anyway.

The ladies came downstairs, and Rex thought Tess looked beautiful in a forest green dress. Mary Kay and Susanne also wore green but each in a different, lighter shade. He briefly wondered about the seamstress who had made such lovely clothes. Rex's mother had been a dressmaker many years before in remote Grand Forks, North Dakota. Rex had grown up amid buttons, bobbins, and bolts of material. Of all the men in attendance this day, he alone understood that sewing might be women's work, but it was also an exact science. Mathematical skills were involved, and precise measuring was essential. Rex remembered his mother sewing by candlelight far into the night. Hers had been their only source of income, because like many families, his dad was long gone. Nick would have understood Rex's mathematical theories about sewing had he ever given sewing a thought. He had not.

Rex was not the only one thinking of home, old times, and lost families. Tess was naturally reticent, but today, on her wedding day, she was quieter than usual. She too was thinking of her parents and ached for them today. It should have been her mother clasping the pearls around her neck. Her sister should have been there handing her the bouquet. And her dad should be waiting to walk her down the aisle. How happy that would have made him! He had performed this ritual once before when he escorted Jeannie down the church aisle to Billy. Tess wondered what her dad's thoughts must have been that day because he had disliked Billy. He must have felt uneasy giving his daughter away to a man he disdained, but Jeannie had insisted on marrying this shiftless Southerner. She loved him; she told her parents. She told them that she had done everything they had ever asked of her, and now she was of the age to make her own decisions. She was correct. She was of age and could make her own choices, even if they were wrong. Her dad knew he could not stop her, could only warn her. Nor could he stop Billy four years later from taking her and Jodie away. Things had turned out pretty much the way her dad had expected they would.

Tess wished with all her heart that her dad were with her today to give her away to Nick, a man he would have approved of and liked. Tess closed her eyes and forced herself now to think of other things. She could not be morose on her wedding day! Today she would not dwell on her old family but would concentrate on her new one.

She smiled when she recalled Mary Kay's reaction to Rex's acceptance. Mary Kay's mind often went places that Tess's mind would never consider. *I am a mundane thinker*, she realized. *Mary Kay thinks differently. Her thinking is on a higher level than mine.*

"What do you mean Rex is going to give you away?" Mary Kay had demanded. "You aren't chattel to be given from one man to another. From a father to a husband. These are not the Dark Ages. I am happy that Rex will walk you down the aisle, but he can't give you away. You are not his to give."

Tess had listened in wonder to Mary Kay. She was right, of course. Women were not property to be traded. Until she met Mary Kay, Tess had not given a thought to the way women were treated. Mary Kay was consistent in her view that women were greatly mistreated. They were not allowed to make serious decisions. They held no high offices, nor could they vote. Even their opinions were dismissed as trivial. Women deserved to be treated better than that. Certainly, they were men's equals.

Mary Kay often reprimanded Nick for his misogynistic views, but Tess knew that Nick, in his heart, did not disparage women. He liked and respected them. He just liked to get Mary Kay's goat was all. It was a game the two played. He also played games of one-upmanship with Jodie. For his own amusement, he said. Nick did not play mind games with Tess, although he did like to tease her. Nick was the kindest man she knew. In just a few minutes now, she would marry him, have children with him, and live out her life with him. "Thank You, God!" she whispered.

* * * * * * * * * *

Outside, in the yard, Nick was also whispering, "Thank You, God." He was well aware that he was fortunate to be marrying Tess, his soul mate, the love of his life. These were trite expressions, he knew, but he used them when thinking of Tess. They explained the way he felt about her. Over the years, he had courted a few women, but he had never felt the connection with any of them that he felt with Tess.

The yard had been transformed from a dry, dusty plot of land into an inviting wedding site. The Manor men had taken this on as their project. Thornton had built a trellis and had flowers woven in and out and overhead. He supplied a small Turkish carpet for the bridal couple to stand on. Wiley, Coosie, and Lex had bushes and trees brought in in large wooden tubs. They had borrowed benches from the Miner's Union Hall and had brought them to the Manor for the guests to sit on. They had planned to buy a long piece of white fabric for the bride to process in on, but Tess had said no— she wanted nothing to do with white, so they had discarded the idea. They were pleased at the changes they had made though. All was ready.

Two days earlier, Nick's parents, Earl and Rose; and Mary Kay's parents, Ben and Ellen, had arrived from Grass Valley. Rose and Ellen brought two matching yellow dresses for the flower girls. Nessie was excited to see her grandparents, and Annabelle was happy to meet them. She had never known a grandparent before and was elated to be introduced to relatives who already loved her. The grandparents swept the little girls up in hugs. Then they went looking for Tristan, so they could hug him too. Jodie hung back, not expecting an embrace, but he was hugged tightly too. Earl and Ben showed the boys the fishing rods they had brought them and offered to take them on a fishing trip the day after the wedding.

The girls had a major role in the wedding, but Tristan was not to be left out. This was his Uncle Nick's big day, after all. Neither he nor Jodie had expected to be part of the wedding party, so they were surprised and pleased when Nick took them to his tailor and had them fitted for suits.

"You two will always be my best men. I wouldn't consider getting married without you both standing up there with me. Lord knows I need you for moral support!" Both boys were happy to be included in this big event. Nick smiled to himself when he realized that cake choice was not the only decision he had been allowed to make. Controlling women indeed!

And then another change was made to the wedding party. Nick mentioned at dinner one evening that his brothers would be able to attend the wedding after all. They owned large almond and walnut orchards and only now had been able to find someone to cover for them. After dinner, Coosie took Nick aside.

"I am resigning as your Best Man. It was different when your brothers were unavailable. So, choose the brother you are closest to, and ask him." When Nick protested, Coosie added,

"No, Nick, I am right about this. Brothers trump friends. Family should always come first. If you had a friend stand up with you instead of a brother, there would be hard feelings, unspoken, but there under the surface. Your mother would be the first to be unhappy. So, although I am your biggest fan, I will not be your Best Man."

Nick acknowledged that Coosie was right, and he had then asked his brother Pete to stand up with him. Pete had readily accepted, and a family problem was averted.

Nick's family was here with him today. Family was important to the Pratts, and they would be nowhere else. All three of his brothers had come, and one had brought his wife and daughters. Both Nick's sisters had come.

It was Chloe, Nick's youngest sister, who had embroidered the quotations that hung on Nick's shop walls. When Jodie had asked Nick months earlier if Nick had stitched them, Nick had impulsively told him yes; it was his own work. Because Jodie had looked horrified at this disclosure, Nick had never told him differently. It amused him that Jodie considered him a wimp. Nick asked Chloe to keep his secret, and she had laughingly agreed.

His family was enchanted by the beautiful, poised woman who had won Nick's heart. Even his mother liked her. However, Rose still had a few questions about Tess's background. Nick refused to answer any of her queries and told her to drop it. He wondered why his mother could not be more like Mary Kay's mother. Ellen was like a second mother to him; he had practically grown up in her kitchen along with Mary Kay. Unlike Rose, Ellen was not judgmental, nor was she was passive aggressive. She was good natured and accepting, and Nick was happy that she and Ben were with him on this special day.

And so, the stage was set. Guests milled around chatting and trading compliments. Nick was unexpectedly nervous and did not know why. These were his people, his tribe, his friends. All were there to wish him well, raise a glass, and kiss the bride.

Nick was eager to get this show on the road. He had not seen Tess all day and he missed her, but tradition dictated that they could not see each other before the wedding. It was almost three o'clock, the appointed time. Father Cassin looked at his time piece and then directed Nick, Pete, Tristan, and Jodie to stand at the front, to the right of the trellis. Nick remembered to keep his hands out of his pockets, but by Jove, he was nervous! The guests took their seats and a hush fell over the crowd. Any minute now, the front door of the Manor would open, and Rex would escort Tess across the threshold and down the aisle to Nick. Nick leaned over and hugged both Tristan and Jodie. He shook hands with Pete. He adjusted the boutonniere on his jacket. Just as he was removing his hand from his pocket one last time, he caught sight of Liam standing at the back, behind the seated guests. Nick was momentarily confused. What was Liam doing here? Hadn't they been looking for him?

CHAPTER 39

Had the stars been aligned, no one would have gotten hurt that day. They were not aligned; however, and Del had not been home to tell Liam that yes, Nick Pratt was getting married, but he was not marrying Susanne. Instead, Del would have told him that Nick was marrying that prostitute who lived on Bonanza Street. Then Liam and Del would have had a good laugh and more whiskey. But Del hadn't been home to set Liam straight, so by the time Nick noticed Liam standing in the back, it was too late.

Before Nick could shout out a warning, Liam lifted a gun and fired it. The bullet caught Nick in the left shoulder and the impact forced him backward. He fell into the trellis and went down. Then Jodie saw his dad, and without thinking, he raced down the short aisle and tackled him, knocking the gun out of his hand. When Liam realized that his shot had failed to kill Nick, he grabbed Jodie and hurled him out of his way, trying to locate the gun. He couldn't find it, and in a temper now, he grabbed a shovel that someone had left leaning against the shed. He ran forward and whacked the shovel over Nick's head. Liam had it raised again to smash it down on Nick when Pete and Casey were on him, holding him back, and preventing him from doing more harm.

Coosie picked Jodie up and carried him into the house. He was badly bruised, and although his arm throbbed, it was not broken again. The wedding guests were shaken up but knew enough to stand back out of the way. Some were more vocal than others in their outrage.

Yes, there was a doctor in the house! John Wagner had brought his wife to the wedding. Doc Wagner dealt first with the gunshot wound. The bullet had gone clear through Nick's shoulder, which was good because no fragment remained to cause infection. Doc Wagner dressed the wound and instructed Mary Kay and Tess to change the bandage daily.

The problem was the traumatic head injury that Nick had sustained from the blow with the shovel. Had Liam been able to hit him twice, Nick would have died on the spot. Mary Kay's dad, Ben, immediately sent for a specialist who boarded the next train. Nick was unconscious and unresponsive and had been that way for two days when the specialist arrived. This doctor told the family it would be a waiting game. He could not guarantee that Nick would ever wake up, or if he did, that he would have normal brain activity. The doctor did not use the words, "brain damage," but everyone got the message. Nick's condition could be temporary and reversible, or it could be permanent. The doctor told Tess that if she had rosary beads, this would be a good time to get them out.

The doctor suggested that Nick's bed be moved downstairs to the main part of the house to make it easier on his caregivers. It might also benefit Nick to be near family whose activities might stimulate him. Research showed that many who came out of a coma reported hearing voices while they were unconscious.

On Tuesday, as the doctor was preparing equipment that would provide nourishment to his comatose patient, Nick gradually began to awaken. Little by little, Nick thrashed around and then finally opened his eyes. He was confused and did not know anyone at first. Gradually, that wore off and he recognized faces. He had a throbbing headache and was nauseous. The doctor called for more pillows to boost Nick up, as they could not afford for him to drown in his own vomit. Nick was sensitive to both light and noise, and those issues were resolved.

The wedding guests stayed on until they were assured that Nick was awake, but then they had to return home to family and jobs. All wanted to be kept informed of any changes in Nick's condition. Earl and Ben stayed on a few more days, but eventually they too had to get back home as they had businesses to run. They promised Tristan and Jodie they would take them fishing another time. Rose surprised everyone by announcing that she was not leaving. She needed to stay by her son's bedside, she explained. After a quick word with Ben, Ellen decided she too would stay on. She hoped she could be useful, and she promised to stay out of the way. Perhaps she could help with the correspondence, sending word on Nick's condition to the many friends who were waiting to hear. She and Rose would stay on at the hotel.

Liam had been moved to an undisclosed town where he sat in jail awaiting trial for attempted murder. His lawyer told him to pray that Nick did not die because then the charge would be increased to murder. Several witnesses had seen him attack Nick, so Liam Burke was clearly guilty. Bodie's town leaders worried that the local vigilante group would hang him before he could stand trial, so Bodie lawmen had quickly spirited him away. No one at the Manor knew where he had been moved, including Jodie.

The specialist told the family that although Nick was out of the coma, he would continue to sleep most of the time. "Sleep heals;" he told them. Before leaving town, he provided a supply of morphine for Nick's pain. "Morphine and sleep should do the trick," he advised. "Time heals," he reminded them. Doc Wagner would check on Nick daily.

Jodie wasn't saying much these days. He was injured physically but was also depressed. The doctor had not recast his arm but had told him to take it easy for a week. Jodie was anguished about Nick and wanted to cry every time he looked at him lying still on the bed near the stair case. Thornton and Wiley had brought the bed in and placed it away from the window. Nick's face was battered, and he had a black eye. His head was bandaged, as was his shoulder. Jodie hoped Nick would get better soon and had even talked to God about it, but there was no change. Nick's recovery would take a while.

Jodie was deeply ashamed that it was his father who had hurt Nick. Only his family at the Manor knew Jodie was Liam's son, and no one there blamed him for his dad's actions. Nick was a popular resident of Bodie, so Jodie suspected that many out on the streets were saying unkind things about Liam Burke. It did not matter what others were saying; however, because Jodie blamed himself for Nick's condition. Had he gone home months before— when his dad had wanted him to, none of this would have happened. It was all his fault. Coosie disagreed and explained that the quarrel between Nick and Liam had nothing to do with him.

"No, Jodie. The fight was not about you," Coosie told him. "It was about Susanne."

"What do you mean?" Jodie asked. "Nick and Susanne are just friends. Why would Dad be jealous of Nick?"

"I reckon it had to do with Susanne claiming that the baby was Nick's. Susanne told Liam that. Do you remember?"

Jodie nodded.

"Since your dad thought Nick was the father, he also thought the wedding was for Nick and Susanne. He didn't know anything about Tess, but he came to prevent Susanne from marrying Nick."

"Wow! Do you suppose Susanne feels bad that she asked Nick to claim the baby?"

"Probably. She hasn't said much, but it must be on her mind. I wouldn't mention it to her because she has enough to think about."

So, the fight had been over a woman! However, Jodie could not shake off the idea that he was also somehow to blame, and so he was riddled with guilt. He missed Nick. Normally, he would have talked all these problems over with him, and Nick would have given him his best advice. Nick was unable to help anyone now as he lay inertly on the bed, and Jodie blamed himself.

A string of visitors came to the Manor, one at a time. Saloon-owner John Wagner arrived one morning with hat in hand. He introduced himself to Mary Kay who opened the door for him. She had not met him at the wedding but had noticed him as his wife tended to Nick. Mary Kay now led him past Nick who was sleeping and past Rose who was dozing in the chair next to the bed. In the kitchen, Mary Kay poured him a cup of coffee and invited him to sit at the table.

"You know that Nick and I are friends," he began.

"I know you two spend every waking minute together, bless your hearts." Mary Kay grinned as she said this, and John laughed. Nick had told him she had a sense of humor.

"I do not want to offend you or your family in any way," John said now, "but I have come to offer my assistance."

Mary Kay looked at him. He continued.

"Financial assistance. Nick is not working now, and I thought I could lend a helping hand until he gets back on his feet."

"Thank you, Mr. Wagner, but we certainly could not take a loan from you."

"No, Mrs. Pratt. I am not speaking of a loan. I want to help you with your bills, free and clear. No loan. Nick does a lot to help this town, and frankly, I know he would be on my own doorstep now talking to my wife if the tables were turned. We are good friends. Please allow me to help." He handed her an envelope. "Tell Nick I will be back when he is up for a visit."

And because Mary Kay did not know how to say no without offending him, she accepted his gift. That evening, her mother told her she had done the right thing.

"It is always easier to give than to receive," Ellen said.

"Yes," Mary Kay acknowledged, "but I don't like taking charity."

"No, don't consider it charity. People instinctively want to do the right thing, and we must allow them to do so. You must give others the chance to be kind."

Next, came a man from the Miners' Union. Yes, he realized that Nick wasn't a miner, but the miners had gotten together and collected a "little something" for Nick's family until Nick was back on his feet. The miners all appreciated the many things Nick did to help them. The man did not mention that Nick was also a drinking buddy of most of them. He handed Mary Kay an envelope.

Fred Bechtel, the postmaster came. "We are a community, and as such, we take care of each other."

He was followed by Harvey Boone and Silas Smith, both store owners. It was the least they could do for Nick, they said, as they too handed Mary Kay envelopes.

Last to arrive were two fellows from the volunteer-fire-bucket brigade of which Nick was a member. Yes, they too wanted to help Nick's family because they considered Nick to be a splendid chap. Mary Kay and Tess counted their blessings.

Because Jodie was in a funk, he had no desire to go to school; and at first, without Nick's watchful eye, no one thought to make him go. Finally, Lex took him aside.

"Your arm is better now, so I am wondering when you plan to return to school."

"I hadn't thought about it, but not yet."

"Wrong answer, Buddy. You know Nick would be disappointed if he knew you were skipping school."

Jodie looked down at his shoes and did not reply. Lex continued. "Look, Jodie. Nick has told me repeatedly that he has great plans for you. He knows you are intelligent, and he expects you to be successful in life. He thinks you will make a big difference in people's lives someday, but none of that can happen without schooling. Education is essential. You don't want to let Nick down, do you?"

"No," Jodie replied, "I have let him down enough." Then he smiled. "But I do know that when Nick feels better, he will have my hide if I am not in school."

"Are you willing to chance his wrath?" Lex asked.

"No way! I will go back to school tomorrow. Thanks, Lex."

Perhaps Jodie had been waiting to see if anyone noticed he had skipped school. Perhaps inertia had grabbed him. The Manor was a sad place right then, and no one had the energy or ambition to do much. If only Nick could get rid of the blinding headaches that tormented him. Everyone talked quietly to him as they came or went, and they held his hand, so he could feel their touch. Cindy lay on the end of his bed most of the time, watching Nick with sad eyes. She left only to eat or to walk. Lex had taken on the job of exercising her.

The morning after Lex's talk, Jodie was up early and walked the short way to school with Tristan. Word had gotten around that

Jodie had disarmed the gunman at the wedding, and so Jodie was a schoolyard hero. Jodie wanted nothing to do with such nonsense and had stalked off, leaving his adoring cult behind. He was unapproachable for a few days until the children found other interests, and then it was business as usual. He would miss playing baseball though.

Now that Liam was no longer a threat to Susanne, she was free to move back to her apartment above her studio. However, Mary Kay and the others told her they preferred she stay at the Manor. A long, severe winter was expected, and they thought it safer if she were to have the baby there with them. Susanne was quite willing to stay, so they again had a shuffle of rooms. Thornton moved home and took his room back. The boarders fixed Nick's room up for Susanne. Everyone realized that Nick was never again going to occupy that room. Either he was going to get well, or he was not. If he recovered, he, Tess, and the children would move next door to the Annex.

The Annex sat empty. A family meeting was called, and it was decided to leave it empty. Had they been gracious, they would have invited Rose and Ellen to move in there to save on hotel expenses. But truth be told, the sooner Rose went home to Grass Valley, the happier they would be. She was driving them all crazy.

Unlike Ellen, who was both helpful and considerate, Rose grated on everyone's nerves. She spent her days sitting by Nick's bedside quietly reading her bible. When she spoke to anyone, it was to request another blanket, or perhaps a cup of hot tea. Would they mind? She provided no help and sat weeping most of the time. Tess wanted to hold Nick's hand and talk lovingly to him but would have been embarrassed to do that with Rose looking on. Jodie did talk earnestly to Nick one morning but felt the older woman's intrusive presence all the while. Nick had been unconscious, so Jodie didn't know if he had gotten through to him. So, Jodie chose instead to read books and poetry to him, so Nick would hear his voice. Rose offered no help preparing dinner or dusting the furniture. She simply was a presence in their lives, and they did not feel comfortable around her. So, the Annex sat empty.

Mary Kay confided in her mother their feelings about Rose. Ellen understood but was in no position to help. The best she could do was to urge Rose to go home with her, but Mary Kay wanted her mother to stay, so that was not a possible solution.

Nessie and Annabelle were concerned about Uncle Nick. They had never known him to be so quiet, and they had certainly never seen him lie in bed all day. Fortunately, the girls had been in the house on the day Nick was hurt, so they had missed the drama. At first, the girls were amused as they watched Coosie exercise Nick's legs, moving them up and down. Coosie had explained to the girls that Nick's legs needed to be healthy when Nick was ready to go.

"Remember how Nick used to walk everywhere? Well, we need to keep him in shape, so he can walk again."

As the weeks passed, Doc Wagner encouraged Nick to be out of bed as much as possible to prevent pneumonia, and eventually Coosie had him up and sitting in a chair. Nick's head hurt so badly that he couldn't attempt to make conversation. He sat with his head in his hands. Nessie and Annabelle tried singing to him, thinking music would cheer him up. He did not have the heart to tell them that their high girly voices made his pain worse. The morphine helped.

Tess tried to look on the bright side. Nick was conscious, and he knew her. He was often out of bed, and the doctor expected the headache pain to lessen. Tess counted her blessings and continued to pray her rosary.

CHAPTER 40

Thornton and Wiley found themselves busy that autumn. As supervisors, they had to deal with several accidents that beset the mining community. A friend of Nick's, Andy Hagerday, had been crushed to death in one of the shafts, and Tom Dorsey died in a cave-in. Another miner fell from a hoisting cage and dropped seventy feet to his death. Officers of the Miner's Union were there grieving with the families and offering them help with burial costs and household expenses. This was long before the days of welfare and other government assistance. Now, people took care of their own.

Bodie was now considered a large city, one of the largest in California as the population reached nearly 10,000. There had been a rich strike at the Standard Mine in June, and miners continued to pour into town despite the danger in the mines and the violence on the streets. Main Street, probably the widest street in the nation at 100 feet across, was crammed with scores of mule teams and with wagons loaded with mining equipment and supplies of all kinds. New businesses opened— every other one a saloon, it seemed. Seven breweries now operated. Beer was made from the pure water of Potato Peak, located just four miles west of town. Nick would have enjoyed this delicious beer had he been well enough for his usual after- shifter with Lex and Casey. Nick was still not up for a beer, however. He was not out of the woods yet.

December sixth arrived, Jodie's twelfth birthday. It was a Friday, and after school, Jodie came straight home. Because it was the Feast of St. Nicholas, Jodie believed that Nick would be feeling better and be alert for his birthday. It would be a sign that Nick would regain his health. Jodie had counted on it, but when he walked in the door, there was no change. Nick was sitting up in a chair but with his head in his hands, suffering from the continuous headache. It had been nearly two months. Jodie put his schoolbooks away, sat and talked with Nick for a few minutes, and then went into the kitchen to offer to help Mary Kay and Tess.

Coosie was sitting at the table peeling potatoes. Tess was frosting a birthday cake, and Mary Kay was preparing meat loaf for Jodie, his favorite. Actually, it was his second favorite dinner, but he knew he would never request lasagna ever again. Memories of birthdays with his mother were still too raw. The kitchen smelled of onions and fresh rosemary. It was a comforting place, and Jodie was happy to be there.

"Thank you for all this," he said to his friends. "You really are the best."

Tess put her arm around him and said, "I bet you're hungry."

"You bet," Jodie replied as he grabbed an apple. "I'm famished."

"How was school?" Coosie asked.

"It was good. It was my turn to recite a passage from Longfellow's, "Song of Hiawatha." I chose the part that begins with 'By the shores of Gitche Gumee.' I think I did fine. Longfellow will always be my favorite poet."

"Mine too," Mary Kay agreed.

"Then, we began reading *Leaves of Grass*," by Walt Whitman. It's about Whitman's belief in the common man."

Mary Kay spoke up, "I have also read *Leaves of Grass*. Just to be clear, Whitman believes in the common woman, as well." She gave Jodie the look he was beginning to know so well. Then she added, "Jodie, tell Tess how you knew about Whitman before today."

"Nick made me memorize his "Oh Captain, My Captain." I did like that poem though because it was a metaphor for the death of President Lincoln.""

"My President!" Coosie murmured. He never forgot the deeds of this good President.

From the kitchen then, they could hear the brakes of a wagon as it ground to a stop in front of the house. They walked out to the porch and saw that it was one of the ranchers. He climbed down from the wagon seat. Coosie knew the man and stepped off the porch and shook hands with him.

"Hi there, Ted. Nice to see you. What brings you by this time of day?"

"I am looking for a boy named Jodie. Anyone here answer to that name?"

Coosie pushed Jodie forward. "I am Jodie, Sir." He extended his hand as Nick had taught him to do.

"Howdy, Son." He shook Jodie's hand. "I have a present for a fellow named Jodie. That seems to be you, so follow me to the back of my wagon."

Jodie followed the man who said, "I hear that today is your twelfth birthday. A couple of months back, Nick came by my ranch and ordered a birthday present for you. He said he would come back on December sixth to pick it up. Well, Sir, I know what goes on in this town, and so I know Nick could not come by today. Is he any better?"

Jodie nodded his head. "Yes, some, but he has terrible headaches."

"Darned shame! He's a nice fellow." The rancher then grabbed a crowbar. "Just give me a minute to open this crate. I'll be right with you."

The rancher lifted the lid off the crate and reached in and pulled out a small, black cocker spaniel puppy. He handed the frightened dog to Jodie who willingly took him. The puppy whimpered and began to lick Jodie's face. It was love at first sight for them both.

"Yep! Nick knew my hound was having puppies, and so he ordered 'the pick of the litter' for his friend Jodie for his birthday. This pup is six weeks old, just old enough to leave his mama. He is all yours, Son. From Nick. Happy Birthday."

Jodie thanked the rancher and then knelt down in the dirt and set the puppy down beside him. He scratched the pup's ears and examined the white marks on his paws.

While Jodie was playing with his new dog, Coosie took Ted aside and asked him if Nick had paid him for the dog. Ted assured him that he had been paid. No money needed!

When asked if he would like to come in and share in the birthday dinner, Ted declined, saying he needed to get back to the ranch. He still had chores to do. Mary Kay brought an apple pie out to him, wrapped in a flour sack.

"Take this, please. You have made our boy so happy, and we are so grateful for your kindness."

"Thank you kindly, Ma'am. The pleasure was mine." He chuckled as he climbed onto his wagon and drove away. Jodie would never see him again, but he would remember him and this day always. Imagine Nick planning ahead like this to ensure that Jodie got the dog he had long wanted!

After dinner and presents, Jodie carried his puppy over to Nick's bed and lay the pup next to Nick. Nick lifted his hand and petted the dog's head.

Thornton asked, "Jodie, have you thought of a name for your dog?"

"I am naming him Duffy."

"You are naming your dog after an Irish poet?" Wiley was amused.

"Yes, Nick would like that, don't you think? Duffy is his favorite poet."

"Sure, he would. He would be mighty pleased."

"You talk about me as though I am not in the room," Nick complained. "Duffy is a fine name."

Jodie had more to say. "In Ireland, Duffy also means Black."

"How do you know that?" Thornton asked.

"I read," Jodie replied quietly, and then he began to cry. He leaned over and put his head next to Nick's. "Thank you, Nick. Thank you for remembering that I wanted a dog."

Cindy lay at the foot of Nick's bed. She began to thump her tail because she too was happy about the puppy. The only unhappy one in the room was Nick's mother who constantly tried to keep Cindy off the bed— to no avail. The minute she turned her back, Cindy jumped up and resumed her place.

"Dogs are unsanitary," Rose tried to tell anyone who would listen. But Nick wanted Cindy there, so no one would listen. And now Jodie was here with yet another dog. Rose got up and left the room.

Two weeks passed, and Christmas was coming. It was time for Rose and Ellen to get back to their families. Rose was reluctant to leave, but Earl came to Bodie to escort the ladies home. He was relieved to see Nick sitting up, taking nourishment, and walking a bit. The reports he had received from Rose had been bleak, so seeing his son recuperating gave him hope. Nick was progressing; even his headaches were less severe.

Earl stayed one night and then ushered the ladies on to the northbound stage. Rose cried all the way home. Ellen would miss Mary Kay and her extended family but was eager to get home. She had missed Ben, her husband of thirty-six years. Christmas with her Grass Valley family beckoned. She had pies to bake, a tree to trim, and children and grandchildren to hug.

* * * * * * * * * *

It was also Christmas time at the Manor. Nessie and Annabelle chattered endlessly about Santa's upcoming arrival. Thornton and Wiley traveled south and chopped down a large tree, which they brought home and placed in the corner of the front room. The ladies of the Manor helped the four children decorate it with shiny glass balls and silvery tinsel but also with strings of popcorn and homemade paper stars. The tree smelled of spruce and lifted everyone's spirits. Mary Kay added to the festivities with baked goods from the kitchen. The smells of cinnamon, chocolate, and applesauce filled the rooms.

The poet Robert Browning had expressed it eloquently: "God is in His heaven; all is right with the world." God was indeed there looking out for all His children, even a relapsed Methodist who hadn't seen the inside of a church in years. Doc Wagner had been right; Nick's headaches were less painful now, and his overall health was improving. He was sleeping less and sitting up more. Coosie had him up walking twice a day, and he had stopped taking the morphine.

Jodie had given serious thought to the perfect Christmas gift for Nick. This was their first Christmas together, and he was determined to make it meaningful. Jodie had his walking-around- money and could have gone to Boone's Store and bought Nick a gift, but a store-bought gift didn't seem good enough for the man who had taken him in and given him a home.

Finally, Jodie happened on an idea that he thought would work. He enlisted Tess's help and began making an embroidered wall hanging for Nick's shop, similar the ones he thought Nick had sewn himself. It was a time-consuming task, and so Jodie had to work on it steadily to complete it in time. To do so, Jodie had to work on it downstairs where Tess could help him but also where Nick resided. So, Nick knew about it. Nick was regaining his sense of humor and found Jodie's project endearing but also laughable. He couldn't help but poke the bear.

"Say there," he would call out to Jodie. "What are you working on over there?"

"None of your business."

"Is it a present for me?"

"Maybe."

"Show me."

"No, you will have to wait for Christmas morning."

Nick would laugh, but he knew Jodie would be both angry and hurt if he ever found out that Nick had not sewn the other wall hangings himself.

The Manor men knew better than to tease Jodie about his "girly work." Actually, they were touched by Jodie's thoughtfulness. They noticed the change in the boy, and what a change it was! Gone was the angry, boastful bully who had first come to live with them. They gave Nick the credit, but in reality, they too had strongly influenced Jodie by their own behavior. Jodie was learning how to be a man by following their lead and Nick's.

Nick also enlisted Tess's help with his Christmas presents.

"Please go buy penny candy, lots of it. I have a piñata to fill. The idea is to hit the piñata with a stick until it breaks, and the candy falls out. Then the children scoop up the candy and eat it. They will like it, don't you think?"

Tess nodded. "And you, Sir?" she asked him. "What would you like for Christmas?"

"A wife," Nick told her earnestly. "Let's get married. No hoopla this time. Put on your pretty dress and send for Father Cassin. That's all I want."

Tess paused as she heard Nick's words, "Put on your pretty dress." She had longed to hear those very words from Connor who had dishonorably never said them. How happy she now was that he had not.

However, Tess disagreed with having a wedding at this time. "No, Nick. It's the holidays. Christmas is about the children. It's about cooking special dishes, trimming the tree, singing carols, and attending church services. It's Christ's birthday. I don't want the focus to be on us instead. Let's wait until January."

Nick conceded that Tess was right, and they contacted Father Cassin and arranged for a quiet wedding on January eleventh. Manor residents only. Coosie would once again be the Best Man.

* * * * * * * * * *

The winter solstice brought snow and a visitor. Jodie answered the door on the Sunday afternoon before Christmas to find a tall well-dressed man there. The young man asked for Susanne, and Jodie invited him in. When Susanne saw who was there, she broke into tears and ran and hugged him tightly.

"Oh, Tom! Is it really you? What on earth are you doing here?"

"I came to spend Christmas with you, Sis. I went to your studio. It was locked, but the jeweler next door directed me here."

Susanne introduced her younger brother to everyone. Yes, he had come all the way from St. Louis.

She hadn't seen him in a long time because he had been away at university when she was home last, but he was her most faithful correspondent. And here he was, and she couldn't be happier! As luck would have it, her apartment above the studio was empty. He could move in there tonight. How long could he stay? Yes, she was expecting a baby. No, she had no husband. She would explain it all to him later.

Mary Kay told Tom she wanted him to regard the Manor as his own. He was to come and go as he pleased, and yes, she expected him for dinner every evening.

"Someone, go find another chair, please," Mary Kay directed. "Tom, do you sing? Please tell me you can carry a tune. It's Sunday, and we always have a singing session on Sundays. Tonight, we will be singing Christmas songs. Wait until you hear Coosie sing! You can sing! Oh, that is such good news!"

Lex might have been concerned about Mary Kay's enthusiasm for this newcomer if Tom hadn't been at least six years younger than she. Lex hurried to find Tom a chair. Everyone at the Manor was happy that Susanne had family with her this Christmas, and they all hoped Tom could stay a while.

CHAPTER 41

"Oh no, Ma'am," Tom began, "this hostess gift is indeed for you."

Mary Kay stopped him. "Do not call me Ma'am. It makes me feel old."

"Yes Ma'am," Tom started again. And then realizing his mistake, he said, "My apologies. What I meant to say was, 'Of course, I would bring you a gift. That's the way I was reared.'"

"Reared?" Jodie laughed.

Tom looked at him. "Reared, certainly. Children are reared. Cattle and horses are raised. I grew up on a horse farm, remember? I know the difference."

Oh my, Mary Kay thought. *Another Nick! Another word purist.* She looked at Tom who now produced a rolled-up piece of parchment paper. Tom untied the string and revealed a colored-pencil drawing of a young woman standing next to a food-laden dining room table.

"Is this a drawing of me?" Mary Kay asked.

"Yes, Ma'am," Tom replied, not catching his word-choice error. Mary Kay let it go.

"Susanne described you all in her letters. She mentioned your fiery red hair and your excellent cooking."

"This is quality work. Who drew this?"

"A young fourteen-year-old friend of mine named Charley Russell. I sat next to him at a wedding reception a couple of years ago, and we became fast friends. He has real talent, I believe. I asked him to draw two pictures for me before I came West. The other drawing is for Susanne. I will give it to her on Christmas." Tom unfurled the other drawing. It depicted a pretty blonde woman on a horse.

"It looks much like Susanne," Tom said. "Charlie lives in St. Louis, but all he talks about is coming out here. He wants to be a Western artist. I hope someday he gets the chance."

Charlie Russell would soon get the chance. He would move to Montana and become a famous artist. These two pencil drawings would one day be worth a fortune, but neither art piece would ever leave Mary Kay's or Susanne's families. Mary Kay would frame hers and hang it on the kitchen wall next to her framed paper bag from Nessie. Later in life, both pieces would remind her of happy times at the Manor and of old friends she once knew in Bodie.

Tom was a welcome addition to the family. He told engaging stories, and the children looked on with awe as he spoke. One evening at dinner he told them of some of his adventures at the university.

"Jean must have been a popular baby name about twenty years ago because many of the young women I met at school had that name. There was Mary Jean, Karol Jean, and Barbara Jean. Another student arrived— this one was simply named Jean. She looked over the crowd of Jeans and declared herself, 'Supreme Jean.' And that was that! No one ever called her anything else. Believe it or not— she is now engaged to marry a fellow student named Eugene."

Tom smiled at Nessie. "I shall call you 'Nessie Jean,'" he declared. Nessie smiled happily. "And I hereby dub you, 'Annabelle Jean,'" Tom said. Annabelle wiggled excitedly in her chair.

Tom talked about a tavern he frequented near the university. He had become friendly with the owner who confided in him a business trick. Behind the bar, three ornate glass bottles sat in front of the mirror. Each had a different metal tag labeling it. One read,

"Weddings." Another read, "Birthdays." The third simply read, "Celebrations." Customers gladly paid the extra price for this quality liquor when celebrating an event. What the customers did not know was that the proprietor filled each bottle with exactly the same liquor from a large jug. It was the same whiskey he sold across the bar daily. The customers were tricked into paying extra.

Mary Kay was pleased when the children objected to this story. Tristan thought the barkeep was a cheater, and Jodie called him a swindler. Tom fibbed as he assured the children that, of course, he and the tavern owner were no longer friends.

After the song fest that first evening, Tom moved his belongings to Susanne's apartment. The next morning, he took Susanne to breakfast, so they could talk. She explained about Liam and her poor choices. She told him of Nick's offer to marry her and her refusal. Tom agreed that things had worked out for the best because Nick and Tess seemed happy.

"What a good guy to offer to help you! I can see why you are so close to these friends."

Over the next few days, Tom learned the life stories of everyone at the Manor. He shook his head in dismay when Susanne told him of Liam's attack on Nick. He felt incredibly sad for Jodie who had recently lost his mother and had such a dishonorable father.

On Christmas Eve, Tom bluntly asked Susanne the question that had been on his mind. "Do you plan to tell Mom and Dad about the baby?" he asked her.

"Someday. But not until the baby is born. When I finish my photo project, I may take the baby and go home. We'll see. Honestly, I don't know what I want to do."

Tom had a suggestion. "What if I stay here with you until after the baby is born? I eventually need to go home, but I could wait, and we could go together. If you decide not to go home, I will understand that too. I know you would hate to leave your Manor family. You can decide after the baby comes. In the meantime, I will be here for you."

"Yes, yes. Thank you, Tom. I would like to have you here."

And so, Bodie gained a new resident.

* * * * * * * * * *

Christmas morning arrived amid much activity and fuss. The children were up early and made quite a racket, hoping to encourage the adults to emerge from their rooms. Mary Kay was up, of course, and busy in her kitchen. The smell of bacon wafted throughout the rooms. Nick had gotten himself up and dressed. He felt well and was wondering when he would be up to carpentry work. He felt that he couldn't stay in bed one more minute.

Jodie had finished his wall hanging just the afternoon before, and Tess had wrapped it for him in shiny gold paper and had attached a large red bow. It lay under the tree now, and Jodie was impatient for Nick to open it. He wondered where Nick would hang it in his shop.

With Tess and Mary Kay's help, Annabelle and Nessie had left milk and cookies on the hearth for Santa the evening before. In the morning, the girls were thrilled to find the glass empty and the cookies gone. Santa had been there! Annabelle had tried to stay awake so she could listen for him on the roof but was disappointed that she had fallen asleep. For once, Tristan had his nose out of a book and had willingly joined the others downstairs. He no longer believed in Santa Claus, but he played along, admiring the empty cookie plate. He told the girls he had heard reindeer hoofs on the roof right before falling asleep himself last night. The girls were excited by this news. They both would make certain to stay awake next Christmas Eve.

Jodie's puppy almost caused trouble when he discovered the end of the string of popcorn that was used as a tree decoration. He began chewing on it and nearly toppled the tree. Thornton caught it in time and set it upright. He did not reprimand little Duffy for doing what came naturally. Maybe the dog, like Jodie, was always hungry.

Finally, breakfast was over, and it was time to open gifts before church services. The piñata was saved for the afternoon. There was no sense in showing children a paper-mache gift and then making them wait to play with it. Better to give it after dinner. Nick also saved another gift to give later. He had asked Coosie to fetch a large brown envelope from the desk drawer in his shop. Nick had put it there weeks ago. It was for Mary Kay. Tess's rocking chair was still there, waiting for the wedding.

And then, Nick opened Jodie's gift. "Fast Service, No Matter How Long It Takes." Nick read the words on Jodie's embroidered wall hanging and laughed. "This is the perfect piece to hang in my shop, Lad. And look at your neat stitches! A lot of work went into this. I thank you, Jodie."

Jodie smiled. The wall hanging had been worth all the time and effort he had spent on it because he had made Nick happy. Nick was touched by Jodie's gift of love.

Nick hoped Jodie would never find out that he had lied about embroidering the other wall hangings In his shop. Nick wanted no more lies between them but was afraid Jodie would be both embarrassed and angry if he knew that Nick had actually never sewn anything. By not admitting his deception to Jodie, Nick felt he was once again doing the wrong thing for the right reason. Because Jodie would be upset to know that he had been duped again, Nick rationalized that he was saving Jodie from embarrassment. Mary Kay privately suggested to Nick that perhaps he should actually create a wall hanging himself. Then it would be less of a lie. Nick decided he would do just that.

Susanne, Tom, Tess, Annabelle, and Jodie attended Christmas Mass together. The day was bitterly cold; but nevertheless, a large crowd had gathered at the Miner's Union Hall. Later, services were held there for the Methodists. Nick expressed his great disappointment in not being well enough to attend services with Mary Kay. Everyone humored him; they knew he was kidding. Past Christmas services had not seen Nick in attendance either.

"Do not worry about it, Nick. Lex will accompany the children and me. And yes, we will all pray for your sad, forsaken soul, bless your heart." Mary Kay smiled sweetly at him.

"No, you don't understand," Nick said. "I am a church-going man, and I would certainly go with you if I were up to it." He looked at his friends gathered around the table. "As you know, I was at Death's Door. Death's Door, I tell you!" He waved his arms for emphasis.

He's back! Mary Kay thought. *Here's the old Nick. Welcome back, Nick.*

Nick continued, "I give Jodie full credit for my recovery. Not the specialist, not Doc Wagner, not loyal Tess who changed my bandages daily. No, these people are insignificant compared to Jodie. Jodie gets all the credit for my recovery."

Jodie was confused. "What are you talking about?"

"There I was, lying in that bed next to Death's Door, and here came Jodie. Not once, not twice, but daily. He would lean down and whisper in my ear, 'Buck up, Nick. You've got to buck up.'" Nick sighed and looked at Jodie as if greatly disappointed.

"So, that's it, folks! Without Jodie's pep talks, I would still be in that bed! Tess's sweet voice whispering in my ear did nothing to save me. No, instead there was that nasal voice two or three times a day saying, 'Buck up, Nick. Buck up.' I would be at my low point, and my headaches would be devastating, and here would come THAT voice. I recovered in record time just to get away from that irksome voice."

Jodie grinned at his friends. "None of this is true, you know. I did tell Nick to 'Buck up,' but only once, and that was when he was unconscious. Only once."

"Ah, Lad, you are one of the most annoying people I know." Nick reached over and grabbed Jodie and put him in a head lock. "But thanks for saving me from Death's Door."

* * * * * * * * * *

Later that afternoon, the children took turns hitting the piñata and succeeded in scattering candy all over the floor. Thornton held Duffy, so he couldn't get at the candy. The children loved the Santa-shaped piñata. They had never seen such a present. The adults allowed them to eat as much candy as they wanted. After all, it was Christmas.

Tristan voiced what the others were thinking, "Uncle Nick, could you get us one of these piñatas every Christmas?"

"I make no promises. This one came from San Diego, the only place I know that sells them besides Mexico. But I'll tell you what— Jodie and I will be going to San Diego at least once a year. If we can, we will bring a piñata back then."

Mary Kay was sitting in her favorite chair, tired from the many activities. She had spent the last two weeks cleaning, cooking, and baking— preparing for this day. She was pleased because Christmas for the children had gone off without a hitch. All had received presents they wanted and liked. She enjoyed watching both Jodie and Annabelle— neither of whom had ever had a holiday like this one with so many "honorary aunts and uncles" trying to make the day perfect for them. She was humming "Greensleeves" to herself when Nick approached her.

"I have a present for you, Mary Kay." He handed her the large brown envelope.

Mary Kay's eyes grew large as she read the contents of the envelope. She looked at Nick.

"Really? In my name? You did this for me? Oh, Nick! I couldn't be more pleased! Thank you." She held the papers to her chest, and tears rolled down her face. Then, she turned the official document around to show the others.

"A four-year scholarship in the name of Mary Katherine Pratt will be given to a young woman who will attend Iowa Wesleyan University in the fall. A candidate for this position must be a practicing Methodist whose actions are intended for the glory of God. She must be dedicated to social justice and human welfare, and she must strive to make a difference in the lives of others. She must have and maintain a high grade-point average. This is an annual scholarship."

Wiley was interested. "Where exactly is this university?"

Mary Kay answered him. "In eastern Iowa, in a town called Mount Pleasant."

Nick spoke up, "The university is the first co-educational institution of higher learning west of the Mississippi River. It is affiliated with the United Methodist Church. We know so much about it because this was the college Mary Kay planned to attend after high school."

Everyone in the room turned and looked at Mary Kay.

"I didn't know you ever considered college," Thornton told her. "What changed your mind?"

"Marriage changed my mind. I wanted to marry Ed, and I couldn't be both a co-ed and a wife. I chose wife. It was a simple decision." Mary Kay smiled sadly. "It was the correct one."

"The first woman lawyer in the United States graduated from there – Belle Babb Mansfield," Nick told them. "Mary Kay wanted to be just like her."

"You wanted to be a lawyer?" Tristan looked at his mother. He had never thought of her as anything but a mother, but now he was impressed. "You should go to the college, Mom. You would be a great lawyer because you are very good at arguing."

Everyone laughed. Mary Kay certainly could hold her own in an argument.

"No, Sweetie," Mary Kay told him, "it's too late for me, but I am hoping that both Nessie and Annabelle will one day go to college."

"I would be a law lady if I knew what it was, Mama," Nessie offered.

"You and Annabelle will have the opportunity to be anything you want to be, Sweetheart.

"That reminds me. . . seven young women from Wesleyan University formed a club a couple of years ago with the goal of providing opportunities for women to receive higher education."

"Women helping women," Lex said.

"Yes, indeed." Mary Kay smiled at him. "This organization is called 'PEO,' which stands for 'Philanthropic Educational Organization.' It raises money to help women pay for education." Mary Kay smiled at Nick. "And now with this scholarship, Nick has given me the opportunity to also help young women." She walked over and gave Nick a kiss on the cheek. "Thank you, my sweet friend."

"Yeah, yeah." Nick said. "I'm just doing the best I can. This scholarship is my way of letting you know that I do value women and even believe they should have the right to vote. I've given this a lot of thought, thanks to Jodie."

"Thank you for all you do for me and for all of us, Nick. I love you." Mary Kay smiled at him.

Jodie looked shyly at Nick. "Thank you for all you do for me too. I love you."

"Are you actually saying something nice to me?" Nick looked at him.

"Maybe." Then Jodie looked Nick in the eye and said, "The answer is 'Yes.' I am actually saying something nice to you. I love you and want you to know it."

"I love you too, Jodie." Nick put his arm around his young friend and smiled happily. He knew Jodie's entrance into his life had been anything but random.

"But do you know why I love you?" Jodie persisted.

"Why?"

Jodie looked earnestly at Nick and said, "I love you because you are nothing like my dad."

EPILOGUE

So, Christmas came to the Manor where its residents would celebrate it this year of 1878, and again the year after, and for a few
years after that. Their time in Bodie was not endless, however. Like
Virginia City, the treasure would eventually run out, and Bodie's
citizens would move on. Tearful goodbyes would be said, and letters
would keep friends and family in touch, but life in Bodie as they
knew it in its heyday would end.

Many people would come into the lives of Nick and his family
before they too called it a day and moved on. They would not know
Lottie Johl but would know of her. Mary Kay would shop at her husband Eli's market. However, there she would deal only with Charlie
Donnelly who stood at the counter in his clean, white apron. Eli
would be in the back, doing the real work of butchering. Charlie's
wife, Annie Donnelly, would become part of society there. However,
few people liked her or her arrogant ways. Pat Reddy would come
to town and become an instant friend of Nick's, as would Jim Cain.
Nick and Jim would be seen around town pulling the occasional
prank together. Nick would get to know Hank Blanchard, the toll-
road owner. Both avid readers, they would often be seen having a
beer together and discussing books.

Jodie would also make a lifelong friend. A few months into
the new year, a young boy would settle in Bodie with his parents.
Grant Smith, two years older than Jodie, would get a job delivering
telegrams all over town, and Jodie would often go with him. Duffy
was always there too, right on Jodie's heels. Jodie and Grant would

share many good times together, and this would make Nick happy because he couldn't have found a better friend for Jodie. As an adult, Grant would become a prominent lawyer. Jodie would have a distinguished career as well, although he would not study law.

Some people who were important to Nick and his family would leave Bodie far too soon. One of these would be William O'Hara, affectionately known as Uncle Billy. When he died in April of 1880, Jodie would be among the saddest of the town's mourners. Jodie would have gotten to know Uncle Billy and would have appreciated his fine character, just as he had learned to appreciate Coosie's admirable qualities. Uncle Billy would be eulogized in Bodie's newspaper as "The Foster Father of Bodie," and people would turn out in droves to honor this well-respected businessman and longtime resident of Bodie.

Nick would still be there as the town grew rowdier and deadlier. He would witness James De Roche's killing of Thomas Treloar although he would not be part of the vigilante committee that settled the matter afterward. Nick would still be there when Pioche Kelley shot Charlie Jardine. Yes, Bodie would become a violent place, and Nick would know to stay home after dark.

By then, Nick and Tess would be working on their dozen, and Nick would have other priorities. His business would thrive, and he would be pleased when the Bodie Railway was built that would provide both lumber and fuel to Bodie. This would be Nick's town with both its good and evil elements. Nick would love it to the end. Only his friend Jim Cain, who would eventually own the town, would love it as much.

Nick would always know there was nothing random about the life he had made for himself in this wind-swept mining town on the California border. There was also nothing random about the family and friends he met there. He would smile when he would think back to the old timer he had once met in a bar in Nevada who had asked him, "Have you ever heard of a place called Bodie?"

ABOUT THE AUTHOR

Catherine Jasek is a retired English and history teacher who claims a fetish for the five-paragraph essay. This is her first foray into fiction writing, and she found that she enjoyed both the research and the weaving of characters onto the page. She hopes someday to claim that her books have been translated into fifty different languages and have sold millions of copies. Until then, she continues to live in San Diego with her long-suffering husband and demanding cat.